INFAMIA

ITS PLACE IN ROMAN PUBLIC AND PRIVATE LAW

GREENIDGE

London

HENRY FROWDE

OXFORD UNIVERSITY PRESS WAREHOUSE

AMEN CORNER, E.C.

New York

MACMILLAN & CO., 66, FIFTH AVENUE

INFAMIA

ITS PLACE IN ROMAN PUBLIC AND PRIVATE LAW

BY

A. H. J. GREENIDGE, M.A.

HERTFORD COLLEGE

Oxford

AT THE CLARENDON PRESS

LONDON: HENRY FROWDE

OXFORD UNIVERSITY PRESS WAREHOUSE, AMEN CORNER

AND

STEVENS & SONS, LIMITED

119 & 120 CHANCERY LANE

1894

Oxford
PRINTED AT THE CLARENDON PRESS
BY HORACE HART, PRINTER TO THE UNIVERSITY

PREFACE

SOME few enquirers, gifted with sufficient imagination, may perhaps be able to realise, almost at the outset, the nature of any particular task which they are undertaking. This has not been my fortune in writing the history of the Infamia. Starting under the impression that, in following up the traces of this singular institution, I was dealing with a somewhat narrow juristic question, I soon found myself confronted by a subject, the juristic aspect of which was quite secondary to its moral and social significance. In its ethical aspect, Infamia is in touch with almost every department of Roman life; in its juristic aspect it is difficult to say what department of Roman law—public, criminal, and private—it did not to some extent control.

A subject which has so many branches is liable to partial treatment. Infamia has been no exception to this rule. One department of it, generally known as the censorian infamia, has often been treated by writers on constitutional law. Another department—the Infamia known to us from the legal books of Justinian—has been the almost exclusive property of writers on private law; and unfortunately, through a series of accidents which will be fully traced in the course of this work, this second branch of the subject has come to usurp the exclusive title of Infamia.

But the first duty of a historian is to restore to their due proportions the different parts of a subject or the various epochs of a period. From a historical stand-point Infamia must be studied as a whole. This is the reason why I have ventured to go over such well-worn ground as the history of the censorship in the Republic and even to trace the feeble survivals of this institution which are met with in the Empire, before investigating the codified institution of imperial times, which has hitherto generally borne the exclusive title of Infamia, but which is in reality only the palest reflection of that 'rule of manners,' which supported the *dignitas* of the free state, and gave it strength to win what the new Monarchy and the later Empire found it so difficult to retain.

A. H. J. G.

HERTFORD COLLEGE, OXFORD,
April, 1894.

CONTENTS

[*The references are to the pages.*]

CHAPTER I.

CHAPTER II.

Chapter III.

CHAPTER IX.

APPENDIX.

ERRATUM.

Page 169, line 20. Omit the words 'From an interpretation' to 'receiving under a testament,' and the reference in note 3.

Greenidge: Infamia

INFAMIA

CHAPTER I.

ON THE MEANING OF 'EXISTIMATIO.'

THE object of the present treatise is an attempt to investigate the history of a conception of Roman Law, which, for want of a better English equivalent, may be termed that of 'civil honour.' The difficulty of nomenclature, however, is unfortunately not confined to the search of English equivalents for conceptions alien to English law. Such a difficulty might conceivably be met by the employment of a new terminology, or might more easily be dispensed with by the use of the technical Roman terms themselves, without any attempt at translation. The difficulty lies deeper than this, and arises from the fact that, though the conception of civil honour was brought home to the Romans by some of their most important political institutions, and underlay many—if not most—of the events of the citizen's daily life, yet there is a striking absence of any strictly technical terminology to express the condition itself, or, what is more important, the mode in which this condition might be destroyed. In the forensic speeches of a Republican lawyer, in the *responsa* of Roman emperors, and in the writings of the classical jurists, we meet only the vague expressions, never accurately defined, which were current in the ordinary Latin language and literature. The two terms by which the conception was most usually expressed were those of *existimatio* and *dignitas.* Both of these convey the notion of the outward respect in which a man is held, which is based upon his deserts and measured by his position in society. As a rule, the only authority which can thus take the measure of a man and assign him his fit and proper place is society itself, and the conception is merely one of 'positive morality.' When, however, the State steps in, not in a penal capacity, but simply with the desire of regulating the position of the individual with reference to what it conceives to be State-functions, whether in public or in private law, in accordance with what it believes to be that individual's deserts, then the conception becomes juristic, and social respect develops into civil honour. Although this is, perhaps, the nearest approach that can be made to a general description of what the Roman jurist meant by *dignitas* or *existimatio*, yet it would be misleading to suppose that, by the 'regulation' of the individual's position by the State, it is meant that the State actually 'assigned' that position. On the contrary, the point of view of the Roman law is that that position is one already existing, that the State interferes to diminish it (*minuere*), sometimes in exceptional cases to restore it (*restituere*), but never, so far as the conception is a universal one, applicable to all Roman citizens without distinction of rank, does it interfere to increase it. Leaving out of sight all the distinctions of privileged and unprivileged classes in Rome, of *dominus* and *servus*, *ingenuus* and *libertinus*, *patronus* and *cliens*, with which we have here no concern, and fixing our attention on the *civis romanus*, we shall find that civil honour at Rome is known to us entirely under its negative aspect. This at once accounts for the absence, noticed above, of a positive definition of the conception; a procedure which is purely negative can hardly give rise to a positive terminology: and further that terminology can be neither definite nor accurate when that procedure is concerned with diminishing the varying degrees of *existimatio* belonging to different classes of individuals and with reference to very distinct needs of the State. The complexity will be greatly increased if we find that the procedure itself was not simple. In this particular case we shall find that it was extremely complex. The authorities who wielded at Rome the power of lessening the civil honour of the individual were many in number, and they exercised this power for very different purposes. These considerations render it no matter for surprise that this subject is the most unsettled in the whole province of Roman law, and one on which, with reference to certain points, any historian, on the evidence which we at present possess, must be content with merely probable conclusions[1]. The historian is fortunate who is able to show that these points are of comparatively minor importance: and that a juristic conception which appears before us in the laws of the Twelve Tables, grew with the growth of the Republic, assumed a somewhat different but hardly less important form under the Roman Empire, and gathered fresh strength with the new disabilities which necessarily accompanied the recognition of Christianity as the State-religion, can be restored in something of its old continuity. What appears to be the most signal proof of incompleteness of knowledge—but one that is by no means so serious as it looks—is that modern historians are not agreed as to what was the

[1] As two of the most important links in the chain of evidence are epigraphic—the *Lex Julia Municipalis* and the *Lex Acilia Repetundarum*—there is yet hope that this evidence may be added to.

general name given by the Romans to this derogation of *dignitas*, or whether it had such a general name at all. It will be provisionally spoken of here as the Roman *infamia*; although the right to use this word in this extended sense is one that will have to be proved during the course of the work[1].

It will now be necessary to point out, with such degree of accuracy as is attainable, the limits of the present subject—a task especially necessary in this case, since the treatment of *infamia* here will be somewhat wider than that which has been allotted to it by most writers on the subject. It has been observed above that the Roman State and the Roman jurist always looked on *existimatio* as a condition of which the citizen was already in enjoyment.

[1] *Infamia* and its variants:—*Infamia*; Liv. xxvii. 11 (of the *censoria notatio*), 'erant perpauci, quos ea infamia adtingeret:' cf. Cic. pro Rosc. Amer. 39, 113; pro Quinctio, 14, 46. In the legal books *infamia* is the usual term, with such variants as 'infamiae detrimentum' (Cod. ii. 11 (12) 1), 'damnum infamiae' (ib. 5), 'famae damnum' (ib. 8), 'infamiae macula' (ib. 20), 'detrimentum famae' (Cod. i. 40, 8). *Ignominia:* Cic. pro Quinctio, 15, 49, and often; *probrum:* ib. 2, 9, and often; these two words are generally applied to the *censoria notatio*. The expression used for the pronouncement of *infamia* is in the Edict (Dig. iii. 2) 'infamia notare;' this is the most usual expression. *Notare* is often used alone, and generally of persons; but we also find 'factum notare' (Dig. ii. 3, 13). But the modes of expressing the fact of *infamia* are very numerous, especially in the imperial rescripts. Amongst them may be cited 'infamiam irrogare' (Just. Inst. iv. 18, 2), 'ignominia irrogari' (Dig. ii. 3, 20), 'damnare ignominia' (Tertull. de Spect. 22), 'ignominia notare' (Cod. ii. 11 (12), 15): 'ignominiae maculam inrogare' (ib. 13), 'labem pudoris contrahere' (Cod. ii. 11 (12), 15): 'existimationis macula' (ib. 17), 'existimationem laedere' (Dig. ii. 3, 2), 'jactura existimationis' (Cod. x. 32 (31), 31); 'opinionis imminutio' (Cod. ii. 6, 6). Besides the usual *infames* of persons (or more rarely the fuller 'infames personae,' Cod. x. 59 (57)), we find 'famosus,' 'inter infames haberi' (Cod. ii. 11 (12) *passim*): 'famosum facere' (Dig. ii. 3), 'quos infamia ab honestorum coetu segregat' (Cod. xii. 1, 2), 'notabilis esse' (Cod. ix. 8, 5). In Gellius (xiv. 7, 8) we find the expression 'facere existimatos': and in Capitolinus (Vit. M. Anton. 12) we find 'famae detestandae' used of the *infamia* incurred by a man who had fought as a gladiator.

Existimatio is, in fact, defined for us as *dignitatis illaesae status*[1]. It was so far a conception similar to that which the old Roman law knew as *caput*, and which the later jurists generally described as *status*. The limits of the present subject may best be defined by showing the relations which these two conceptions, *existimatio* and *caput*, bore to one another. It is clear, on examination, that the conceptions differ from one another in two respects. *Caput* denotes the whole condition of the Roman citizen as the subject of all kinds of personal rights, and is therefore necessarily a much wider and more comprehensive term than *existimatio*. They differ further in the respect that *existimatio* possesses a connotation which is on the whole wider than that of *caput*. It conveys the notion of moral censure as well as that of legal punishment: it is the *status legibus ac moribus comprobatus*[2], whereas *caput* might be described as a *status legibus comprobatus* alone[3]. If we accept the ordinary Roman subdivisions of *caput* and assume that it

[1] Callistratus in Dig. l. 13 (*de extraord. cogn.*) 5, §§ 1–3.

[2] Callistratus (l. c.) 'existimatio est dignitatis illaesae status, *legibus* ac *moribus* comprobatus, qui ex delicto auctoritate legum aut minuitur aut consumitur. *Minuitur* existimatio, quotiens, *manente libertate*, circa statum dignitatis poena plectimur—vel cum in eam causam quis incidit, quae edicto perpetuo, infamiae causa, enumerantur. *Consumitur* vero, quotiens *magna capitis* deminutio intervenit, id est, cum *libertas* adimitur.' The use of the positive conception *existimatio* and its equivalents in a juristic sense may be illustrated from Cic. pro Quinct. 15, 49 ('fama et existimatio'), cf. 16, 51; 23, 73; 31, 98 and 99. In the same speech we find (31, 79) 'integra sua fama' and (15, 49) 'existimatio est integra'; in pro Rosc. Com. (5, 15) 'bona existimatio'; ib. 6, 16 'summae existimationis.' 'Integra fama' is found in Dig. xxvi. 10, 4, 2. Cf. Cod. x. 11 ('integram existimationem illibatamque conservat') and ib. § 21 ('inviolatam existimationem obtinent'). For variants see Cic. pro Rosc. Amer. 39, 114: 'honestas' and Cod. x. 59 (57) 'integra dignitas.'

[3] This is true even in the rare cases where *capitis deminutio* ensues from a lapse of duty to the State: as in the case of the person who does not appear to be registered at the census (the *incensus*) Cic. pro Caec. 34, 99), or who attempts to evade military service (Ulp. *Reg.* xi. 11). These are both strictly penal measures.

consists in freedom (*libertas*), in citizenship (*civitas*), and in membership of a *familia*, it is clear that the *existimatio* of an individual may be affected without his being involved in either of the three kinds of *capitis deminutio*. For purposes of illustration we may anticipate for a moment facts which will be treated of in detail later on, and take the instance of the Roman censor who, on moral grounds, suspends for a time the individual citizen's right of voting (*jus suffragii*). Yet all the other rights implied in *civitas* still remain intact, and the citizen has not suffered the *media capitis deminutio*. And, even if we take what seems the most extreme disqualification in civil law, the rendering of an individual *intestabilis* (a word the history of which will be traced further on), whether this means incapable of being a witness, or incapable of having a witness, to a testament, or both[1], this disqualification destroys an important right connected with the *familia*, but does not produce the *minima capitis deminutio* or loss of *familia* itself. These partial derogations of the citizen's rights never do, in fact, involve a real *capitis deminutio*, and hence the consideration of the modes in which *caput* may be destroyed or restored lies entirely outside the scope of this work. The distinction between a change in *dignitas* and *status* is in fact drawn for us in the legal writings of Justinian[2]; a change in the former produces no *capitis deminutio*: and although we often find in Latin authors disqualifications of different degrees and for different purposes spoken of as a loss of *caput*, yet this terminology was due to a more or less superficial analogy, natural enough in non-juristic writers, to whom

[1] Gaius in Dig. xxviii. 1, 26.

[2] Inst. i. 16, § 5, 'Quibus autem dignitas magis quam status permutatur capite non minuuntur: et ideo senatu motum capite non minui constat.'

the conception of *caput* was as vague as the term itself[1]. Sometimes indeed the analogy was very close. When the censor took from the citizen the right of voting, it did seem as if *civitas* and *libertas* were snatched away[2], for all the active manifestations of political life were now withheld. Still more was this the case if each succeeding censor did, as is probable, accept in certain cases the ruling of his predecessors, and rigorously exclude from all active political rights men disgraced by certain professions such as that of an actor[3]. This permanent disqualification seemed to entail a modified *capitis deminutio*[4]: and hence we are not surprised to find that this terminology crept into a province to which it was, strictly speaking, inapplicable.

Here, therefore, is one limitation on our discussion of the subject which is not only justifiable but necessary. With the consideration of *caput* or *status*, with the conditions on which it depends, and the circumstances by which it may

[1] For instances of this usage see Liv. xlv. 15; Cic. pro Quinct. 9, 32: 13, 44, 45; pro Rosc. Com. 6; Tertull. de Spect. 22. These passages will be examined in detail later on.

[2] Liv. l. c. 'civitatem libertatemque eripere.'

[3] Tertull. l. c. 'scenicos manifeste damnant ignominia et capitis deminutione.'

[4] Still more was this the case when the disqualification was hereditary, as it was in the exceptional instance of Sulla's proscription list. Here the disqualification in some respects resembled the Greek ἀτιμία. The disabilities imposed by Sulla on the children of the proscribed, and to which a retrospective legal sanction was granted by the *Lex Valeria* (Plut. Sulla, 32; Cic. de Leg. Agr. iii. 2, 7), and which were perhaps further confirmed by a law of the dictator himself, were illogical and arbitrary. The pretext for them was that those so disfranchised were the children of *hostes* (Cic. pro Rosc. Amer. 43, 126). As such they should have suffered complete *capitis deminutio*. But we know that they were disfranchised only for certain purposes. The general effect was to debar them from all chances of a public career ('a republica summoveri' Cic. ap. Quinct. ii. 1, 85). But this was not strictly a *capitis deminutio*. This exceptional legislation does not belong to the general history of civil honour at Rome, for many reasons, and above all because, as we shall see, the Roman *infamia* was not hereditary.

be lost, we have nothing to do. Other limitations, which it is necessary to mention, may best be seen, if we proceed to sketch rapidly the main course which this discussion will take, and the chief questions which, during the course of it, will have to be answered.

The history of the Roman Infamia is a history of special disqualifications, based on moral grounds, from certain public or quasi-public functions: by the latter are meant those functions, such as postulation in the praetor's court, which, though based primarily on the rights of the individual in private law, yet necessarily bring him into contact with an official of the State. The easiest manner of classifying these disqualifications will, therefore, be to divide them into two main categories of (i) those disqualifications which have reference primarily to public rights (*jura publica*) and (ii) those which have reference primarily to the procedure necessary for the exercise of private rights (*jura privata*)[1]; although it may be boldly said, in the latter case, that the disqualification ultimately has reference to private rights themselves, since any limitation on procedure is inconceivable without some limitation of the rights which are reached by such procedure.

The disabilities which were connected with the public law of Rome will necessarily be considered first. Whatever may be our theory as to the origin of the term *infamia* in Roman law, there can be no doubt that the disabilities

[1] The word 'primarily' is particularly necessary as regards the second category, since at Rome a limitation in procedure in the matter of private law might affect a man's capacity to act on behalf of the State. E. g. the limitation on the right of postulation imposed on the *infamis* in the praetor's edict prevented a man so declared *infamis* from sustaining a *popularis actio*—one in which a money penalty was exacted on behalf of the State; since in such a case he appeared as a *cognitor* or *procurator* of the State.

which it implies were concerned primarily with the exercise of public rights by Roman citizens. By the side of these mere questions of procedure in civil law, even considered as affecting the majesty of such a magistrate as the Roman praetor, sink into comparative insignificance. But, not only, as will be shown, is the conception of *existimatio* and its violation, *infamia*, prior in respect to public to that which we meet with in respect to private law; it is also a far more striking conception in the former case than in the latter. Equality in private law is an idea which arouses little interest or wonder: but nowhere, save in a state like Rome, which on the whole recognized perfect equality amongst the citizens in matters of public honour and public duty, could the conception of *existimatio*—of a moral standard to which all citizens alike should conform—be fairly exhibited. So far as the disabilities implied in *infamia* affected public rights, they may again be conveniently subdivided into two classes; (i) those affecting the *honores* of the State, by which, as will be seen, are meant strictly the magistracies of the State, and (ii) those affecting the *jura publica* of all citizens other than magistrates—the most important of these *jura* which the State cared to control being the right of voting, and the right (for it was a right as well as a duty) of serving in the Roman legions. This is a simple and in the abstract perhaps an exhaustive classification of what were meant by 'public rights'—they are generally summed up briefly as the *jus honorum* and the *jus suffragii*. In practice however they formed, as we should expect, but a portion of the functions of State which might be exercised by the individual citizen. By the side of them we find a class of offices, which were never regarded as *honores*, and can as little be looked on as *jura publica*, since they could not be claimed of right by any and every Roman citizen. They were offices other than the regular magistracies, for which certain special qualifications were necessary. One of these was the position of a senator, and the special qualification for this during a great portion of the Republic and during the Empire was the previous holding of a specified magistracy. With this special qualification we have here no concern; but what does concern us is this: that, in consequence of this special qualification, and of the importance of the duties of a senator to which it led, developed the notion of a *dignitas* peculiar to that position. Not only society but the State demanded a standard of conduct conformable to that rank: and here for the first time we are introduced, not to *existimatio* as a simple and universal conception, attaching to *honores* in general or to *jura publica* in general, but attaching to a class or *ordo*, which is presumed to have a life-long tenure of its position, and to which necessarily but few of the citizens can belong. Amongst classes the *senatorius ordo* claims the first place with the historian as it claimed the first place with the censors in their revisions: and we need but give a passing notice, and only with reference to our subject, to that strange anomaly of the Roman constitution—the existence of a body, hardly recognized by constitutional law at all (if indeed we can speak of constitutional law in connection with a government such as that of Rome), but which was long obeyed as the *de facto* sovereign of the State, and which the State accordingly took excessive care to preserve from every stain which might weaken the influence and the power not secured to it by statute-law. To the senate *existimatio* was everything, and that this truth was fully recognized by the State will be clearly shown when we come to treat of the exercise of the censorian power in relation to that body. Amongst *ordines* more distinctly recognized by public law were the *equites*, who, whether regarded as a military body or as a civil order, required special monetary qualifications, and others which varied from time to time as the condition for admission to their ranks. Here, again, the only point that we need dwell on is that the conception of a *dignitas* and an *existimatio* was established, applicable to that order and differing (sometimes, it is true, according to the caprice of the magistrate whose duty it was to regulate the citizen's position) from that of the magistracy, the senate and the voting populace. More artificial—because less stable—was the *ordo* of the *judices.* A special *existimatio* attached to these as well. Only as the *album judicum* was often created afresh by *leges judiciariae*, the conception of this *existimatio* could be—and apparently was—embodied in law. At least one of the earliest notices we possess of the legal recognition of *infamia* is contained in the *Lex Acilia Repetundarum* of 122 B.C., the clauses of which containing the qualifications for the jurors, who were to be employed on that special *quaestio*, were undoubtedly copied from the *Lex Judiciaria* of C. Gracchus.

However the moral qualifications of the different classes in the State were determined in each particular case, the main fact about *existimatio* is now clear. It differed according to the needs of the community. And, simple and obvious as the fact may seem, it is yet the one which it is most important to bear in mind when we are studying the Roman *infamia*. *Infamia* could not have been a uniform procedure if *existimatio* was not a uniform conception.

Before leaving the subject of qualifications for State-functions, another and very necessary limitation of the subject may now be pointed out: and that is, that we cannot consider here the qualifications for magistracies (*honores*) or other offices of State any more than we can consider the qualifications for citizenship generally.

Although the Roman State might ordain that a man must be of a certain age before he can hold office at all, that he must exercise some functions before exercising others, or even that he must not be disqualified physically for office, yet none of these conditions touch the question of *existimatio*. There was, however, one condition requisite for holding office at Rome which does present a difficulty to us, because it seems to lie on the borderland between the ordinary qualifications and that of *dignitas* or *existimatio* with which we are here concerned. It was certainly a rule at Rome that any one who exercised a trade or profession for payment should not be eligible for the magistracy: and a historic instance of the application of this rule is furnished by the case of a certain Cn. Flavius, a *scriba* of the aediles, whom the magistrate presiding over the election for the curule aedileship refused to receive as a candidate for that post until he had formally abandoned his profession[1]. There can be no doubt that this principle was based on the consideration that it was beneath the dignity of a Roman magistrate to be engaged in such an occupation: and was the outcome of a conception somewhat similar to the Greek idea of *βαναυσία*, which in this case, as in some Greek Republics[2], found open legal expression. It, therefore, is, to some extent, connected with our subject: although the disqualification was here not based on moral grounds, and the man so disqualified would certainly not have been described as *infamis*. A more difficult question will meet us later on in the case of certain professions which disqualified for municipal offices, and which were evidently considered disgraceful[3]. The individuals

[1] Mommsen, Staatsrecht, i. p. 497. Gell. vii. (vi.) 9. Liv. ix. 46.

[2] Arist. Pol. iii. 5, 7, p. 1278 a.

[3] Those namely mentioned in the *Lex Julia Municipalis*, l. 104. For this form of disqualification, see ch. ix. § 2.

holding these also would hardly have been described as *infames*: although we cannot argue from our modern notions to the singular prejudices which even the most democratic portions of the ancient world entertained towards certain modes of life. The other disqualifications with which we are concerned were all based on a moral stigma, and all affected *existimatio* through *infamia*.

When we turn from the public law effects of this censure to its application in the procedure of the civil law we leave all such grades behind us. The juristic formula, *omnes homines aequales sunt*, although extended almost as widely from the original sphere to which it applied by the Roman jurists themselves as it has been by modern thinkers, was yet in its narrowest sense strictly applicable to the *jus privatum* of Rome. This equality necessarily embraced procedure—which, in the special case we shall have to consider, was the capacity for *postulation* in the praetor's court. And the equality could only be disturbed by some special disability, which might be that of age or sex, of physical or moral incapacity. Amongst the kinds of moral unfitness which produced disability in this given case, that known as the *infamia* holds the first place.

The nature of the subject which we have to treat in detail is now tolerably clear. It is the subject of the special disqualifications based on an injury to reputation (*laesa existimatio*). The questions to which it gives rise are partly moral, partly juristic: since the institution itself depended on the theory that a moral taint involved a civic disability. It was this civic disability, conceived consciously as based on a moral imperfection, that was generally spoken of by the Romans as *infamia*.

Before proceeding to the proof of this point, which is, after all, not of very great importance (for it is little more than the justification of a nomenclature), it will be convenient to close this introductory chapter by giving a sketch of the main points which will be touched on in the discussion, more especially as many—if not most—of these points have been the subject of long-sustained controversy, and it is important to set the precise issues clearly before us.

Next to the conception itself, the main point which we shall have to consider is the nature of the machinery by which the civic disqualification based on it was secured. It will be found that there were three modes by which it could be brought about.

(i) By the performance of their duties by the magistrates who had the right of admitting citizens to *honores*, to the *ordines*, and to the exercise of the *publica jura* generally. These magistrates were, to some extent, the consuls or other magistrates who presided at elections to office, but more particularly the censor. The working of this kind of disqualification is known to us entirely from facts recorded by historians, and not from public documents. A question that must necessarily be answered in this connection is, how far the caprice (*arbitrium*) of these magistrates was limited by recognized rules of procedure or by legal prescriptions.

(ii) By the performance of his functions by a magistrate who had the control of procedure in the civil courts, that is, the praetor. The mode in which this disqualification was brought about is known to us from legal documents; namely, from the portions of the praetor's edicts dealing with this subject which have been preserved for us (no doubt incompletely) in the Digest, from the amplifications of the commentators, and from further interpretations in the Codex.

(iii) By legislation. The laws dealing with this subject are known to us from official documents which have been preserved in inscriptions, from the legal books of Justinian, and to some extent also from scattered notices preserved in other writers. Such laws were statutes embodying principles of constitutional law[1], certain statutes of the criminal law (the *leges judiciorum publicorum*), perhaps certain civil laws themselves, and decrees of the Roman Emperors. In one particular case we find a civic disability imposed by the only great charter that Rome possessed, the laws of the Twelve Tables.

It is at once clear that the first two classes mentioned above bear a much greater resemblance to one another than either of them bears to the third class. What may be, for purposes of convenience, termed the censorian and the praetorian *infamia*, are both exercises of the *auctoritas* of a magistrate. It is the resemblance and the difference between the modes of exercise of these two kinds of authority that have given rise to most of the controverted points with which we shall have to deal. The disputed questions are concerned both with the causes and with the effects of these two kinds of disqualification. If we ask, 'Did the grounds of the censorian and the praetorian *infamia* coincide?' our answer will be, on the whole, in the affirmative; the chief difference that we shall observe being that the grounds in the latter case were necessarily of a somewhat narrower compass than in the former. If we ask further 'Did the consequences of the two kinds of *infamia* coincide?' we shall certainly find that the effects in either case were different, each procedure being regulated strictly with reference to its own object. But we shall also find that the attempt which has been made to distinguish *infamia* as a permanent disqualification from political rights, from the *censoria notatio* as a temporary disqualification, is a failure, in the extreme form in which this theory has been stated by many eminent authorities. It is untenable, that is, for the period of the Republic, where alone it can be properly tested, for it was only then

[1] As the *Lex Julia Municipalis* and to a less extent the *Tabulae Bantinae*.

that the *censoria notatio* was in full working and was in the nature of a living and progressive political institution; although it will not be denied that, at some period during the Empire, as a consequence mainly of the decline of active political life and definite political progress, *infamia* did become a fixed and rigorous conception and did disqualify permanently from certain political functions.

The third class of disqualifications mentioned above ought to be of a comparatively simple character. The mandate of the law ought, we might think, to be of a more uniform character than the *arbitrium* of the magistrate. Here again we shall find that on the whole the grounds of the *infamia* created by statute tend to coincide, only differing, as we should expect they must differ, from the scope of the particular laws. The narrowness or the fulness of the grounds embraced depended naturally on the object which each law had in view: and therefore we must conclude, that, in the case of laws, as in the case of magistrates, it is impossible to expect uniformity in the effects they ordained. But, although the law might ordain that certain effects should follow certain causes, at Rome, where during the Republic the machinery necessary for enforcing a law was notoriously inadequate, and the discretionary power of the magistrate extremely great, a question noticed above necessarily suggests itself in this connection, namely, how far the magistrate in power—the consul presiding at the elections or the censor making out the list of the Senate—felt himself absolutely bound by such legal prescriptions. There were no doubt many modes of ignoring them, and hardly a single definite regulation for bringing the facts before the notice of the magistrate. In the case of the censorian power especially we shall therefore find that it is hardly possible to give a simple answer to this question.

In the course of this discussion it is proposed to treat the modes by which *infamia* could be brought about, and its consequences when effected in the following order. First, the censorian procedure of the Republic, which is, on the whole, the oldest and certainly the most important; and in close connection with this procedure, the developments which it subsequently attained, as applied mainly to the construction of the higher orders of the State, in the Principate and in the later Empire. Secondly, we shall concern ourselves with the praetorian *infamia*: and in this (the most difficult portion of the subject) the following questions will arise for settlement: (1) the rules of postulation in the praetor's court and the structure of the three edicts referring to postulation; (2) the grounds of the disqualifications resulting from these rules: and in connection with these grounds we shall have to consider the various attempts which have been made to reconstruct the edict dealing with the *infames*, which has come down to us in a fragmentary and disjointed state; (3) the consequences, mainly in civil law following on this restriction of postulation. We then reach the developed conception of *infamia*, as it is known to us in the legal books of Justinian. This, and the modified forms in which *existimatio* could still be affected in the later Empire, and which fell short of the developed conception of *infamia*, form the conclusion of the history of Civil Honour, so far as its chief possessors, men, were concerned.

A further subject which will demand treatment—and one which, because on account of its anomalous character, it could not be classified with the others, has not been noticed in this introductory chapter—is the conception of *infamia* as attaching to women. We shall have to consider this exceptional stigma in its probable connection with the praetor's edict and with the Julian laws.

CHAPTER II.

ON THE MEANING OF 'INFAMIA.

It is now necessary to redeem a promise made in the preceding chapter, and to attempt to give a history of the word *infamia*, so far as it bore a juristic or quasi-juristic sense. Verbal discussions of this kind have of themselves little interest or importance: more especially with reference to a conception, which, as has been already shown, was expressed in no strictly technical terminology. It is, however, rendered essential in this case on account of the attempts which have been made to narrow the term down to a very special juristic signification—an attempt which has resulted in falsifying and obscuring the whole history of Civil Honour at Rome.

To every reader of classical Latin literature it is obvious that *infamia* is used of the ill report which accompanies moral turpitude of almost every kind—a use which is so frequent as not to require illustration. It may be worth noticing, however, that it is used as synonymous with words, which we know, from direct evidence, bore a quasi-legal by the side of their ordinary signification. It is thus found conjoined with *probrum* [1], which, as we shall see, was the term regularly employed to denote the offence which led the censors to 'mark' (*notare*) an individual: and with *ignominia* [2], which we know was the name usually given

[1] Cic. pro Coel. 18, 42; cf. pro Quinct. 2, 9 and 14, 46.
[2] Cic. Tusc. iv. 20, 45.

to the dishonour attaching to an individual in consequence of the censorian *notatio*. It need not surprise us, therefore, if *infamia*—certainly the widest of the terms descriptive of ill-repute—bore the widest quasi-juristic sense. One further consideration will make it almost certain that this was the case. We have seen from the passage of Callistratus (p. 5) that *existimatio* came to have almost a technical juristic sense which we have attempted to translate by the words 'civil honour.' In the pleadings of Cicero which have reference to disqualification based on loss of reputation we find *fama* and *existimatio* used constantly as synonyms. In a passage of the speech pro Quinctio, for instance, he asserts that 'cujus bona ex edicto possidentur, hujus omnis fama et existimatio cum bonis simul possidetur[1]'. There was no convenient negative form for the term *existimatio*, which was becoming technical: but there was for its synonym *fama*: *infamia*, in fact, must have been the technical equivalent to *laesa existimatio* or *minutio existimationis*. If we find a narrower juristic sense attaching to this word in very late developments of Roman law, this is no proof that the narrower signification always attached to it, especially if we can show that, from historical causes, the restriction of the term was in the long run natural and perhaps inevitable.

Even if we believe, however, that *infamia* was the juristic term usually employed for loss of civil honour, we cannot be always certain where it denotes a legal disqualification, and where a merely moral censure. We may take a rather extreme instance in illustration. Asconius tells us, with reference to the trial of Catiline for extortion in 65 B.C.,

[1] pro Quinct. 5, 50; cf. 23, 73: 24, 76: 31, 97 and 98; pro Rosc. Com. 5, 15 ('bonae existimationis'), 6, 16 ('summae existimationis'); pro Rosc. Am. 39, 112 and 114 ('infamia' opposed to 'honestas').

'ita quidem judicio est absolutus Catilina, ut Clodius infamis fuerit praevaricatus esse: nam et rejectio judicum ad arbitrium rei videbatur esse facta[1].' Now we know from more than one source that *praevaricatio*, if proved, was followed by disqualifications both in public and private law: but he would be a bold commentator who would positively assert that *infamis* in this passage is used of the effect of legal disability and not of moral censure. Even in an official document it is by no means always certain where *infamia* is used in a juristic sense. In the 'oratio' which M. Antoninus sent to the senate on the suppression of the conspiracy of Avidius Cassius the following words occur[2]: 'Ego vero a vobis peto, ut conscios senatorii ordinis et equestris a caede, a proscriptione, a timore, *ab infamia*, ab invidia . . . vindicetis;' *infamia* may here mean 'ill-repute' simply, or it may have the later technical sense of exclusion from service to the State, which, by the time of the Antonines, was becoming more definitely attached to the word. Mommsen probably goes too far when he asserts that *infamis* was in the time of the Republic neither a legal expression nor a legal conception[3], although he is no doubt correct in the assertion that the conception was variable, and not restricted to the special signification given it by Savigny and others. It was, probably, partly a juristic conception during the Republic: one of those that have become narrowed during the course of history,

[1] Ascon. in or. in tog. cand. p. 113.

[2] Vit. Avid. Cass. 12.

[3] Mommsen (Staatsr. i. p. 496, n. 2) says, with special reference to the question he is treating, i. e. qualification for office, 'Die Bezeichnung *infamis* wird meines Wissens in republikanischer Zeit nie auf den als bescholten von der Wahl ausgeschlossenen Bürger angewandt: freilich aber wüsste ich auch keinen anderen technischen Ausdruck anzugeben, der die rechtliche Stellung zum Beispiel von Cicero's Clienten P. Sulla ausdrückte—vielmehr ist *infamis*, wie unser ehrlos, zunächst weder ein Rechtsausdruck noch ein Rechtsbegriff, sondern ein Ausdruck der gewöhnlichen Rede und darum von schwankender Begrenzung.'

and which are unfortunately far better known to us in their later than in their earlier stages.

The chief justification for the extended use of the term must, however, be derived from a criticism of those who hold that it bore, throughout the greater part of its early history and chiefly in Republican times, a narrow and special meaning. Most modern views of *infamia* have been derived from the treatment of it by Savigny in his 'System des Römischen Rechts' (§§ 76 sq.). His conclusions in that work are briefly as follows. After reviewing the causes of *infamia*, as they are expressed in the document from which they are best known to us, the praetor's Edict as given in the Digest, and after noticing that the object of the praetor's infamy is clearly shown, i. e. that it is merely a means of regulating procedure *dignitatis tuendae causa*, he raises the question, 'Did the praetor create this infamy?' He answers this question in the negative, and holds that the praetor 'presupposes the idea of infamy to be an old recognized legal notion, the limits of whose application were not by any means doubtful to him.' He considers that that application belonged essentially to public law: that the notion of infamy consisted in the loss of all political rights in regard to a subsisting citizenship. The *infamis* became an *aerarius* and lost the *suffragium et honores.* The definition of such a person was as follows: 'That Roman is called *infamis*, who in consequence of a general rule (not of censorian caprice), in regard to a subsisting citizenship, has lost the political rights belonging thereto.' His view of the final history of the conception is that 'this signification of infamy lost its importance under the Emperors, as the political rights of citizenship fell into the background. From this period, then, infamy only remained visible in secondary effects; and this accounts for the obscure form in which it appears in our law sources.' But, perhaps, the most remarkable point in his conclusion is that this disqualification, while in the height of its political vigour, 'operated immutably through life.' *Infamia*, according to Savigny, is a perpetual disqualification from all public rights, regulated according to general rules.

This theory involves three main contentions, the evidence for which must be examined in some detail. They are, firstly, that there was a sharp and definite conception of *infamia*; secondly, that *infamia* was consciously distinguished from the *censoria notatio*, the only procedure which, so far as we know, dealt extensively with political rights during the Republic, in enjoining a definite exclusion from *dignitates* and the *suffragium*; and thirdly, that the disqualification entailed by *infamia* was permanent. The two latter contentions are to some extent identical, since we know that the *censoria notatio* might be, and perhaps in most cases was, merely temporary in its effects; they may, therefore, be discussed together.

As regards the first point, it is remarkable that this definite and terrible disqualification left so few traces in Roman law that there is hardly a passage which can be interpreted as a distinct reference to it in the writings of the classical jurists; but, even from these few traces left by the legal writers, the kind of definiteness demanded by Savigny's theory (i.e. definite exclusion from public rights) is by no means proved. In Dig. xlviii. 7 (*ad legem Juliam de vi privata*) we find the following words of Marcian used with reference to those *de vi privata damnati*: 'Cautum est, ne senator sit, ne decurio, aut ullum honorem capiat, neve in eum ordinem sedeat, neve judex sit: *et videlicet omni honore quasi infamis ex senatus consulto carebit*.' It is possible that the last line adds no new penalty, but simply sums up the consequences enumerated just before;

even, however, if we suppose the *senatus consultum* to have increased the penalty, *quasi infamis* is only added to show the ground of the disqualification: the words are equivalent to 'on account of the *minutio existimationis* involved in condemnation.' A passage of Modestinus at the end of the same title (§ 8) seems to furnish a better instance of definiteness. It runs, 'Si creditor sine auctoritate judicis res debitoris occupet, hac lege tenetur et tertia parte bonorum multatur *et infamis fit*.' Here the last words do seem to extend a principle to a new case: but the principle so extended is simply the *infamia of the law*, or of its *interpretation* by the *senatus consultum*; and we cannot argue from the *infamia* following condemnation in a single *judicium publicum* to the conception generally. For it will be shown later on that the kinds of disqualification created by various criminal laws differed from one another. Consequently, so far as these passages are concerned, we need not admit the recognition of a definite *infamia* debarring from all *honores* even for the time of the classical jurists.

The proof of the second contention—that *infamia* differed from the *censoria notatio*, and excluded from all public rights, rests on passages which certainly do contrast the arbitrary discretionary power of the censors, in the usual exercise of their functions, with certain principles which entailed a more definite, perhaps a more permanent, disqualification. But nowhere in these passages is the term *infamia* applied to the latter form of disability and denied to the former. The reasons which led Savigny to restrict the term to the one class of cases were: that in the Digest we find that the praetorian *infamia* is an immediate effect of certain causes; and that some of these causes are mentioned in Republican literature as producing consequences more serious than the ordinary *ignominia* of the censors. Therefore, it was argued, the individuals so affected must have been called *infames*, and distinguished from those who were merely *notati*. This is an unconvincing argument with respect to the history of a term so vague as that of *infamia*, and proves nothing as to its early usage.

The more important question, however, is one that is not concerned with a mere name but with the procedure. Was there, in fact, a system running parallel with the censorship, which entailed more definite and permanent disabilities than were entailed by that office itself? Savigny and the writers who follow him answer the question in the affirmative: admitting, however, that the censorship was the only medium through which both kinds of disqualification were effected, but thinking that in the one case the magistrate was bound by fixed principles, in the other exercised his own discretion. That this distinction is drawn for us by our authorities there can be no manner of doubt; it is only on the question of *interpretation* that we venture to differ from Savigny. The view that will be here maintained is that these fixed principles of disqualification, so far from being imposed on the magistrate from without, were created by him, at least in the main. We know that there were certain laws at Rome which enjoined disqualification for certain offices; these, no doubt, the magistrate was bound to respect. But the historical evidence is, on the whole, in favour of the view that the permanent categories which we find in the *Lex Julia Municipalis* and in the Digest were themselves the creation of magisterial authority, that the rules observed by the censors were to some extent tralaticiary, like the rules observed by the praetor in his edict: but that, in consequence of the mode in which these rules were created, any magistrate might violate them without entailing on himself the consequences of the law. It is merely this distinction between a principle that should be observed, and one that might be neglected, by each succeeding censor that is drawn for us by Cicero in his speech 'pro Cluentio' (42, 119). He is arguing that, if the *censoria auctoritas* be a true *judicium*, then its consequences should be permanent, and 'therefore,' he says, 'ut ceteri, *turpi judicio damnati, in perpetuum omni honore ac dignitate privantur*, sic hominibus ignominia notatis neque ad honorem aditus neque in curiam reditus esset.' The particular instance given here of a *turpe judicium* is *furtum*. It was, therefore, improper for the consul or other presiding official to admit a man condemned for *furtum* to the magistracy, perhaps for the censor to admit him to the Senate. But that the former admission at least was not impossible we know from an actual historical instance, drawn from Cicero's own writings. In the speech 'In toga candida' he taunted a certain Mucius with having 'compromised' (*pactus, depectus*) in an *actio furti*—a proceeding which the Roman law regarded as equivalent to condemnation. This Mucius whom he addressed was at that time tribune of the Plebs[1]. The notion of exclusion

[1] Ascon. in or. in tog. cand. p. 112 'Q. enim Mucius tr. pl. intercedebat—hunc Mucium in hac oratione Cicero appellans sic ait—"cum tecum furti L. Calenus ageret, me potissimum fortunarum tuarum patronum esse voluisti—nisi forte hoc dicturus es, quo tempore cum L. Caleno *furti depectus sis*, eo tempore in me tibi parum esse auxilii vidisse."' That the conception of *pactio* as equivalent to condemnation was an early principle in Roman law is shown by the *Lex Jul. Munic.* l. 110 'quei furtei quod ipse fecit fecerit condemnatus pactusve est erit.' Cf. Dig. iii. 2 (*de his qui not. inf.*) 'qui furti, vi bonorum raptorum, injuriarum, de dolo malo et fraude suo nomine damnatus pactusve erit.' The principle itself is explained by Paulus (Dig. iii. 2, 5), 'quoniam intellegitur confiteri crimen qui paciscitur.' The only manner in which the case of Mucius could be regarded as exceptional would be on the principle mentioned by Ulpian (l. c. § 6) 'qui jussu praetoris pretio dato pactus est, non notatur.' But the words of Cicero sufficiently show that this was not the case.

as based on a *turpe judicium* must, therefore, have been a principle created by the magistrates and capable of being neglected by them[1]. Perhaps one of the earliest codifications and legalisations of this, as of other, principles of disqualification is that which we find contained in the *Lex Julia Municipalis*, by which these principles were extended to municipal offices. In this law, and in the praetor's Edict, we find other private delicts[2] producing *infamia* of different kinds; but it cannot be shown that any of these delicts *ipso jure* produced disqualification for office; still less could they have necessarily involved the loss of the *suffragium*.

If we pass from these private delicts to the next category given in these two documents we find that *infamia* followed condemnation consequent on certain obligatory relations[3], such as *fiducia*, *pro socio*, *tutela*, *mandatum*. It has been consequently argued that condemnation in these produced disqualification for the *honores* and the *suffragium*. That some serious breach of *existimatio* did follow condemnation in these actions we learn from Cicero, who tells us (pro Rosc. Com. 6, 16) that 'si qua enim sunt privata judicia *summae existimationis et paene dicam capitis*, tria haec sunt, fiduciae, tutelae, societatis,' the reason being the peculiar moral turpitude involved in such breaches of faith: 'aeque enim perfidiosum et nefarium est fidem frangere, quae continet vitam, et pupillum fraudare, qui in tutelam pervenit, et socium fallere, qui se in negotio conjunxit'; and *mandatum* he describes as a *turpissimum*

[1] In the case mentioned by Cicero (pro Cluent. 42, 120 'quos . . . censores furti et captarum pecuniarum notaverunt') the *notatio* preceded the *judicium* and was naturally of less weight than one based on a verdict.

[2] In the Lex Jul. Munic. *furtum*, *injuriae* and *dolus malus*; the Edict adds *vi bona rapta*.

[3] *Fiduciae* (in Edict *depositi*), *pro socio*, *tutelae*, *mandati*.

judicium[1], one in which condemnation involves the loss of *honestas omnis.* Yet, if we try to discover what the loss of this *existimatio* involved, we shall find it very difficult to do so. He actually speaks, for instance, of Roscius the actor, who, according to Savigny's theory, was *ipso jure* deprived of all political rights, as being in danger of losing *bona existimatio* in an action *pro socio*[2]. In the speech pro Quinctio he speaks of a writ of *bonorum possessio* as a *causa capitis*[3], one which, if we take his language strictly, must have excluded from all political rights[4]. That this was most certainly not the necessary consequence of a writ of *bonorum possessio* we know from the case of an individual with whom Cicero himself was brought into very close contact. Antonius, his competitor and eventually his colleague in the consulship, had been excluded from the Senate by the censors on the ground, amongst others which they mentioned, that his goods were *proscripta.* Yet he was afterwards restored to that body, and finally raised to the highest magistracy in the State[5].

[1] Cic. pro Rosc. Amer. 39. 113, 114.

[2] Pro Rosc. Com. 5, 15.

[3] On this language see above, p. 7, and cf. Modestinus (in Dig. l. 16, 103) 'licet "capitalis" latine loquentibus omnis causa existimationis videatur, tamen appellatio capitalis mortis vel amissionis civitatis intellegenda est.' In this particular speech pro Quinctio Cicero's abuse of legal phraseology is directed by the argument to which he wishes to lead up. This argument is contained in the words (9, 33) 'judicium esse, C. Aquili, non de re pecuniaria, sed de fama fortunisque P. Quinctii vides. Quum majores ita constituerint, *ut, qui pro capite diceret, is posteriore loco diceret:* nos, inaudita criminatione accusatorum, priore loco causam dicere intelligis.' This argument, eminently applicable to a criminal cause in which *caput* was involved, does not in the least hold good for a case in which an individual has to show cause why a writ, the consequence of which involved some loss of *existimatio,* should not be made absolute.

[4] Pro Quinct. 13, 42 'quid igitur pugnas? an, quod saepe multis in locis dixisti, ne in civitate sit, ne locum suum, quem adhuc honestissime defendit, obtineat? ne numeretur inter vivos? decernat de vita et ornamentis suis omnibus?'

[5] Q. Cicero, De pet. cons. 8 'eorum alterius (sc. Antonii) bona proscripta

The solution of the riddle is that these cases involved no definite *infamia*, but might be used by the magistrates as a ground of exclusion from public functions. Where disqualifications were imposed by law at Rome they seem to have been invariably of the nature of appendices to special *leges*[1]. We should, therefore, expect to find them an ingredient in the criminal law which grew up in the last century of the Republic, and to some extent appended as a sanction to administrative law. We should not look for them as a legally recognised element in the civil law: and the instances that have been cited show that this expectation is verified.

But, when we turn to the criminal legislation of Rome, we find that there is ample evidence for a legal control over the powers both of the presiding magistrate and of the censor. The disqualification pronounced by a criminal law, and which followed condemnation in a criminal trial, was one that affected *existimatio*, and therefore produced *infamia:* and this *infamia* was one which the magistrate was bound to see executed. When, however, we consider the character of the *judicia publica* or *quaestiones perpetuae* of Rome, we are not surprised to find that this disqualification was not of a uniform character. The criminal courts at Rome were of a gradual growth: and one of their most distinctive marks was that each court (*quaestio*) depended on a special *lex*[2], which defined the

vidimus.' Ascon. in or. in tog. cand. p. 111 'hinc Antonium Gellius et Lentulus censores . . . senatu moverunt causasque subscripserunt, quod socios diripuerit, quod judicium recusarit, quod propter aeris alieni magnitudinem praedia mancipārit bonaque sua in potestate non habeat.' Cicero's word *proscripta* seems to show that bankruptcy proceedings are meant.

[1] Such laws are those spoken of by Cicero (pro Cluent. 43, 120) 'quibus exceptum est, de quibus causis aut magistratum capere non liceat aut judicem legi aut alterum accusare.'

[2] Cic. pro Cluent. 35, 97: Phil. i. 9, 23; Lex Acilia Repetundarum, l. 17;

offence, the procedure, the punishment, and the disqualification (presuming that one was attached) which should follow condemnation. Thus we are told that the *Lex Cornelia de Ambitu* enacted that those condemned under that law should not be candidates for office for ten years, and that this was followed in 67 B.C. by a *Lex Calpurnia* dealing with the same offence, which enacted that the condemned should be excluded perpetually from all offices and from the Senate[1]. It is doubtful, however, whether either of these disqualifications is a quite fair instance of the later relation in which *infamia* stood to criminal condemnation; they are described by our authority as the *poena*; one was the whole, the other a part of the penalty, rather than a consequence following on condemnation. This seems to have been the essence of the early disqualifications accompanying criminal laws; they were in every case part of the penalty. The *Lex Julia Repetundarum*, besides ordaining exclusion from the Senate, seems to have enacted that any one condemned for an offence under this law should be incapable of being a *judex* or even of giving evidence in a court of law[2]. A very far-reaching, but probably late, extension of the principle of disqualification is found in the attachment to the *Lex Julia de vi privata* of exclusion from all office, from the Senate and from the bench of *judices*. This was effected by a *senatus consultum*, and the person so

Dig. xlviii. 1, 1 'non omnia judicia, in quibus crimen vertitur, et publica sunt, sed ea tantum, quae ex legibus judiciorum publicorum veniunt.'

[1] Schol. Bob. in Cic. pro Sulla, 5, 17, p. 361 Orell. '(ambitus) damnati lege Cornelia hoc genus poenae ferebant, ut magistratuum petitione per decem annos abstinerent. Aliquanto postea severior lex Calpurnia et pecunia multavit et in perpetuum honoribus carere jussit damnatos.' For exclusion from the Senate, Dio Cass. xxvi. 21.

[2] Dig. i. 9, 2 'judicare vel testimonium dicere.' That it excluded from the Senate may be gathered from a comparison of this passage with Suet. Caes. 43.

disqualified is said to be excluded from these privileges *quasi infamis*[1]. Criminal laws which contained such sanctions no doubt agreed in excluding from the magistracy and from the Senate. When minor disqualifications alone are mentioned we must probably apply the later legal principle given by Pomponius, that 'qui indignus est inferiore ordine, indignior est superiore'. This principle, reasonable in itself, was recognised in the *municipia* of the Empire, and municipal law is often but a reflection of that of the Republic[2].

Hitherto we have been dealing with the later period of criminal legislation at Rome; but, even before the complete growth of the *quaestiones*, and their replacement of the old criminal procedure of the *judicia populi*, we find a striking instance of the general application of the principle of disqualification. In the year 104 B.C. we are told that a *lex Cassia* was passed which limited to a considerable extent the discretionary power of the censor; for it enacted that 'quem populus damnasset cuive imperium abrogasset in senatu non esset[3]." It is a striking proof of the chaotic nature of the Roman *infamia*, so far as it depended on legislation, that the most sweeping measure of the kind was connected with the *judicia populi* which were rapidly becoming obsolete, and that, so far as we

[1] See p. 22.

[2] Pomponius in Dig. i. 9, 4. For municipal offices, Dig. xlviii. 22, 7, 22 'si cui honore uno interdictum sit, non tantum eum honorem petere non possit, verum ne eos quoque, qui eo honore majores sunt'; but on the other hand interdiction from *honores* did not necessarily imply interdiction from *ordo*, Dig. xlviii. 22, 7, 20 and 21; cf. Dig. l. 2, 2.

[3] Ascon. in Cornel. p. 78. Mommsen (Staatsr. i. p. 492, n. 1) argues that, although disqualification for the Senate alone is mentioned, yet the law must have implied exclusion from office, since the two were so closely connected. This is probably correct (see last note); but it is obvious that, if this was the case, the implication was not contained in the law itself. Only the more striking provision has been preserved by our authority.

know, only a few of the *judicia publica* contained clauses of a similar kind.

At the same time we do meet with traces of a class of laws which recognised a disqualification, based on condemnation, which was a nearer approach to the later *infamia.* In the *Lex Acilia Repetundarum* of 122 we find it enacted that the praetor is not to assign as *judex* in this court, or as a *patronus* to the prosecutor under this law, one who has been condemned in a certain kind of *judicium publicum*[1]; but this is only disqualification from certain causes and for a special purpose. Documentary evidence is, on the whole, in favour of the conclusion that criminal condemnation did not disqualify from office at the end of the Republic. In the *Lex Julia Municipalis* only condemnation involving *exsilium* is mentioned; in the praetor's Edict (a reflex, as we shall see, of the censor's rulings) only condemnation involving loss of *caput* produces the praetorian *infamia.*

But gradual legal interpretation (an instance of which is given us in the clause appended by a *senatus consultum* to the *Lex Julia de vi privata*) tended to establish the principle that *infamia* should follow condemnation for criminal offences; that it was finally established we know from the words of Macer in the Digest (xlviii. 1, 7), 'Infamem non ex omni crimine sententia facit, sed ex eo, quod judicii publici causam habuit. Itaque ex eo crimine, quod judicii publici non fuit, damnatum infamia non sequetur, nisi id crimen ex ea actione fuit, quae etiam in

[1] Lex Acilia Rep. l. 111 'queive quaestione joudicioque publico condemnatus sit, quod circa eum in senatum legei non liceat.' The words 'quod circa,' &c. imply that only certain *judicia publica* necessitated exclusion from the Senate. As a fact, however, only three *judicia publica* appear to be known previously to this date: that *repetundarum* (of which this law is a re-enactment), a *quaestio de sicariis* (Cic. de Fin. ii. 16, 54) and possibly a *quaestio de ambitu* (Plut. Mar. 5).

privato judicio infamiam condemnato importat, veluti furti, vi bonorum raptorum, injuriarum.' When it was finally established it was, although the completion of a process, little more than a juristic survival. Codification had led to the association of the disqualifications pronounced by criminal law with those attendant on civil actions, which, as we have seen, were not originally regulated by law. But this codification was effected earliest, for Rome itself, by the praetor's Edict, which had no reference to exclusion from state functions—the primary object of *infamia*—but only to a limitation in civil procedure. It is no doubt this praetorian *infamia*, with its minor disabilities, which Macer has, at least chiefly, before his eyes. It is true that the cases specified in the edict came again to involve disqualification for political offices, and there are not lacking indications that this principle was gaining recognition as early as Hadrian and his immediate successors; but exclusion from functions of state is neither mentioned nor assumed as a necessary consequence of *infamia* of any kind in the writings of the classical jurists; the very fact that they mention the disqualifications created by special laws shows the absence of any such general consequence attending criminal condemnation at least. But a definite and uniform conception of *infamia*, developed from that of the praetor's Edict, was being reached; and by a rescript of Constantine this *infamia* is made a ground of exclusion from all offices and honours[1]. There must, however, have been a considerable interval between the extension of the

[1] The most universal rule is that of Constantine (Cod. 12. 1, 2), 'neque famosis et notatis, et quos scelus aut vitae turpitudo inquinat, et quos infamia ab honestorum coetu segregat, dignitatis portae patebunt.' Earlier and more partial constitutions are found in Cod. x. 32 (31), 8 (Valerianus) Cod. x. 59 (57) (Diocletianus and Maximianus). In another part of the work we shall trace the growth of this change further back still—to the time of Hadrian and the Antonines.

praetorian *infamia* to criminal condemnation and the recognition of the principle that exclusion from *dignitates* was a necessary consequence of this stigma.

It is obvious, from the foregoing review, that the criminal law of Rome knew of no one perpetual disqualification attendant on a *minutio existimationis* brought about by conviction. Above all, loss of the most distinctive political right of citizenship—the *suffragium*—is never mentioned in these cases. Sometimes these laws disqualify from *honores* and from the Senate, sometimes from the *album judicum*, sometimes they go so far as to inhibit the evidence of the condemned; but nowhere are the disabilities uniform, and nowhere do they imply the loss of all political privileges. It was the same with ordinary laws; although some Roman statutes included loss of *dignitas* amongst the penalties mentioned in their sanction[1], it is quite possible that we have in such cases the exception rather than the rule: and there is no evidence that the disqualifications pronounced in these sanctions showed any more uniformity than those of the criminal law.

We may now pass on to the cases in which all political privileges seem to be destroyed in consequence of *infamia*. The most extreme disqualification known to us in Roman public law was in most cases due wholly to the exercise of his power by the censor, and seems seldom to have been recognised by a law which controlled his authority. Nowhere do we find more strongly marked at once the power of this magistrate and the mode in which this power was controlled by precedents, which developed into rules, than in

[1] See the *Lex Agraria* (of 111 B.C.) l. 41 'neve ei ob eam rem magistratum quem minus petere capere gerere habereque liceto'; and the long list of disabilities appended to the fragment known as the *Lex Latina Tabulae Bantinae*.

the practice of 'excluding from the tribe.' It was in the power of the censor, if he saw sufficient cause, to remove an individual from the tribe, or to 'relegate him to the *aerarii*,' expressions the full meaning of which will be investigated in the next chapter, but which, when used in their strict and original sense, meant to deprive an individual, so censured, of his vote. Sometimes this procedure was arbitrary, and, when so employed, the censure was so grave as naturally to arouse a protest against the employment of such a power by a magistrate on his own discretion[1]. But in other cases this discretionary power disappeared before the unwritten rules of his office, which had been sustained for centuries. In some cases it was felt incumbent invariably to exercise this power of exclusion from the franchise. We find the principle recognised in the case of the profession of an actor. As we have already seen the exercise of any profession disqualified for a magistracy, and justified the presiding magistrate in refusing to accept the name of the individual associated with it. This disability, like the similar ordinance which forbade trade to senators[2], only affected *existimatio* to a limited extent: but it was otherwise with what was considered a positively disgraceful profession such as that of a *scenicus*. Tertullian tells us[3] 'quadrigarios scenicos manifeste damnant ignominia et capitis deminutione, arcentes curia, rostris, senatu equite ceterisque honoribus;' and Augustine[4], quoting Cicero, 'cum artem ludicram scenamque totam probro duxerunt, genus id hominum non modo honore civium reliquorum carere, sed etiam tribu moveri notatione censoria voluerunt': a passage, the

[1] Liv. xiv. 15.

[2] A principle perhaps recognised rather than established by a *Lex Claudia* of 218 B.C.

[3] De spect. 22.

[4] De civ. dei, ii. 13.

technical terminology of which (as exemplified by the words *probrum*, *tribu moveri*, *notatio censoria*) shows that this exclusion was due wholly to the tralaticiary rules of their office established by the college of censors[1]. This is also implied in the language of Livy[2], where he accounts for the fact that the religious acting brotherhood of the *Atellani*, established to check the plague of 364 B.C., was not subject to these severe political disabilities. He says 'eo *institutum manet*, ut actores Atellanarum nec tribu moveantur, et stipendia, tamquam expertes artis ludicrae, faciant.' This conception of the *ars ludicra* as involving disgrace was naturally taken up, together with the others, when various necessities dictated the attempt to codify the idea of *infamia*. It appears in the *Lex Julia Municipalis* and in the praetor's Edict. But the chief point which we must notice here is that where the content of *infamia* is at its widest, where it means—what some would have it always mean—exclusion from all political rights, there its application is at its narrowest. It applies, so far as we know, chiefly to the case of one profession which was considered disgraceful, and to the very exceptional instances in which censors chose to exercise their power of producing a complete suspension of all public rights, which might be reversed by their successors in office.

This review is unfavourable to the belief that a definite and uniform conception of *infamia* existed in the Republic or even in the Principate. A summary of results may best

[1] This principle is not contradicted by the case of Laberius described by Macrobius (Sat. ii. 7, 3). He claims to have lost his position as an *eques* the moment he appeared as a mime; and so firmly was the principle established that the censor never admitted such to active citizenship that there was some justification in the claim. But, had the incident occurred in the Republic, Laberius might no doubt have retained his position both as an *eques* and as a voting citizen until the next census.

[2] vii. 2.

be made by referring again to the sketch which has been given in the first chapter (p. 14) of the various ways in which *infamia* might be pronounced. More definite answers can now be given to the questions stated there. Of the special kinds of *infamia* we see that—

(i) One was pronounced by the presiding magistrate who had the right of admitting to *honores*, and who might refuse to nominate unworthy candidates; or by an official who had the control of the *ordines*, and might degrade members from the ranks. Exclusions of this kind were based, chiefly towards the end of the Republic, on a minimum of statute-law; but the evidence is very strongly in favour of their having been based most largely on customary law, created by the magistrates and sanctioned by the tacit consent of the community.

(ii) Another *infamia* was pronounced by the praetor, with reference to a narrow object of his own, the control of his court. By a strange accident of history, due to the early codification of the praetor's Edict, this became *the infamia* of later Roman law. It came eventually to have a political signification attached to it, justified by its character (for the grounds of the praetorian *infamia* were borrowed from those of exclusion from political rights), but quite disproportionate to its original object, and as the ground of deprivation of civil rights has influenced modern systems of law.

(iii) Very many different degrees of *infamia* were established by the criminal legislation of Rome, and to some extent by administrative law. But the gradual growth of this legal *infamia* may be tested by the fact that it took some centuries of interpretation to evolve even the simple principle that criminal condemnation in a *judicium publicum* produced disqualification for the exercise of public rights. How from these various conceptions one ruling idea of *infamia* developed, it will be the main object of this work to show. The scattered threads can only be collected when we have dealt with the *infamia* of the praetor's court, which became the dominant legal form of this disability.

Now that we have reviewed the chief modes in which *infamia* operated during the greater period of its growth, we are in a position to judge how very ill-defined this institution was both in its causes and in its consequences, and how impossible it is to gain any clear conception of it apart from an examination of the specific modes of its exercise. When we know it at the latest stages of its development it was an institution regulated according to certain rules, but the formation of these rules was the work of centuries; and hence a definition applicable to the conception at every stage of its history must be so general as to be almost valueless. From this general point of view we may perhaps repeat the definition which we have given elsewhere and say that the Roman *infamia* was 'a moral censure pronounced by a competent authority in the State on individual members of the community, as a result of certain actions which they had committed, or certain modes of life which they had pursued, this censure involving disqualification for certain rights both in public and in private law [1].'

But ill-defined as the actual working of the institution may be, its general relation to the personal rights of the individual is sufficiently clear. *Existimatio*, or the moral approbation of the State, which was one of the grounds on which the full exercise of personal rights was based, is a conception applicable only to the individual, and has reference only to the capacities he may be possessed of during his lifetime. Hence the *minutio* of it does not

[1] Art. *Infamia* in Smith's Dictionary of Greek and Roman Antiquities (3rd edition).

extend beyond the lifetime of the individual, and *infamia* is not hereditary; it does not destroy *status*, and therefore cannot be perpetuated[1]. Again the instances already cited are sufficient to show the truth of Savigny's remark, that *infamia* always follows as the result of a personal act. *Infamia* always involves the idea of personal responsibility, and thus, from a moral standpoint, rises far above the mere conception of *status*. The law, it is true, makes little distinction between the degrees of individual responsibility; as in Aristotle's conception of distributive justice, the end in view is too great a one to make it possible to scrutinise closely the moral claims of the individual. The State deprives the man who chooses to remain an actor of his vote, it debars the auctioneer and the undertaker from municipal magistracies; it may sometimes omit to impose such severe disqualifications on a man guilty of crime or breach of faith. But, although the degrees of moral censure are not perfect, and indeed cannot be, when we are dealing with the interests of the State, yet the idea of responsibility is apparent throughout. It is clear also that the personal act which produces *infamia* may do so in two ways; it may lead to it either directly or indirectly; to quote again Savigny's admirable analysis of the conception, *infamia* depends either on a judicial sentence or on an extra-judicial matter of fact; it is, to use the technical terms invented by modern commentators which do not appear in our ancient texts, either mediate or immediate: mediate when it follows on a judicial sentence, immediate when it is the consequence of a matter of fact. This distinction is not of sufficient importance to make it an adequate *fundamentum divisionis* for the discussion of the whole of the subject: but it will be found

[1] This was the principle of the early *infamia*; we shall find one instance in which it was modified during the Empire, p. 149.

a convenient basis for classifying the actual grounds of *infamia*, as they are known to us in their fullest extent.

In connection with this distinction, however, and with the general estimate of *infamia* discussed in this chapter it will be convenient to mention the conditions laid down by the classical jurists and recognised by the legislation of the emperors, which were requisite to enable *infamia* to take effect. With respect to immediate *infamia* nothing is said, because no further definition was needed to complete the conception. It depended simply on a matter of fact, and to make this *infamia* effective, nothing more was needed than sufficient evidence of the fact before the magistrate who admitted to office or before the praetor. With respect to mediate *infamia* the case was rather different. It was the result of a sentence: and what was meant by a sentence had to be clearly defined by the jurists. The first condition laid down is that the author of the sentence must be a judge. The decision of an *arbiter* did not produce *infamia*[1]. Secondly, the decision of the judge must be pronounced as the result of a trial (*causa cognita*). A mere remark or interlocution introduced by a judge during the course of a trial did not have the same effect. Thus *calumnia*, if proved after a trial, produced *infamia*, but if the judge turned to one of the parties during an action and intimated that he was guilty of *calumnia*, no results followed this statement of belief[2]. Equally ineffective was the expression of opinion on the part of a judge that the evidence to which he was listening was false[3].

[1] Ulpian in Dig. iii. 2, 13, 5.

[2] Ulpian in Dig. iii. 2, 13, 6; Cod. iii. 11 (12) 17 (Gordian A. D. 242): 'etenim cum non causa cognita dictum est συκοφαντεῖς (i. e. *calumniaris*), sed ad postulatum patroni interlocutione judicis responsum sit, nequaquam hoc infamiam inrogat.'

[3] Paulus in Dig. iii. 2, 21.

Again, a sentence in a criminal court was invariably followed by some form of punishment. But *infamia* is always the result of a sentence, never of any particular form of punishment. A punishment in itself disgraceful, such as scourging, does no injury to *existimatio*[1]. We shall see the peculiar importance of this principle when we come to discuss the modes by which *infamia* was extinguished, and the curious relation which was established, in the procedure of the Empire, between a sentence and a punishment, when it was thought fit to reestablish a man in the full possession of his civil honour.

[1] Marcellus in Dig. iii. 2, 22: 'ictus fustium infamiam non importat, sed causa propter quam id pati meruit, si ea fuit, quae infamiam damnato inrogat. In ceteris quoque generibus poenarum eadem forma statuta est.' Cf. Cod. ii. 11 (12), 1 and 14.

CHAPTER III.

THE CENSORIAN INFAMIA AND ITS DEVELOPMENTS.

§ 1. *General characteristics of the censorian infamia.*

In the year 443 B.C. a magistracy was established in Rome, which was 'a small thing in its origin, but grew so great that it came to hold in its hands the guidance of the manners and of the training of Rome[1].' The primary duty of this new magistracy, the censorship, was that of numbering the people—one that had originally belonged to the supreme magistrate, the consul: but which, like the financial business of the State, was gradually felt to be incompatible with the exercise of the active functions of that office. The duties of the censor, though apparently multifarious, really spring from a common source. With the registration of citizens was intimately connected the assignment of the pecuniary burdens which the State imposed on individuals; hence the connection of the censor with Finance. With registration was still more intimately connected the consideration of the moral worth of the individual citizen, as a guarantee of the proper exercise of even the most subordinate public duties: hence the censorian 'rule of manners' (*regimen morum*). So closely were the three functions associated that we shall see how the censors sometimes employed the powers given them by the control of taxation

[1] Liv. iv. 8.

as a means of emphasizing their disapprobation of a moral offence.

The separation of these duties from the consulship and their attachment to the new office must have had a very important influence on the history of the Roman infamia. The idea itself, of a rejection of individual citizens from service to the State based on moral grounds, cannot have been a new one. It must have been as closely associated with the consular registration of the mass of citizens as it was without doubt one of the grounds on which the consuls exercised their right of selecting or rejecting the members of their own peculiar advising body—the Senate. But, just as the rules for selecting senators became for the first time definite and formulated when this duty was transferred to the censors, so the principles which regulated the infamia must have become more precise, when they were in the hands of a magistrate, of whom they were felt to be not only the special but the chief function. To the average consciousness the significance of the censorship as a means of moral control completely overshadowed the other attributes of that office. There came a time in the history of the Republic, during the period succeeding Sulla's reform of the constitution, when it seemed possible to dispense with all the duties of registration connected with this office. The abolition of the *tributum* had taken away their powers of taxation; the centuries of Roman knights, which they were in the habit of revising, had almost ceased to exist as a distinct body: and the Senate was filled up by a fixed and self-working principle of admission. Yet the cry for the *censorium nomen* was raised; but raised only as a demand for an authority which could punish outrages on justice, with which at times the criminal law could or would not deal[1]. This was the only pretext

[1] Cic. Div. 3. 8 'judicum culpa atque dedecore etiam censorium nomen,

for its restoration during the closing years of the Republic, and one sufficient to quicken it into occasional life, as long as there was a real meaning in the institution. When the rule of the free burgesses at last gave place to the administration, under imperial guidance, of the twin bureaucracies of the senatorial and equestrian orders, this department of the office still survived, sometimes under the same, sometimes under other names, for the purpose of preserving the purity of the lists of these two governing classes.

It would on *a priori* grounds be inconceivable that an institution which had such a history as this, and in which the procedure was so uniform and so invariably directed to the same issues, should not have developed a code of its own, setting forth both the grounds and the consequences of disqualification with some adherence to a logical classification. Even documentary precedents were at hand on which successive censors could model their judgments. We shall see that the censors were in the habit of issuing edicts, and each succeeding holder of the office had at least before him his predecessor's list of names, under which were written the grounds of disqualification. We may elicit from Cicero, an unwilling witness, the fact that succeeding censors had begun to give a permanent character to decisions pronounced by those who had previously held office. But we cannot help a feeling of disappointment

quod asperius antea populo videri solebat, id nunc poscitur, id jam populare atque plausibile factum est.' The senatorial *judices* were criminally liable for judicial corruption: the *equites* were exempt by a clause of a law of C. Gracchus which was constantly upheld (Cic. pro Cluent. 55, 154: ad Att. ii. 1, 8). The law of C. Gracchus seems even to have limited the power of the censors to take cognisance of this offence (Lex Acil. Rep. l. 28). Cicero's remark in the passage quoted is justified by the fact that the censors often took it on themselves to degrade for offences which had not been proved in a court of law. Cf. Cic. pro Cluent. 42, 120.

when we turn to the specific instances of censorian severity with which our authorities have furnished us. It is true that to a large extent they do bear out our expectations, for they often show us constantly recurring acts punished in a constantly recurring manner. What we have really to guard against is the supposition that we have here anything like the true relative proportions of the moral offences they visited, or anything approaching an exhaustive catalogue of such offences.

Mommsen has well remarked that our authorities possibly present us with more exceptions than rules. A historian like Livy, who loves to chronicle exciting incidents, tells us of a censor who disfranchised almost the whole Roman community for an alleged abuse of its power of voting; but he would form a strange impression of the censorship who imagined that it often proceeded on the lines of such official insanity. *Raconteurs* and scholars like Plutarch and Gellius single out, as we should expect, only the strangest and most amusing instances from the mass before them—perhaps in some cases they were the only ones that had survived. And meanwhile all forget to mention cases, which must inevitably have occurred at every census, but which were too ordinary to attract attention. We may anticipate for a moment and take as a case in point one of the simplest and most obvious duties known to the Roman, and enjoined no doubt by the pontifical law of Rome—that of mourning for the dead. A violation of this mourning, in a modified form, is visited with infamia by the praetor's Edict, as known to us in the Digest; a violation of it in the extreme form which it assumed in the Republic, must *a fortiori* have often been visited by the guardian of morality and religion: yet no instance appears in our authorities. Such simple instances have naturally given place to the more exciting stories of Roman knights who were struck from the list for making witty but indiscreet remarks to the presiding magistrates, or of a senator whom Cato degraded for kissing his wife before his unmarried daughter.

It is also a singular and rather an unfortunate coincidence that the most detailed account which we possess of the theory of the censorian supervision, given us by a capable authority who lived at a time when the office was in full—though not its fullest—vigour, should come from what all must admit to be a prejudiced source. The object of Cicero, speaking as a barrister in defence of Cluentius, is to throw discredit on the whole censorian system, and to elicit the sympathy of a jury with whom this system was never very popular. The passage is, no doubt, of the greatest importance for our subject, and may be safely used, if only we remember that we have here a characteristic instance of the mode in which the orator 'threw dust in the eyes of a jury.'

Such considerations should be borne in mind by those who object to the attempts to fill up the gaps between the earlier and later stages of the infamia by pointing to the fact that there are discrepancies between the historical instances of the one and the documentary evidence for the other. It will be shown that in all probability every case that we find in the praetor's Edict had its prototype in the censorian procedure—only that these more ordinary, although not less serious cases—have not been transmitted to us, in connection with the censorship, on account of the peculiar nature of our evidence. The function of the censors with which we are concerned, is generally summed up briefly as the rule of manners (*regimen morum*): it is also described as the apportionment of honour and dishonour, as the mode in which position (*dignitas*) was assigned, and moral disgrace punished[1]; and, although the consideration of the complex functions of the censorship, which made it the most anomalous of Roman magistracies, is outside the scope of this work, yet it is necessary to examine some of the attributes of the office which were peculiarly associated with this *censoria potestas*. Both the extent and the limitations of the powers involved in it are the only adequate explanation of its development, which was an outcome both of its weakness and of its strength. There are four attributes of the office with which we are concerned. The first is one which secured its power and freedom, namely, its irresponsibility; the three others are modes in which some limitation of this power was effected; they are, the short tenure of office, the impossibility of re-election, and the collegiate principle.

(i) The censorship is spoken of by Dionysius as an irresponsible office (ἀρχὴ ἀνυπεύθυνος)[2]: and the irresponsi-

[1] Cic. De Leg. iii. 3, 7 'censores mores populi regunto; probrum in senatu ne relinquunto.' Liv. iv. 8, 2 'in senatu equitumque centuriis decoris dedecorisque discrimen sub dicione ejus magistratus esset.' Cf. Liv. xl. 46; xli. 27; xlii. 3.

In Cicero (pro Cluent. 46, 128) the functions of the censors are summed up as consisting 'in delectu dignitatis et in judicio civium et in animadversione vitiorum,' cf. § 129 'tu es praefectus moribus, magister veteris disciplinae ac severitatis.' De Prov. Cons. 19, 46 'illud morum severissimum magisterium.'

[2] Dionys. xix. 16. The scandals connected with the censorship of 204 B. C. (Liv. xxix. 37) led to an attempt to call the censors to account ('Cn. Baebius tr. pl. diem ad populum utrique dixit'), which was resisted by the Senate who declared these magistrates irresponsible (Liv. l. c.; Val. Max. vii. 2, 6). Attempts of the same kind were made by the tribunes both before (in 214 B. C. Liv. xxiv. 43) and after this *senatusconsultum* (Liv. xliii. 16). This latter was successful: and although the trial of Gracchus and Claudius in 169 B. C. arose from their financial business with the *publicani*, yet the special charge brought by the tribune against Claudius ('quod concionem a se avocasset') might apply equally to any exercise of the *censoria potestas* which infringed the *majestas* of the tribune. The same cause led to the very violent attempt of the tribune C. Ateius

bility was marked by the fact that they could not be called to account judicially for any act done in connection with the *census*. This principle seems never to have been strictly recognised by law: at best it was guaranteed by a decree of the Senate of the year 204 B.C.; yet so important was the principle felt to be, that every attempt to enforce responsibility, which was made by the tribunes, was either staved off by the Senate or remitted by the good sense of the magistrates themselves, and ended in failure. It was not until the year 58 B.C. that a definite attempt was made to render the censors responsible. One of the effects of the Clodian *plebiscitum* of that year would certainly have been to render the censors judicially liable for a breach of any of the provisions contained in that law. But this law was soon repealed, and even had it remained valid, came too late in Republican history to alter the development of the *regimen morum*. Not only were the censors exempt from all liability for their past actions; they were also free from the usual fetters of a Roman magistrate during their tenure of power: and it is quite clear that the tribunician *veto*, the only one which could have affected this office, was not applicable against the specific *potestas* exercised in connection with the *census*[1]. It is difficult to form a judgment on this aspect of the office; but the belief is at least permissible that the Roman censorship would have been a more valuable contribution

Labeo to secure the responsibility of the censor Metellus by carrying him off to the Tarpeian rock (Plin. H. N. vii. 44). Although Metellus' life was saved, yet, according to Pliny, he was condemned for *majestas* and his goods confiscated.

[1] The powerlessness of the tribune with respect to the *census* is shown by many passages of Livy; see amongst others Liv. xliv. 16 'multis equi adempti, inter quos P. Rutilio, qui tr. pl. eos violenter accusarat: tribu quoque is motus et aerarius factus.' The *obnuntiatio* could, however, be used against the summons of the people to the *census* and *lustrum*, as against any other *contio* (Cic. ad Att. iv. 9, 1).

to the moral history of the world had its powers been limited in some more definite way. Had the office been a responsible one, it would either have evolved of itself more definite rules of conduct, or have had such rules imposed on it from without, which would appear with some distinctness in our authorities. But it is only by the historian in his search for records that the regret can be entertained. As early codification is in every case a misfortune—and one that may be gauged in this particular instance by a comparison of the later with the earlier infamia—it was in strict accordance with the progressive political institutions of Rome that she recognised a progressive moral code as equally in harmony with her national life.

(ii) The limitation of the censors' tenure of office to eighteen months—a tenure which, even as thus fixed, exceeded that of the other Republican magistrates—was an assertion of the principle that the censorship was merely an occasional office: nor is it probable that the office was ever coextensive with the quinquennial period of the lustrum. Since it is probable that the *cura morum* came eventually to be exercised at other times than when the *census* was actually in progress, this rule was an effective guarantee against the possibility of the peculiar moral notions of two men being imprinted on the life of the State for an uninterrupted period of five years[1].

[1] In Liv. iv. 24 we find the mention of the law of the dictator Mamercus Aemilius (434 B.C.) by which the censorship was limited to eighteen months, and in Liv. ix. 34 Claudius' attempted violation of this law. Mommsen (Staatsr. ii. p. 349) thinks the original quinquennial period of the office a mistake due to a confusion between the duration of the validity of the censorian ordinances and the duration of the office itself. He suggests that this *Lex Aemilia* first made the censorship an independent magistracy with a fixed tenure. The words that Livy (iv. 24) assigns to the dictator, 'grave esse, iisdem per tot annos magna parte vitae obnoxios vivere,' although true of the later powers of the censor,

(iii) Re-election to the censorship was forbidden, and on the same grounds which dictated the last-mentioned limitation. But this prohibition was still more important in fostering a free and powerful, because unconscious, development of the infamia[1]. Since succeeding colleges had always the power of reversing the actions of their predecessors, it was essential that these officials should not have a chance of stereotyping their decisions or reverting to an antiquated procedure. The swing of the pendulum from conservatism to liberalism in moral notions must no doubt have been an interesting subject of contemplation in connection with this office; but like the changes of parties and of programmes it was healthy, and while the high-water mark of conservatism has left its trace everywhere on our records, the more moderate holders of the office are concealed in consequence of the more modified views they took as to the average demands that might be made on human nature.

But by far the most effective limitation on censorian caprice arose from the collegiate nature of the office, and the mutual power of veto which this principle involved. In accordance with the theory of the Roman collegiate system the censors act independently of one another, and the negative in every case overrides the positive decision. Thus the senator whom one censor erased from the list might be retained by his colleague, the new candidate

are an anachronism with reference to the time at which they are supposed to have been uttered.

[1] Liv. xxiii. 23 'nec censoriam vim uni permissam, et eidem iterum.' In Plut. Cor. 1 we find a reference to Marcius Censorinus and his law against re-election to the censorship. Cf. Val. Max. iv. 1. 3 'Marcius Rutilus Censorinus (Censor 294 and 265 B.C.) . . . populum . . . oratione corripuit, quod eam potestatem bis sibi detulisset, cujus majores, quia nimis magna videretur, tempus coartandum judicassent.' Mommsen remarks that the law could not have been the work of Censorinus, as the censor had no power to introduce laws (Staatsr. i. p. 520).

whom one placed on the list of the Senate might be rejected by the other. When Cicero attempts to exhibit this power of the censors' to annul one another's actions as one of the inherent weaknesses of the office, which destroyed the respect that might be paid to its decisions[1], he ignores for the moment the fact that the same argument might be used with greater force of the highest civil magistracy of Rome, the praetorship; and that this conflict in the censorship is not necessarily one act of caprice overriding another, but may be due to the opposition of two rules of procedure, or to the assertion of a rule of procedure over an act of caprice. Nowhere was this conflict of authority more necessary than in cases where principles had to be maintained and minute questions of personal evidence investigated by magistrates, who also pronounced a penalty varying in its degrees, and which was supposed to be nicely adjusted to the gravity of the offence. Those must indeed have been remarkable years mentioned by Livy—remarkable, that is, for the blackness of their criminals in high places—in which there was perfect agreement between the censors as to the individuals to be excluded from honours and as to the form which this exclusion should take[2].

The quasi-judicial position of the censor is at once

[1] Cic. pro Cluent. 43, 122 'atque etiam ipsi inter se censores sua judicia tanti esse arbitrantur, ut alter alterius judicium non modo reprehendat, sed etiam rescindat: ut alter de senatu moveri velit, alter retineat et ordine amplissimo dignum existimet: ut alter in aerarios referri aut tribu moveri jubeat, alter vetet.'

App. B. C. i. 28 *τιμητὴς* Κοίντος Καικίλιος Μέτελλος (censor 102 B. C.) *Γλαυκίαν τε βουλεύοντα καὶ Ἀπουλήιον Σατορνῖνον δεδημαρχηκότα ἤδη τῆς ἀξιώσεως παρέλυε—οὐ μὴν ἐδυνήθη· ὁ γάρ οἱ συνάρχων οὐ συνέθετο.*

[2] Liv. xlii. 10 (173 B. C.) 'concors et e republica censura fuit. Omnes quos senatu moverunt, quibusque equos ademerunt, aerarios fecerunt, et tribu moverunt: neque ab altero notatum alter probavit.' xlv. 15 (168 B. C.) 'omnes iidem ab utroque et tribu remoti, et aerarii facti.'

apparent from this review of his most essential attributes. The framing of the edict by successive colleges of magistrates, the mutual *veto* within the college, operated here as they did in the praetor's court. And, as the praetor was bound to embody statute-law in his edict, so the censors must have been morally bound to recognise and carry out the sumptuary laws and the laws repressive of particular forms of immorality[1]. The chief difference was that the actual procedure in the censor's court was less vigorous and less uniform, and the question raised for us by Cicero 'how far was the censorship a *judicium*?' depends for its answer on the extent to which the censors can be shown to have recognised the formalities which were usual in the ordinary process of law.

The censorian process is often spoken of as a trial (*judicium*), or as a trial concerned with morals (*judicium de moribus*)[2]: sometimes more generally as a cognizance (*notio*)[3]. Cicero's arguments against its being a *judicium* are that none of the accompaniments of a regular trial, such as sworn evidence or records, were essential to the exercise of what he calls the censorian *auctoritas*, and that the decisions of the censors did not command that universal respect which was accorded to judgments pronounced by a competent court[4]. Both these arguments

[1] An instance of activity of this kind is furnished by Appius Claudius, censor in 50 B.C. Cic. ad Fam. viii. 14, 4 'Scis Appium censorem hic ostenta facere? de signis et tabulis, de agri modo, de aere alieno acerrime agere?'

[2] Liv. xxiii. 23 'judicium arbitriumque de fama ac moribus,' cf. Cic. pro Sest. 25, 55; de Prov. Cons. 19, 46; in Pis. 4, 10; Tac. Ann. xi. 25 'judicium censorum.' *Judicatio* is also employed by Cicero (de Repub. 4, 6), and in Gellius (iv. 20) we even meet the expression 'in jure stare' used of a man appearing before the censors.

[3] 'Notio,' Cic. pro Sest., de Prov. Cons., in Pis. ll. cc.; Liv. xxvii. 25.

[4] Cic. pro Cluent. 45, 126 'Quid igitur censores secuti sunt? ne ipsi quidem, ut gravissime dicant, quidquam aliud dicent praeter sermonem atque famam. Nihil se testibus, nihil tabulis, nihil gravi aliquo argu-

are no doubt theoretically valid; as regards the first, it is clear that the censor's acts are legally a pure exercise of discretion (*arbitrium*) and independent authority (*auctoritas*): they seem to have been spoken of usually as *animadversiones*, a word which does not necessarily convey, although it does not deny, the connotation of regular forms of procedure. It is hardly necessary to add the main point which differentiates the censor's court from a criminal trial at law, and that is that the consequences of the procedure in the former were never regarded as strictly penal. Although it might disqualify, it did not punish, and the result of the censor's judgment was only *ignominia*[1]. The process was spoken of as a *notatio*, from the mark (*nota*) which the censor made under the name of the person affected, to which was appended a written record of the cause or causes for which he had been degraded (*subscriptio*)[2]. It is evident that this record might take either one of two forms, in accordance with the nature of the grounds on which it was based. It might be either a record of an already proven fact or a statement of the belief of the censors[3]. In the former case, in which nothing required to be proved, the necessity for judicial procedure would clearly be obviated: it was

mento comperisse, nihil denique, causa cognita, statuisse dicent;' 42, 117 'Sequitur id, quod illi judicium appellant, majores autem nostri numquam neque judicium nominarunt, neque proinde, ut rem judicatam, observaverunt, *animadversionem* atque *auctoritatem* censoriam' (cf. 44, 123; 46, 128); 42, 119 'Hic primum illud commune proponam, numquam *animadversionibus* censoriis hanc civitatem ita contentam ut rebus judicatis fuisse.

[1] Cic. de Repub. 4, 6 'ut omnis ea judicatio versatur tantum modo in nomine, animadversio illa ignominia dicta est.'

[2] Liv. xxix. 42, 6 'ut censores motis e senatu adscriberent notas.' Cic. pro Cluent. 45, 118 'subscriptiones'; ib. 42, 119 'causam subscribere.' A good instance of a *subscriptio* written under a senatorial name has been preserved by Asconius (in Or. in tog. cand. p. 111); see p. 27, note 5.

[3] Cic. pro Cluent. 44, 123 'ac primum illud statuamus, utrum, quia censores subscripserint, ita sit, an, quia ita fuerit, illi subscripserint.'

in the latter case that it required to be, and, so far as we can determine, was in most cases resorted to.

We possess, in fact, abundant evidence that, in the latter case, all the main outlines of a *judicium* were present: and that a censor endued with a full conception of his duties, refused to act even on his strongest convictions of guilt, unless these were supported by independent accusation and evidence. Thus we find Scipio Africanus, censor in 199 B.C., expressing his firmest belief that a knight who stood before him had committed perjury, and inviting evidence of the crime. When this evidence was not forthcoming, he said 'Lead your horse on: I will not act the part of accuser, of witness, and of judge[1]'. The summons to the supposed delinquents to plead their cause (*causam dicere*), the accusation by a third party which was sometimes invited, sometimes offered spontaneously, the evidence of witnesses who were summoned in his favour by the accused, and the defence which was permitted him, all conduced to create in the procedure before the censor a strong resemblance to the ordinary process of law[2]. We must bear in mind, however, that these forms, although they might have been usual, were by no means necessary: and that, above all, the censors could not

[1] Cic. pro Cluent. 48, 134; Val. Max. iv. 1, 10 'Traduc equum, inquit, Sacerdos, ac lucrifac censoriam notam, ne ego in tua persona et accusatoris, et testis, et judicis partes egisse videar.'

[2] Summons: Liv. xxiv. 18 (214 B.C.) 'jusso deinde eo ceterisque ejusdem noxae reis causam dicere, quum purgari nequissent, pronuntiaverunt'; accusation: Liv. xxix. 42 (Cato's censorship 184 B.C.) 'longe gravissima in L. Quinctium oratio est, qua si accusator ante notam, non censor post notam, usus esset, retinere Quinctium in senatu ne frater quidem T. Quinctius, si tum censor esset, potuisset'; accusation and defence: Plut. C. Gracch. 2 *κατηγορίας αὐτῷ γενομένης ἐπὶ τῶν τιμητῶν κ.τ.λ.*; witnesses: Cic., Val. Max. ll. cc. In Gell. (iv. 20) we find the story of a witness, summoned for the defence, who excited the censor's displeasure by yawning, and only escaped degradation by pleading that it was a physical infirmity.

wait for the formal accusation of a delinquent. They were, by the very nature of their office, necessarily influenced by a prevailing rumour growing out of a prevailing scandal[1]. If the rumour was prevalent that a bench of *judices* had been bribed, the censors would be on the look out for these *judices* at the *census*, and, as in the case of the *consilium Junianum*, if they could not punish all, would at least punish the most guilty. From an adverse point of view it might easily appear as if the censorship were swayed by the *ventus popularis*, and as if they adopted the procedure of visiting their displeasure on certain individuals of a class, 'to encourage the others.' But this latter defect could not be helped, and is indeed a proof of the caution with which the censors directed their animadversions.

With regard to the second point made by Cicero, that the judgments of the censors did not command the universal attention of those of the courts of law, it is true that the censorian infamia was not bound to be respected by other magistrates, except with reference to the particular disqualification pronounced by the censor. Besides the instances of the election of men suffering from *ignominia* of various degrees to a magistracy we are told that the censor's judgments did not necessarily influence the praetor in his selection of the *judices*[2] But Cicero's statements must mark the exceptions, not the rules. If it were true that the censor's judgments were systematically disregarded both by magistrates and people, the continuance of the *regimen morum* would have been an impossibility.

[1] Cic. pro Cluent. 47, 130 'verum omnis intelligimus, in istis subscriptionibus ventum quemdam popularem esse quaesitum—praetermitti a censoribus, et negligi macula judiciorum posse non videbatur.'

[2] Cic. pro Cluent. 43, 121 'Praetores urbani, qui jurati debent optimum quemque in selectos judices referre, numquam sibi ad eam rem censoriam ignominiam impedimento esse oportere duxerunt: cf. 45, 126.

Yet the arbitrary employment of the *notatio* was, in the later Republic, in an age intolerant of discipline, and jealous of any authority which it did not seem to control, regarded as a defect of the office. The attack came from the democracy, but, unlike Sulla's practical abolition of the office, it assumed a wise and moderate form. Amongst the plebiscites passed by the tribune Clodius, in the year 58 B. C., was one enjoining that individuals, before being subjected to *ignominia*, must be condemned by both censors and must be impeached by a third party [1]. The first of these regulations appears at first sight to introduce no innovation: since no *ignominia* pronounced by one censor could at any time have been effective without the tacit consent of his colleague. It shows, however, that, where no difference of opinion was contemplated, the censors were accustomed, for the purpose of expediting business, to act independently of one another: and the meaning of the regulation must have been that in all future cases, the cognisance was to come before both of the magistrates sitting together. This would have rendered their procedure more formal, and have added weight to their judgments. The second element in the new procedure was one that, as we have seen, was never ignored, but was not always observed, by the censors. Its enforcement, by the law of Clodius, would have had the effect of taking the initiative from the censors in every case, and in this respect, as well as in the closer investigation which this change necessitated, it would have brought the censorian process nearer to a process of law. It lessened the censor's arbitrary power in one respect, in that it would have prevented him from taking cognisance of a great many offences

[1] Ascon. in Pison. p. 124: 'ne quem censores in senatu legendo praeterirent, neve qua ignominia afficerent, nisi qui apud eos accusatus et utriusque censoris sententia damnatus esset.' Cf. Dio Cass. xxxviii. 13.

which he would gladly have noticed, and which were perhaps specified in his edict—but this was a clear gain to the censorship as an institution; for it was the one regulation necessary for bringing the office into close harmony with current public opinion. It would also have lessened the censor's discretionary authority in another and still more wholesome manner: in that it would have prevented him from ignoring the disqualifications pronounced by law, the effectiveness of which rested hitherto on his knowledge and his choice of initiative, but on which he would be bound to act when they were formally presented to him by a voluntary prosecutor. It is impossible, therefore, to agree with Cicero when he speaks of this law as destroying the sanctity and effectiveness of the office [1]. It democratised the censorship, but, in so doing, promised it a new and vigorous life, in recognising it as still the wholesomest expression for the public opinion of a free community. But a free democracy was not the gift in store for Rome: and Clodius was the last reformer that the Republic produced. His law was lost in one of those conservative reactions that preceded the downfall of the senatorial government [2]. The censorship itself, the most republican because the most aristocratic of institutions, was soon to disappear before the new monarchy; but insensibly, and without external aid, it had done its work in defining the conception of infamia. As the praetor's edict was tending towards redaction, so the free life of the censorship was giving place to a code. It had long been the tendency of the office: for we find that, in the case of certain offences which involved ignominy, a permanent character had been

[1] Cic. pro Sest. 25, 55 'ut censoria notio et gravissimum judicium sanctissimi magistratus de republica tolleretur.' Cf. de Prov. Cons. 19, 46.

[2] It was repealed by a *Lex Caecilia* carried by Metellus Scipio in 52 B. C. (Dio Cass. xl. 57).

given to the rulings of the censors. This was the case with perjury[1], with condemnation in a disgraceful suit[2], and especially with disgraceful professions, such as that of an actor was accounted[3]. 'The precedent having been established that this disqualified for all civic honours, it was natural that it should continue to be respected, and thus we find how the censorian infamia came to assume in time a tralaticiary character that gives us the permanent categories in the *Lex Julia Municipalis* and in the Digest. Certain standing offences came to be regarded as necessarily involving *notatio*, and as involving a *notatio* that the censors thought fit to make permanent; and we should naturally expect that offences which were thought deserving of a permanent *notatio* would involve the most serious disqualification, that of exclusion from all civic duties. It is possible, therefore, to say with Savigny, that there was a class of offences involving permanent disqualification, and that of the most severe kind, and we may perhaps with safety seek such cases in later documents, such as the praetor's Edict in the Digest[4]'; but that these cases had the exclusive title of infamia, and that this was ever, during the Republic, distinguished from the *censoria notatio*, cannot, as we have seen, be established from the evidence adduced.

This permanent character secured by successive judgments could hardly have asserted itself without the use of written records. It has already been observed that the censors had many such records ready to hand: and we have now to notice the most important, because the fullest and perhaps the most permanent, of them, the censorian

[1] Cic. de Off. i. 13, 40 'eos omnes censores, quoad quisque eorum vixit, quia pejerassent, in aerarios reliquerunt.'

[2] Cic. pro Cluent. 42, 119 'turpi judicio damnati in perpetuum omni honore ac dignitate privantur.'

[3] Augustin. de civ. Dei, ii. 12; Tertull. de Spect. 22; see p. 34.

[4] Art. *infamia* in Smith's Dict. of Greek and Roman Antiquities (3rd ed.).

Edict. The right of issuing commands in the form of Edicts (*jus edicendi*), in connection with the spheres of administration within their own departments, is common to all Roman magistrates, from the quaestor in his collection of the taxes to the consul in the higher branches of administration. All of these Edicts probably corresponded to one another in their general form—they contained commands, prohibitions, and advice: and it is needless to say, when we are dealing with Roman administration, that all of them were modelled on precedents. The differences between them were simply those of more or less regularity and continuity. Some of them, such as those of the consuls and quaestors, were merely occasional, others, such as those of the praetors, curule aediles, and provincial governors, continuous (*perpetua*), and transmitted (*tralaticia*). We have every evidence that the censors' Edict belonged to this latter category, in so far as it was a regular preliminary to the exercise of their office. Our sources do not enable us to state with certainty whether each successive censorian Edict embodied, like the praetor's, all the rulings of his predecessors. What they show us is that the censor, when he meant to make a new departure, and to animadvert on certain evils which had hitherto escaped censure, mentioned these in his Edict and emphasized their importance in the speech (*oratio*) which he delivered on the same occasion. But it is extremely probable that he preceded it with at least a general statement that he would hold as offences against custom and morals (*praeter consuetudinem et morem majorum*[1]) all that had been so held by previous censors with certain exceptions (rare we may believe and mainly due to the change in legal obliga-

[1] 'Haec nova, quae praeter consuetudinem ac morem majorum fiunt, neque placent, neque recta videntur': from the speech of the censors of 92 B. C. (Suet. de clar. rhet. 1; Gell. xv. 11, 2).

tions) which he chose to specify. And, although it can be only a matter of conjecture, it is equally probable that he enumerated in particular certain grave offences, which he would profess to deal with as they had been dealt with by past censors—those namely which have been mentioned as involving the severest disqualification, and which formed the fragment afterwards codified as the infamia of the Empire.

Our actual information about the censors' Edict is as fragmentary and unsatisfactory as that about the censorian infamia itself; but we can discover that it contained three elements: these being, firstly advice, secondly expressions of displeasure, and thirdly actual prohibitions. The advice given seems often to have been of a fatherly character, general directions for securing safety and happiness, and to have had no connection with the *nota*[1]. Exhortations to marriage were perhaps as common as any other form of this advice[2]. On the other hand, expressions of displeasure, introduced by the words *nobis non placere*, directed against new and unhealthy customs, and actual prohibitions, such as those against forms of luxury lately introduced[3], would have had no meaning except they were meant to be followed up by the *nota:* and as in many cases it must have been difficult and would have been often unfair to enforce them by penalties at the *census* immediately fol-

[1] One of the Emperor Claudius' edicts contained the advice that 'nothing is so good for the bite of a snake as the sap of the yew-tree' (Suet. Claud. 16).

[2] It was in a censorian *oratio* that L. Caec. Metellus, censor 131 B. C., uttered his remarkable exhortation to marriage; he urged the citizens to wed, and so show that they preferred the safety of the State to their own happiness, Gell. i. 6; Livy adds (Ep. 59) 'exstat oratio ejus, quam Augustus Caesar, quum de maritandis ordinibus ageret, velut in haec tempora scriptam, in senatu recitavit.' For another censorian *oratio* see Gell. iv. 20.

[3] Many such are mentioned by Pliny, H. N. viii. 51 and 57; xi. 13; xiii. 3; xiv. 14; xxxvi. 1. In his edicts the emperor Claudius inveighed against 'theatralis populi lascivia.' Tac. Ann. xi. 13.

lowing, they must have been meant as precedents to bind succeeding censors. The censors' edict was spoken of, with not more and not less propriety than that of the praetor, as a *lex*[1]. It was the *viva vox*, not of *jus* but of *mores*[2], and the moral code, even when only partially written, was a happy mean between the State-enforced morality of the Greek law-giver and the fluctuating and ill-defined conceptions of modern public opinion.

When we come to the special grounds of censorian censure, which were in the later Republic severally called by the singular name of *opus censorium*[3], but are more usually spoken of as *probra*[4], we should wish to be able to trace historically the gradual development of moral conceptions exhibited by this censure, or rather, as the censorship was always regarded as a conservative institution aiming at the preservation of an ideal *mos majorum*, of the gradually extending spheres of Roman life which forced greater activity on the censorship. But this would be to write the history of Roman morals, and their connection with different epochs in the censorship could only be restored conjecturally, on account of the fragmentary nature of our authorities. It is obvious, however, that its sphere must have gradually increased with the increase of national immorality, if such a name can justly be given

[1] The censorian Edicts are called *leges censoriae* by Pliny (ll. cc.); there is no reason to think with Mommsen (Staatsr. ii. p. 373, n. 2) that the expression was invented by this author. In popular phraseology they would naturally have been spoken of as 'ordinances'; and they could never have been confused with the *leges censoriae* proper, where *lex* bore its old sense of contract. The praetor's Edict was spoken of as *lex annua* (Cic. in Verr. i. 42, 108).

[2] Marcian speaks of the *jus honorarium* as *viva vox juris civilis* (Dig. i. 1, 8).

[3] Gell. iv. 12; xiv. 7. It is probable that the expression was found by Gellius in his authorities; the latter passage suggests its employment in the Commentarium of Varro. From its use by Gellius a man exposed to censure might be said *opus censorium facere*.

[4] For *probrum* see pp. 4 and 18.

to the greater complexity in the relations of life which Imperialism necessarily forced on Rome. In the early period of its history we may agree with Lange in saying that it must have been mainly concerned with what we should call relations of private life. No developed community has ever realised more keenly than Rome did, even in the later stages of her history, the truth that the State has its basis in the family; and in the earlier times, when the family was the real unit, and individual rights as such were hardly recognised, this truth must have been still more keenly felt. We may well believe, therefore, that the evils affecting the position of the family, the neglect of the *res familiares*, questions of celibacy and divorce, misuse of the *patria potestas* and the rights of the *patronus*, neglect of the family *sacra*, prodigality and luxury were the matters that chiefly called in early times for the cognisance of the censors. Some writers have even attempted to go back beyond the history of the censorship, almost beyond that of the State, and have imagined that, in the old patrician community, some methods of animadverting on such abuses were in the hands of the *gens*, an institution, which, as known to us in historic times, possesses hardly any corporate capacity at all. Even, however, if such were the case, it is highly improbable that the sanctions of such corporations could have had an effect on the exercise of the *publica jura* of the State, and therefore their activity, if even it existed, had no bearing on the history of the infamia. If we pass from the circle of the family, and examine the relations existing between independent members of the community, we find that many business relations had no sanction other than good faith (*fides*)—one therefore enforceable by no other power than that which regulated the civil honour of the State; many of the rulings of the early censorship must thus have been directed to the relations of private law: and in this respect the infamia of the Empire is no bad reflection of the earliest stages of the institution, since it was largely directed to the punishment of breaches of trust. Again the transition from the old pontifical jurisdiction with its religious penalties to the sanction of the criminal law, must have left for a time an open space, to be filled up only by the infamia. The early censorship must in fact have been largely concerned in regulating by its sanctions the relations of private life in matters moral, civil or quasi-criminal. There is even good reason to believe that this always continued to be the main aspect of the office, although a disproportionate importance is given to its regulation of political functions by our historical authorities. Its later growth, as regards the control of private life, may be measured by the growth of analogous rules which we can trace: for instance, by the long succession of the sumptuary laws of Rome, which extend from the *Lex Oppia* of 215 B.C. to the close of the Republic[1]. The political evils entailed by the growth of Roman dominion, such as the corruption and misconduct of officials, which entailed disqualification pronounced either by the law or by the censors, are fully noticed by our authorities and will be made sufficiently apparent by the following sketch.

It will be convenient to divide the instances of censorian severity which may be gathered from our texts under four heads: (i) those concerned with family life or the relations of private life; (ii) a category closely akin to this of disqualifications following as the result of certain modes of life, trades, or professions; (iii) instances of censure that

[1] The only sumptuary regulations known to us earlier than the *Lex Oppia* were those contained in the Twelve Tables limiting the expenses of funerals (Cic. de Leg. ii. 23). It is characteristic of the earlier period that the only expense which the law felt itself bound to check was one connected with a religious obligation.

followed political misconduct. All these instances fall under the head of what modern jurists, in dealing with the praetor's edict, have called immediate infamy. The (iv) fourth class of instances of *infamia mediata*—that following condemnation by a judicial sentence—plays but a subordinate part in our authorities.

(i) In considering the censor's control of private life, we must remember that the census was one of full heads of families (*patres familiarum*). Women and sons under power did not appear: the father answered all questions concerning them put by the censor. The father in his capacity as judge and magistrate of the household (*judex domesticus, domesticus magistratus*) was responsible for its conduct[1]. Cicero indeed tells us that the reason why the Roman State never felt bound to appoint inspectors of women (*mulieribus praefecti*, *γυναικονόμοι*), such as existed in Greek constitutions, was that the woman was responsible to the man, the man to the censor[2]. So effective was this control that Dionysius, in a comparison between Athens, Sparta, and Rome, tells us that it was at Rome alone that the State ventured to intrude beyond the threshold of the household[3]. He enumerates no less than seven modes in which this control was exercised, and his account may be verified and supplemented by references in other authorities. The slave was unprotected by the civil law, and until

[1] 'judex domesticus' (Sen. Controv. ii. 3); 'domesticus magistratus' (de Benef. iii. 11); cf. Liv. xxxiv. 1 (the agitation about the repeal of the *Lex Oppia*), 'matronae nulla nec auctoritate, nec verecundia, nec *imperio virorum* contineri limine poterant.'

[2] Cic. de Repub. iv. 6, 16 'Nec vero mulieribus praefectus praeponatur, qui apud Graecos creari solet; sed sit censor, qui viros doceat moderari uxoribus.' Ib. § 18, the word *famosa* occurs applied to a woman under the censure of the *cognati*.

[3] Dionys. xx. 13. The Spartan's home, he says, was his castle, *Ῥωμαῖοι δὲ πᾶσαν ἀναπετάσαντες οἰκίαν, καὶ μέχρι τοῦ δωματίου τὴν ἀρχὴν τῶν τιμητῶν προαγαγόντες, ἁπάντων ἐποίησαν ἐπίσκοπον καὶ φύλακα τῶν ἐν αὐταῖς γινομένων.*

the introduction of the *Lex naturalis* into Roman jurisprudence, there were no rights of men as such which might safeguard him. But the cruel punishment of a slave was visited from the earliest times by the censors. The patron who wronged his client was devoted to the infernal gods[1]: but the pontifical law of the Republic had no power to enforce its sanctions, and the client's protection must have rested mainly with the censorship. It also interfered with what was theoretically entirely under the father's control, the education of his children, and reproved both harshness and over-indulgence[2]. The non-performance of the worship and sacrifices of the clan (*sacra gentilicia*), always looked on as peculiarly a duty owed by the family-unions to the State, and sometimes even imposed on the clan from without[3], also came under its ban. Its activity was particularly remarkable in connection with the marriage bond. Celibacy was discountenanced by the censors as it was by the State[4]: in their speeches they urged the citizens to marry[5], and one of the first questions put at the census was, 'According to the best of your knowledge have you a wife[6]?' The bachelor of mature age always suffered the reproaches of the censor[7], but it has been doubted whether

[1] By the Twelve Tables it was ordained 'Patronus si clienti fraudem fecerit sacer esto' (Serv. ad Verg. Aen. vi. 609).

[2] Dionys. l. c.; Plut. Cat. Maj. 17.

[3] If we may believe Cincius (ap. Arnob. iii. 38) 'solere Romanos religiones urbium superatarum partim privatim per familias spargere, partim publice conservare.'

[4] 'Caelibes esse prohibento' (Cic. de Leg. iii. 3, 7).

[5] Liv. Ep. 59; Gell. i. 6, see p. 59, note 2.

[6] To the question 'Tu ex animi tui sententia uxorem habes?' a citizen once replied 'Habeo equidem uxorem, sed non ex animi mei sententia'; and was immediately made an *aerarius*, 'quod intempestive lascivisset' Cic. de Or. ii. 64, 260 (Gell. iv. 12).

[7] The Emperor Claudius was as usual unfortunate in his questions on this point. Suet. Claud. 16 'quibuscumque caelibatum, aut orbitatem, aut egestatem objiceret, maritos, patres, opulentos se probantibus.'

it was ever made a ground for the *nota*[1]. But here the censor's financial functions came into play, and there is a record of censors attempting to counteract the advantages of celibacy by the imposition of additional taxation[2]. The dissolution of marriage formed, if anything, a still more important matter for the censor's cognisance. The marriage bond had been rendered very lax by the introduction of the plebeian form of union in place of the older *confarreatio*, and the Twelve Tables had sanctioned divorce in such a case by mere repudiation on the part of the husband[3]. The abuse of such a power could only be restrained by *mores*: and we find an instance of a censor visiting a senator with penalties who had divorced his wife without taking advice of the family council (*consilium domesticum*), the permanent check on his arbitrary power[4]. If it is true that, in spite of the laxity of the law, no instances of the abuse of the power of divorce were known until the beginning of the second century B. C.[5], this result must have been largely due to the control exercised by the censor-

[1] Metellus apparently meant to make it a ground for the *nota*. Liv. Ep. 59 'Q. Metellus censor censuit, ut omnes cogerentur ducere uxores, liberorum creandorum causa.'

[2] Val. Max. ii. 9, 1 'Camillus et Postumius censores aera poenae nomine eos, qui ad senectutem caelibes pervenerant, in aerarium deferre jusserunt.'

[3] Cic. Phil. ii. 28, 69.

[4] Val. Max. ii. 9, 2. 'M. Val. Maximus et C. Junius Bubulcus Brutus censores . . . L. Antonium senatu moverunt, quod, quam virginem in matrimonium duxerat, repudiasset, nullo amicorum in consilio adhibito.' Gell. (iv. 3) tells a story of a noble Carvilius Ruga who put away a wife whom he loved, because she was barren, as a matter of conscience, 'quod jurare a censoribus coactus erat uxorem se liberum quaerendorum gratia habiturum.' The family council was only dispensed with by the Lex Maenia of 168; its functions, in the matter of arranging the forfeiture of the marriage provisions consequent on divorce, were transferred to a *judicium de moribus* nominated by the praetor. On the question as to whether a divorce was advisable it may still have been consulted.

[5] Gell. l. c.

ship. Even *mésalliances*, such as unions between free-born citizens and freed-women, involved the notatio of the censor[1]. Bad husbandry and neglect of property were similarly visited[2]; and during the later centuries of the Republic luxurious living was one of the chief objects for which the censorship went in search[3]. Their financial functions gave them a very effective means of checking luxury besides the *nota*: since they could impose an arbitrary and excessive taxation on articles of value[4].

In treating the censor as the controller of the Roman household we might with safety carry our description of this control far beyond the positive evidence which has been handed down to us. For most of the observances once enforced by the *jus divinum* of the pontiffs—such at least as had not come to be protected by the criminal law—must have claimed the control of the censors, at a time when religious had yielded to temporal sanctions. The dead claimed the protection of the magistrate as well as the living. When we find the violation of a sepulchre made a ground of infamia in the later Empire we may regard this as a survival of the censorian supervision of religious and family law: while the duty of

[1] One of the privileges granted to Fescennia Hispalla, revealer of the Bacchanalian conspiracy in 186 B.C. was 'utique ei ingenuo nubere liceret; neu quid ei, qui eam duxisset, ob id fraudi ignominiaeve esset' (Liv. xxxix. 19, 5). The *ignominia* refers to the censorship: the *fraus* seems to show that the marriage was illegal: but whether because she was a *libertina* or a *meretrix* is doubtful. See Rossbach, *Römische Ehe*, p. 466.

[2] Plin. H. N. xviii. 11.

[3] Plut. Tib. Gracch. 14; Val. Max. ii. 9, 4. The censure might be aroused by the hire of a too expensive house (Vell. ii. 10), by an effeminate mode of dress (Gell. vii. 12). For curious censorian edicts about luxury, which show into what details they enquired, see Plin. H. N. viii. 51 and 57; xiii. 3; xiv. 4; xxxvi. 1.

[4] This was Cato's procedure in his censorship, 184 B.C. (Liv. xxxix. 44; Plut. Cat. Maj. 18).

mourning for the dead and the *annus luctus* prescribed for a widow after the death of her husband by the pontifical law, which will deserve a more detailed discussion in connection with the praetorian infamia in which they reappear, must also have been enforced by the censor —vicariously in every case through the head of the household—especially after the pontifical sanctions had disappeared and the expiatory offerings (*piacula*) could no longer be enforced.

In passing from the circle of the family to legal relations between man and man we find the most important obligations almost undefended by legal sanctions in the early Roman law; they were matters of simple honour (*fides*) and depended for their enforcement mainly on *mores*—of which the censor was the representative. It was thus with wardship (*tutela*) which was reckoned as a duty (*officium*) parallel to that which a *patronus* owed to his client[1]. A breach of *fiducia* in all its forms was always visited with infamia, and this sanction must have been all the more necessary in the earlier period, when legal guarantees (*cautiones*) had not been developed as they were in the later law, and when good faith was the bond relied on. When in the *Lex Julia Municipalis* and in the praetor's Edict we find violations of the obligations of partnership, tutory, mandate, and deposit, all involving *bona fides*, entailing disqualifications of various kinds, we may be sure that this is a survival from the censorian infamia.

(ii) Chief amongst the professions that disqualified for offices at Rome were those connected with the stage. The

[1] Gell. v. 13 'ex moribus populi Romani, primum juxta parentes locum tenere pupillos debere, fidei tutelaeque nostrae creditos . . . M. Cato in oratione, quam dixit apud censores in Lentulum, ita scripsit: "quod majores sanctius habuere defendi pupillos, quam clientem non fallere."' For the part played by *bona fides* in the legal business of a Roman's life, see Cicero, de Off. iii. 17, 70.

permanent exclusion of actors from all civic privileges during the Republic has already been noticed, and so strong was the sentiment on the subject that, even in the Empire, when a strict censorship was revived, even amateur performances called forth its displeasure[1]. The arena was naturally under the same ban: and actors and gladiators are excluded by the municipal law of Caesar from seats in the local senates. But here we have an institution connected with the infamia, the history of which can be traced forward into the Empire, and the shifting of sentiment in this respect is worth noting, as showing how far the conception of *dignitas* gradually sank below that of the Republic. The levelling of classes was often the sport of the sole rulers of Rome. The dictator Sulla is said to have given Roscius the actor the gold ring, the symbol of equestrian rank. Caesar forced Laberius the knight to come forward as a mime[2]; Balbus, the humble imitator of his master, gave the gold ring to an actor, Herennius Gallus, and introduced him to the fourteen rows reserved for the knights in the theatre at Gades[3]. At the games which followed Caesar's triumph knights fought in the *arena*, although the dictator had the good taste to restrain an eager senator from joining in the fray[4].

This license was permitted by the Emperors partly to ensure their own popularity, for the *plebs* took a keener interest in the shows when graced by these distinguished combatants[5]. Although in the reign of Augustus a decree of the Senate was passed interdicting such displays, yet

[1] Suet. Dom. 8 'suscepta correctione morum . . . quaestorium virum, quod gesticulandi saltandique studio teneretur, movit senatu.'

[2] Macrob. Saturn. ii. 7. After the performance '(Caesar) Laberio anulum aureum cum quingentis sestertiis dedit.' The latter was apparently a payment; the gold ring restored his knighthood.

[3] Cic. ad Fam. 10, 32. [4] Dio Cass. xliii. 23.

[5] Dio Cass. lvi. 25 δεινῶς οἱ ἀγῶνες αὐτῶν ἐσπουδάζοντο.

before, and apparently even after this, he permitted knights to appear on the stage and in the *arena*[1]. The practice was at first continued by Tiberius[2], but early in his reign a severe decree issued from the Senate prohibiting senators and knights even from close personal relations with individuals connected with the stage[3]. The evil, however, continued under Gaius and Claudius[4], and culminated in the reign of the actor-emperor Nero. Roman knights and senators were seen in the gladiatorial lists[5], while the introduction of the *Neronia*, after the model of the Greek games, helped to break down the Roman disgust for the stage[6]. The last prohibition of the practice that we hear of was made by the Emperor Vitellius, apparently through an edict having reference to the *lectio senatus* and the *recognitio equitum*[7]. Yet in the reign of M. Aurelius men became praetors who had fought as gladiators[8], and it was only by the abolition of gladiatorial shows—which seem to have exercised a stronger fascination over the military instincts of the Roman than the theatre—that the evil

[1] During the triumvirate (Dio Cass. xlviii. 33) and in the aedilician games of Marcellus (liii. 31); for the extent to which the practice gained ground, and for the prohibition of it, see Dio Cass. liv. 2. Suetonius indeed says (Aug. 43) 'ad scenicas quoque et gladiatorias operas etiam equitibus Romanis aliquando usus est; *verum prius quam senatus consulto interdiceretur.*' But Dio mentions the practice in the later years of Augustus, the reason being that the knights cared nothing for the ἀτιμία, and that Augustus despaired of enforcing the rule.

[2] Dio Cass. lvii. 14.

[3] Tac. Ann. i. 77 (A. D. 15) 'adversus lasciviam fautorum multa decernuntur; ex quis maxime insignia, ne domos pantomimorum senator introiret, ne egredientes in publicum equites Romani cingerent aut alibi quam in theatro spectarentur, et spectantium immodestiam exilio multandi potestas praetoribus fieret.' Cf. Suet. Tib. 35.

[4] Gaius (Dio Cass. lix. 10), Claudius (ib. lx. 7).

[5] Dio Cass. lxi. 9; Tac. Ann. xiv. 14 and 15; xv. 32.

[6] Tac. Ann. xiv. 20.

[7] Tac. Hist. ii. 62; Dio Cass. lxv. 6.

[8] Capitol. M. Ant. 12.

appears to have been stamped out. In the developed Roman law there is no longer any question of gladiatorial games, but actors are declared *infames* and as such debarred from office by the Edict of Constantine [1].

Other professions of a more strictly dishonourable character were followed by similar consequences. It is inevitable to refer the disqualification of *lenones*, which appears in the *Lex Julia Municipalis* and the praetor's Edict, to the procedure of the censor. Usury, which was rendered illegal by the Twelve Tables and by a Marcian law of the fourth century B.C., must also have been followed by the *nota*: and we find it again becoming a source of infamia subsequently to the redaction of the Edict. The same consequences attended any small financial business approximating to a dishonest character [2].

(iii) Failures in political duty which called down the censor's *nota* may be considered under two heads—according as they affected special functionaries of the State, or according as they were applicable to the mass of citizens. As regards special functionaries the magistrate might be degraded for a misuse of his powers, for cruelty in his provincial administration, or for insubordination to the Senate [3]: any of the supreme magistrates for a neglect of constitutional formalities [4]. The abuse of the auspices

[1] See p. 32. As an illustration of the different standards of conduct established for the soldier and the *paganus* under the Empire, we may note that, even at the time of Severus, a soldier who went on the stage was punished with death ('si miles artem ludicram fecerit . . . capite puniendum Menander scribit.' Dig. xlviii. 19, 14).

[2] Suet. Aug. 39 'notavitque aliquos, quod, pecunias levioribus usuris mutuati, graviori foenore collocassent.'

In Tac. Ann. xiii. 23 a man is spoken of as 'exercendis apud aerarium sectionibus famosus.'

[3] Plut. Cat. Maj. 17; C. Gracch. 2.

[4] Gell. xiv. 7 'opus etiam censorium fecisse existimatos, per quos eo tempore (i.e. at an improper time) senatus consultum factum esset.'

could be tempered only by the exercise of the censor's power[1]; even the passing of a law likely to do harm to the morals of the State might call down the censure[2].

In other spheres of political activity the *judex* might be degraded for accepting bribes[3]; the soldier and the commander for shirking service, or showing cowardice or disobedience in battle[4]. As regards the mass of citizens, we find in one very exceptional case, which represents the censorship in its worst light, misuse of the right of voting calling down the censor's punishment on the people, as misuse of the power of legislation might bring it on the magistrate[5]. Improper conduct towards the censor himself was often visited with punishment. His control of finance and of morals gave him a power of vindicating the majesty of his office not possessed by any other magistrate. Attempts to limit the power of his office might be met by the aggravated taxation as well as by the degradation of the offender[6]: and there are many instances on record of a

[1] Cic. de Div. i. 16, 29 'Appius . . . censor C. Ateium (tribune 55 B.C.) notavit, quod mentitum auspicia subscripserit.'

[2] Val. Max. ii. 9, 5 'M. autem Antonius et L. Flaccus censores (97 B.C.) Duronium senatu moverunt, quod legem de coercendis conviviorum sumptibus latam tribunus plebis abrogaverat.'

[3] Cic. pro Cluent. 42, 119; cf. 43, 121 'quos contra leges pecunias cepisse subscriptum est'; on the alleged bribery of this 'Consilium Junianum,' see p. 54. Suet. Dom. 8 'nummarios judices . . . notavit.'

[4] See Liv. xxiv. 18; xxvii. 11, for the penalties meted out to those who shirked service after Cannae; amongst them was a quaestor. Cf. what is said of the *equitum recognitio*, p. 95; Val. Max. ii. 9, 7. In the discussion as to the conduct of Livius, praefect of Tarentum, in 208 B.C. (Liv. xxvii. 25) the principle was maintained 'ad censores, non ad senatum, notionem de eo pertinere.' In Dig. xlix. 16, 13, 4 we find 'eum, qui centurioni castigare se volenti restiterit, veteres notaverunt': but this may refer primarily to ignominious dismissal by the general.

[5] In 204 B.C. the censor M. Livius disfranchised (*aerarios reliquit*) thirty-four out of the thirty-five tribes 'quod et innocentem se condemnassent et condemnatum consulem et censorem fecissent' (Liv. xxix. 37).

[6] Liv. iv. 24 (431 B.C.): the dictator Mamercus Aemilius proposed to limit the tenure of the censorship (see above, p. 48): 'censores, aegre

very summary procedure being adopted in case of the contempt of the censor's court[1]. Further, any disgrace that attached to appearance in a court of law was taken cognisance of by the censors. When we find collusion in a criminal case (*praevaricatio in judicio publico*) a ground of infamy in the *Lex Julia Municipalis* and in the praetor's Edict, we may be sure that it had its origin in the censorship. But more particularly was it concerned with false witness and false oaths, because for these there was no secular sanction[2]. Perjury belonged to religious law (*fas*), and if premeditated and intentional[3], was one of the inexpiable sins for which the gods would accept no atonement (*piacularis hostia*). In the older days the pontiffs may have excommunicated such a sinner, and declared him *sacer*, in which case his life was unprotected and his goods perhaps forfeited to the god he had offended. After the old pontifical sanctions had died out, vengeance in such cases had to be left to heaven: and the principle of the Roman law was, in respect to perjury, that 'the gods must avenge their own wrongs' (*deorum injurias dis curae*). But what the civil law refused to deal with the censorship might and did punish.

One form of action, that nearly touched a Roman, and which from this point of view must have been regarded as

passi, Mamercum, quod magistratum populi Romani minuisset, tribu moverunt, octuplicatoque censu aerarium fecerunt.'

[1] Cic. de Or. ii. 64, 260; Gell. iv. 20. A well-equipped-knight appeared before the censor leading a lean and badly kept horse ('strigosum et male habitum'). 'Why,' asked the censor 'are you better cared for than your horse?' 'Because,' answered the knight, 'I take care of myself and my slave takes care of my horse': 'visum est parum reverens esse responsum, relatusque in aerarios, ut mos est.'

[2] Cic. de Off. iii. 31, 111 'indicant (the spirit of former times) notiones animadversionesque censorum, qui nulla de re diligentius quam de jurejurando judicabant.' Cf. Gell. vii. 18.

[3] 'Verbis conceptis pejerasse' (Val. Max. iv. 1, 10).

an offence against the state, remains to be noticed as involving the censorian infamia. The emperor Claudius in his censorship, evidently in this case as in others following Republican precedent, censured a man for an attempt at suicide[1]. Certain kinds of suicide were always censured by the Roman law and gave rise to a form of condemnation of memory[2]. We may imagine that, in these cases, the censors discriminated between the motives which led to the attempt.

(iv) Mediate infamy, or that following on a judicial sentence, does not come prominently before us in the Republic: and, although, as we have seen, a fairly definite conception of it was growing up throughout this period, in connection with certain civil actions, such as private delicts and obligations involving *bona fides*, yet this conception seems to have been created by the censorship, not imposed on it from without: and, as is usually the case with such self-created principles, was not always quite rigorously adhered to. But, even before trial, and therefore apart from condemnation, theft and private delicts had been visited by the *censoria notatio*[3]. To a separate category belongs criminal condemnation in a *judicium populi*, after the passing of the *Lex Cassia*, and in certain *judicia publica*,

[1] Claudius was again unfortunate, 'eo quidem, qui sibimet vim ferro intulisse arguebatur, illaesum corpus veste deposita ostentante' (Suet. Claud. 16).

[2] Women were not bound to mourn husbands 'qui manus sibi intulerunt non taedio vitae, sed mala conscientia' (Ulpian in Dig. iii. 2, 11). This discrimination between the motives to suicide was a leading principle in the later Roman law; see especially Dig. xlviii. 19, 38, 12; xlix. 16, 6, 7; a rescript of Hadrian, referred to in the latter passage, decrees the death penalty on a soldier guilty of an attempt at suicide; but if this attempt was due to a venial motive ('taedium vitae, morbus, furor, pudor') the penalty was reduced to *missio ignominiosa*.

[3] Cic. pro Cluent. 42, 120 'quos autem ipsi L. Gellius et Cn. Lentulus, duo censores . . . furti et captarum pecuniarum nomine notaverunt, ii non modo in senatum redierunt, sed etiam illarum ipsarum rerum judiciis absoluti sunt.'

to condemnation in which disqualifications had been attached by law before the close of the Republic. These consequences the censor was no doubt bound morally to respect, although, since he was irresponsible, there seems to have been no power which could compel him to do so. But the procedure was in accordance with the spirit of the censorship, since, even before these legal sanctions came into force, he had 'marked' individuals in consequence of criminal condemnation[1].

§ 2. *The censorian infamia in its connection with the Senate.*

The selection of the Senate (*lectio senatus*) was, as a formal act, regulated by certain fixed rules, unknown to the earliest Roman constitution. This may be accounted for on either one of two hypotheses; selection would be obviated by the fact of there being a fixed and certain method of attaining to the position of a senator; a regular method of selection would also be rendered impossible if the choice of his councillors rested originally on the arbitrary will of the supreme magistrate of the State. Neither of these hypotheses can be accepted in its extreme form. The fact that the Senate was originally the advising body of the magistrate, and that even after the appointment of members was transferred to other hands, and the mode of appointment had been prescribed by law, selection (*lectio*) continued to be the formal mode of filling up the gaps, shows that the choice of advisers must have rested originally with the magistrate; but there are also evidences that prove (what indeed we should expect) that in this choice he was not quite unfettered by

[1] Liv. xxix. 37 '(Claudius Nero) M. Livium (his colleague), quia populi judicio esset damnatus, equum vendere jussit.'

traditional usage; that the heads of families (*patres*) whom he summoned to his council-board were to some extent representative of the patrician clans (*gentes*). But yet, although tradition tells us that the numbers of the Senate were fixed, it rested with each succeeding magistrate (the king and afterwards the consul) to omit to summon (*praeterire*) some of the members of the body whom he found existing and to summon others in their stead; and the freedom of his choice prevented any stigma from attaching to the rejected members in consequence of this procedure. There must, indeed, have been an *infamia* predicable of senators in the Monarchy and early Republic: but the rejection from the list was in itself no sign of this infamia: since that fate was common to those rejected on moral and to those rejected on political grounds[1]. Here again, as in the case of the *populus* and of the *equites*, we cannot speak of a definite infamia until the right of selecting the members of the Senate was transferred to the censors.

The duty of making out the list of the Senate had no necessary connection with the powers originally possessed by the censor, and was never officially a part of the *census*. Thus we are not surprised to find that, for many years after the institution of this office, the power of creating senators still remained in the hands of the chief magistrates, the consuls. It is possible, indeed, that the *lectio senatus* was actually not transferred to the censors until some year

[1] Festus, p. 246 (quoted next page). Mommsen (Staatsr. ii. p. 418 sq.) states the case rather differently. While holding that the *lectio senatus* was unknown to the oldest Roman constitution, he insists more strongly on the life-tenure of the position in the early Senate. He thinks, for instance (p. 420, n. 3), that those senators not called upon by the magistrate were not definitely excluded, and that the place occupied by the senator, who was not summoned on account of dishonour, could not be filled up while he was alive. This is purely conjectural, and is clearly not warranted even by the belief that the Senate was representative of the *gentes*.

falling between the dates 318 and 312 B.C.; at least we know that in the year 311 B.C. so little official recognition was given to the censors' functions in connection with the Senate, that the consuls of that year actually ventured to set aside the censorian list, and to return to the original practice of summoning their own *consilium*. The censors' powers were finally ratified by a *plebiscitum* known as the Ovinian, of uncertain date, which has been regarded by some authorities as the bill establishing the censors' right of selection, and which has been therefore thought to be earlier than the year 312 B.C.: but which may in fact have been passed considerably later, and may have been a bill, not creating, but merely regulating and modifying the caprice (*arbitrium*) of the censors, which had been possible in previous revisions and indeed marked the continuity between the censorian and the pre-existing consular right of selection. It is at any rate certain that the main point of the *Ovinium plebiscitum*, in the form in which it has been preserved to us, is, not the transference of this power to the censors, but the limitation of the mode in which this power should be exercised by these officials; it was enacted that the censors must choose all the best men (*optimum quemque*) for the Senate: a vague direction, which, however, when interpreted by our knowledge of subsequent censorian procedure, would necessitate the choice of the ex-magistrates, at least those of curule rank. The consequences of this enactment was, as Festus explains, that those struck off the list at each revision, or who, having a legal right to be selected, were not placed on the list, were now *in opprobrio* and *ignominiosi*, which means that the only ground for rejection from the list, after the date of this enactment, was *infamia* [1]. However we may interpret

[1] Festus, p. 246 'Praeteriti senatores quondam in opprobrio non erant, quod, ut reges sibi legebant sublegebantque, quos in consilio publico

the ultimate legal theory of appointment to the Senate [1], the general effect of the *Lex Ovinia* was to establish a life-

haberent, ita post exactos eos consules quoque et tribuni militum consulari potestate conjunctissimos sibi quosque patriciorum et deinde plebeiorum legebant, donec Ovinia tribunicia intervenit, qua sanctum est ut censores ex omni ordine optimum quemque curiatim (*cod.* curiati : *Meier,* jurati) in senatum legerent; quo factum est ut qui praeteriti essent et loco moti, haberentur ignominiosi.' Both Mommsen (Staatsr. ii. p. 418) and Willems (Le droit publ. Rom. p. 189) think that this law first *gave* the *lectio* to the censor, and therefore assign to it the date 318–312 B. C. Mommsen brings it into close connection with the action of the consuls of 311 B. C.: Liv. ix. 30 'Itaque consules, qui eum annum secuti sunt, C. Junius Bubulcus tertium et Q. Aemilius Barbula iterum, initio anni questi apud populum, deformatum ordinem prava lectione senatus, qua potiores aliquot lectis praeteriti essent, negaverunt, eam lectionem se, quae sine recti pravique discrimine ad gratiam ac libidinem facta esset, observaturos: et senatum extemplo citaverunt eo ordine, qui ante censores Ap. Claudium et C. Plautium fuerat.' The *prava lectio,* he holds, violated the rule 'ut optimum quemque legerent.' The words of the plebiscitum *ex omni ordine* have been interpreted to mean 'from every order of the magistracy': an interpretation which can only be accepted in the sense that the censor was obliged to go through the list of ex-magistrates before selecting private individuals at his own discretion. The *quaestorii* could not as a rule have been included in the list. Our earliest definite notice of censorian procedure is in connection with the extensive *sublectio* of 216 B. C. There the ex-curule magistrates, not already on the list, were chosen, in the order of their creation: then the ex-aediles and tribunes of the plebs, and the *quaestorii*: lastly, distinguished individuals who had held no magistracy (Liv. xxiii. 23). That the censors could not have had the right of selection much before the year 312 is shown by the procedure of the consuls of 311 (Liv. l. c.), and is consistent with what we are told of the limited powers which the censors held originally. Mommsen finds a further proof of this in Liv. iv. 24 (319 B. C.), where it is said that Mamercus Aemilius was made an *aerarius,* but it is not mentioned that he was also struck off the list of the Senate.

[1] Mommsen lays too much stress on the theory that the *lectio senatus* was properly an election. He says, e. g., that the keeping in the Senate a person who was already there was treated legally as an exception (ii. p. 421). All that *lectio senatus* meant originally was probably merely the reading of the list of senators; this may even be the main connotation of *sublectio*; *adlectio* conveys more forcibly the idea of selection in accordance with the arbitrary choice of the magistrate who employs it.

tenure of the office of senator, and a tenure that could only be interrupted on moral grounds.

It has already been remarked that the *lectio senatus* had no necessary connection with the *census*. The consequence of this was that, according to the principles of constitutional law, the Senate might be filled up by a magistrate other than the censor. Twice we find a dictator exercising this power. In 216 B.C. M. Fabius Buteo was appointed *dictator ad supplendum senatum*[1], and in 81 B.C. Sulla as *dictator reipublicae constituendae causa* took upon himself the task of reconstructing the Senate on a new basis by the formal use of the *lectio*[2]; so that the power of pronouncing this particular kind of infamia might in very exceptional cases be transferred to other magistrates than the censors, as it had belonged to the consuls even after the creation of the censorship. Yet the exceptional position of the ordinary revising magistrate necessarily brought the *lectio senatus* into some connection with the *census*. Although the choice of senators had no necessary connection with, and was not vitiated by a failure in, the *lustrum*[3], yet the temporary tenure of office by the censor rendered it impossible for gaps to be filled up immediately on their occurrence, and the infamia, which in this case might be based on the rejection of existent, or the refusal to include expectant, members, was brought into connection with the infamia affecting the *populus* and the *equites* by the quinquennial periods at which it was revived.

The revision of the list of a body which formed the actual central government of the Roman State was, as might be expected, regarded as quite the most important of the censors' functions. The cleansing of the sovereign body necessarily took precedence of a similar attention to

[1] Liv. xxiii. 22. [2] Liv. Ep. 89; Plut. Pomp. 14; App. B. C. i. 100.
[3] Mommsen, Staatsr. p. 419, n. 3.

the subjects: and the making out of the senate's list was the first business of the censors after entrance on office. Considerations of dignity forbade the summoning of the Senate as a corporation similar to that of the *equites*; and even the summons to individuals, only possible at the *census*, had here to be dispensed with. There must, indeed, have been facilities offered to a senator of clearing himself of charges which the censors meant to make the ground of erasure from the list: but before the Clodian *plebiscitum* of 58 B.C. the appearance of the suspected individual, and the semi-judicial procedure involving accusation and evidence, which was sufficiently common in the proceedings at the *census*, seem to have been absent from this revision of the senate's list[1]. Nowhere, therefore, was the censor's *arbitrium* more apparent than in this procedure: and nowhere, considering the gravity of the consequences, could it have been exercised with greater discretion or on more certain grounds. The making out of the senate's list was, we know, accomplished as rapidly as possible. It took the simple form of affixing marks (*notae*) against certain names on the senatorial register and omitting these names in the revised list. Then followed the supplementary entry (*sublectio*) of the new names: and the censure might therefore take the form of rejecting (*movere*, *ejicere*) unworthy members from the list, or, as it is sometimes expressed, of passing them over (*praeterire*) in the

[1] We do indeed get evidence for formal procedure in the case of a senator (Liv. xxxix. 42), but the rapidity with which the list was made out must have rendered careful examination impossible. That it was unusual is shown by the fact that Asconius (in Pison. p. 124) makes Clodius' law have reference entirely to the Senate. That this is incorrect, and that the true account, viz. that it was meant to regulate the infamia generally, is given by Dio Cassius (xxxviii. 13), is probable. The statement of Asconius, however, illustrates the point that the chief necessity for the forms of a *judicium* was felt in connection with the *lectio senatus*.

reading of the list (*recitatio*): and also of omitting the names of individuals who, in accordance with the terms of the *Lex Ovinia*, had a claim to a seat at the Senate[1]. The collegiate principle operated very sharply as a check on the arbitrary power of the individual censor. The *veto* might be employed in two ways; names omitted from the list by one censor might be retained by the other, and there is equally little doubt that the election of a new member might be hindered by the opposition of one of the censors[2]. The other two guarantees of the proper use of the censorian power were of special importance in this the greatest of their functions: the *subscriptio censoria*, which implied a permanent record of the grounds on which they had founded their judgment, and the special oath that they would exercise their great discretionary powers without fear or favour. One of the curious anomalies that meet us so often in connection with the censorship resulted in the case (presumably rare) where these officials had ventured to strike from the list a curule magistrate whose rank gave him the power of transacting business with the Senate. Such a magistrate might, during his year of office, still preside at the board, of which he had been declared unworthy to be a member[3]. For over the magis-

[1] *Senatu movere* (Liv. xxxix. 42; Festus, p. 246), *emovere* (Liv. xlv. 15), *de senatu movere* (Cic. pro Cluent. 43, 122), *e* or *de senatu ejicere* (Cic. pro Cluent. 42, 119; Liv. xl. 51; xli. 27; xliii. 15); *praeterire* has reference to the reading of the list (Cic. pro Domo, 32, 84 'praeteriit in recitando senatu'), but may refer either to those already on the list (Cic. l. c.; Liv. xxiv. 44, xxxviii. 28) or to those who had a claim to be placed on it. Both classes may be referred to in Liv. xxvii. 11, xl. 51, and the latter especially in Liv. ix. 30. This latter class would be composed of those 'qui nondum a censoribus in senatum lecti, senatores non erant, sed quia honoribus populi usi erant, in senatum veniebant, et sententiae jus habebant' (Varro ap. Gell. iii. 18; cf. Liv. xxiii. 32; Fest. p. 339).

[2] Liv. xli. 57 'retinuit quosdam Lepidus a collega praeteritos.' Cf. Cic. pro Cluent. 43, 122.

[3] Such a case is mentioned by Liv. (xli. 27) where we find L. Cornelius

tracy the censorship had no control. It was the sphere of political honour, interference with which would have brought the censors into too sharp a collision with the liberties of the whole people; for these liberties were most clearly expressed in the free choice of popular representatives.

The mode in which the censorian infamia was pronounced against men of senatorial rank never varied throughout the Republic, and indeed reappeared under the same form during the constitutional rule of the early Principate. But it was necessarily more far-reaching in its consequences as long as the censorship remained *the* effectual mode of filling up gaps in the Senate: that is approximately during the period extending from 319 to 81 B.C. Sulla did not abolish the censors: but in accordance with his jealous legislation (which in this particular respect may even be pronounced misguided), he did his best to emancipate the Senate from these officials by creating an artificial mode in which the *curia* could be filled from the enlarged body of ex-quaestors. The censorship was indeed resumed again in 70 B.C. in obedience to a popular demand, and reappears at intervals throughout the remaining period of the Republic: and the creation of the office was always accompanied by a revision of the Senate. But the magistrate's functions were now confined more peculiarly to the rejection of individuals already on the list; and he lost the power which he had formerly possessed of passing over the names of individuals from the large body of applicants who had waited for admission

Scipio, praetor peregrinus for the year, excluded from the Senate. The two censors, who disqualified one another (Liv. xxix. 37), might have reversed one another's decisions. The *notatio* of a magistrate is rare; we find instances of a quaestor (Liv. xxiv. 43) and of a tribune (Liv. xliii. 15) made *aerarii*. The same anomaly would have resulted in the latter case as in that of the praetor.

at each recurring *lustrum*. This was not essentially a different power from that granted by the *Lex Ovinia*, but it could not be so strictly called a *lectio*, or making out of the list. An interesting but not easily answered question is whether the censors still retained their power of reversing the infamia. There are no positive evidences of this; but, in the absence of evidence to the contrary, it is probable that if a man, in accordance with the qualification of the quaestorship, had already possessed a seat in the Senate house, and had subsequently been excluded from the list, he might resume his position by the act of the censor. There could, in fact, have been no legal hindrance to his resuming his place, if the infamia was not perpetuated. Usually, however, the mode of regaining admission adopted by rejected members, as being on the whole a more certain one, was to appeal to the suffrages of the people, and to stand again for a magistracy which admitted to the body from which they had been excluded[1].

After the creation of the Principate we find, during the transition period which preceded the true 'birthday' of the new Monarchy, an extraordinary use made of the *lectio senatus* by Augustus. It was regular, in so far as the older constitutional theory had never recognised this revision as being necessarily associated with the censorship, but as capable of being transferred to the supreme magistrate for the time being. It was, however, quite as exceptional as the revision undertaken by the dictator Sulla in 81 B.C., and it could not have proceeded on the lines of, or have added anything to, the history of the infamia: for it aimed at narrowing down the body enlarged by the liberal policy of the dictator Caesar to the proportions of the old Italian council, and at excluding those who were *indignissimi*[2] only from a narrow Roman

[1] See p. 111.

[2] Suet. Aug. 35.

standpoint. Probably on these two occasions on which Augustus personally revised[1] the order the formalities or fictions of the old *lectio* were present: but the institution itself reappears again in its true Republican form under the early Principate, and always in connection with the *census*. With the last *census* under Vespasian it vanished, and the constitutional *lectio* of the early Republic was replaced by the arbitrary *adlectio* of individuals by the *princeps*, which was merely meant to supplement, in the interest of the ruler, the automatic method of creation which the Empire had inherited from the reforms of Sulla.

But two of the early *principes*, Claudius and Vespasian, assumed the censorship in person and, in accordance with Republican precedent, only as a temporary office: and with the exercise of the other powers of the office the formal *lectio senatus* was conjoined. It was marked by the same formalities as the Republican procedure[2], with the exception that under Claudius voluntary retirement was humanely permitted as a means of avoiding expulsion, even in consequence of acts which would always have produced infamia[3]. Eventually the character of the censorship was altered, and the institution itself rendered meaningless, by the assumption by Domitian of the office for life. This principle was not continued, but the *lectio senatus* involved in it was rigidly adhered to by succeeding Emperors, who kept

[1] The great revision was in 29–28 B.C., followed by another in 18 B.C. Suet. Aug. 35 'Senatorum affluentem numerum deformi et incondita turba . . . ad modum pristinum et splendorem redegit duabus lectionibus; prima, ipsorum arbitratu, qua vir virum legit; secunda, suo et Agrippae.' Cf. Dio Cass. liii. 42; liv. 12.

[2] An irregularity is noted in the censorship of Vitellius, the colleague of Claudius. Tac. Ann. xii. 4, 4 'Silanus repente per edictum Vitellii ordine senatorio movetur, quanquam lecto pridem senatu lustroque condito.'

[3] Tac. Ann. xi. 25, 5. Claudius allowed men *famosos probris* to retire 'ut judicium censorum ac pudor sponte cedentium permixta ignominiam mollirent.'

the power of adding to the list and striking from it as they pleased[1]. The censorship had, during the later period of its history, become almost identified with the control of the Senate: but so actual was the Emperor's control in this respect and so well established by other means, that it was not thought necessary to add another fiction, in the shape of a life-censorship, to that strange collection of powers which made up the unity in difference of the Roman Principate.

During the Principate a new mode of expulsion from the Senate was added to those already existing which deserves some notice, since it undoubtedly exercised an influence on the conception of mediate infamia in its application to this order; and perhaps helped to lead to a result which we shall soon have to describe: this result being the application of the rigid system of infamia as a means of excluding from the Senate and from higher offices. The Senate became indirectly a court of justice as the advising body to the consuls, who took cognizance *extra ordinem* of important criminal offences, as one of the two supreme heads of jurisdiction established in accordance with the principle of the dyarchy. A trial before the Senate, as it is often briefly but improperly called, naturally led, where the accused was a senator, and where the trial had ended in condemnation, to the expulsion of the offender from the ranks of his order. The Senate, it is true, claimed no right as such to expel members from its body. The process was always quasi-judicial. But the power seems to have been exercised very freely, and the instances with which we are furnished[2] seem to show that members were expelled, at the discretion of this body, even when loss of senatorial

[1] Dio Cass. liii. 17 καὶ τοὺς μὲν καταλέγουσι . . . ἐς τὸ βουλευτικόν, τοὺς δὲ καὶ ἀπαλείφουσιν ὅπου ἂν αὐτοῖς δόξῃ.

[2] See especially the instances in Tac. Ann. iii. 17, 8; vi. 48, 6.

rank was not a strictly legal consequence of the crime for which they were condemned. Above all it gave the Senate a chance of grappling with one of the growing evils of the Principate, the practice of *delatio*. Where the informer was a senator, and where the information had proved false, the Senate employed the weapon of expulsion. The legal ground for it no doubt was that they interpreted such false accusation as *calumnia*[1]. It was natural to extend the same principle to dishonest procedure on the part of an accuser, the object of which was to shield the criminal (*praevaricatio*). So closely were these evils brought home to the Senate on its becoming a court of justice, that, as a consequence of one such revelation in the reign of Nero, the *Senatus Consultum Turpillianum* was passed, which, by extending the limits of *calumnia* and *praevaricatio*, thereby extended the incidence of the infamia[2].

When we are dealing with the Senate of the Principate we feel that, whatever the decline in its actual powers may have been, the body we are considering bears a formal resemblance to that which had swayed the destinies of the Republic: and that the modifications introduced in the mode of selection to the order were only such as were absolutely required to adapt it to the great powers of the newly-created Republican magistrate, the *princeps*. But when we turn to the Empire of Constantine we feel that we are dealing with a wholly new order of things. The actual Senate was now but the kernel of another order, larger and more imposing than that body itself. This was the senatorial order, composed of the *clarissimi*. Entrance into the inner circle of active senators was still effected

[1] See the instances in Tac. Ann. iv. 31, 8; xii. 59, 4.

[2] Tac. Ann. xiv. 41, 2, where the case of Valerius Ponticus is described. Tacitus says 'additur senatus consulto, qui talem operam emptitasset vendidissetve, perinde poena teneretur ac publico judicio calumniae condemnatus'; cf. Dig. xlviii. 16 (*ad s. c. Turpillianum*).

through the quaestorship and the praetorship, especially through the latter, for by the end of the fourth century A.D. the quaestorship tends to disappear, and dispensation must have been frequently granted by the Emperors from this useless magistracy[1]. The Emperor might still employ the *adlectio*; but, in view of his actual control of the offices through which the Senate was entered, this was only necessary when he meant to dispense a candidate from the expenses of the praetorship. Such candidates of Caesar were *adlecti et immunes*[2]. Entrance into the senatorial order, on the other hand, might be effected in a great many ways. The son of a *clarissimus* is prospectively a possible senator by birth[3]; but his reception even into the order requires a formal *professio*, made when he has reached maturity[4]. It was, however, with entrance to the order, even more than with admission to the actual Senate, that the Emperor's power of *adlectio* was concerned. Many modes were adopted by which the introduction of officials of a lower rank into the order of *clarissimi* might be effected[5]; and in some cases this introduction was accompanied by dispensation from the praetorship, and thereby by admission to the Senate as well.

What the effect of this system was on the infamia in its application to the Senate is not very easy to determine.

[1] Lécrivain (Le Sénat romain depuis Dioclétien, p. 10) conjectures that candidates, who were able to pay the expenses of the praetorship, were probably dispensed from the quaestorship.

[2] Cod. Theod. vi. 23, 1.

[3] Symm. Ep. x. 66 'his copulati sunt quos senatui vestro recens ortus adjecit.' Lécrivain shows (op. cit. p. 12) that 'senatui' here means only the order.

[4] Such are the individuals mentioned by Symmachus as being added by the *professio* to the senatorial *census*. Symm. Ep. x. 67 'ut majestas vestra cognoscat quis in amplissimam curiam collegarum numerus influxerit, et quid censibus senatoriis aut nova professio incrementi dederit, aut exemptio vetus amputarit.'

[5] For these modes see Lécrivain op. cit. pp. 16–19.

The album of the Senate is kept by the prefect of the city, and it must have been the business of this official to keep the Emperor informed of any moral lapses on the part of members which rendered their expulsion desirable. But the system of exclusion was in some respects more rigid and definite than it had been in the earlier periods. It is hardly necessary to remark that Constantine's Edict, which excluded *the infames* from all dignities applied with special force to the Senate and to the order of the *clarissimi*. The praetorian infamia, the history of which it will soon be our business to trace, had, in fact, through interpretation and extension by imperial constitutions, assumed the dimensions of a great and rigid system which could be so applied. But there are passages in the Theodosian Code which prove that general moral considerations were still taken into account, at least in the selection of senators[1]. There is little reason to doubt that similar considerations might lead to their exclusion from the order, of which they were already members: and we may therefore conclude that, besides the application of the systematized infamia, the Emperor exercises a *notatio*, which was no doubt meant to involve permanent disqualification, although it was necessarily capable of reversal by his successor on the throne.

[1] Cod. Theod. ii. 17, 2 (Constantine A. D. 321) 'ita ut senatores apud gravitatis tuae officium de suis moribus et honestate perdoceant.'

Ib. xii. 1. 74, 5 (Valentinian, Valens and Gratian A. D. 371), 'ceterum suae potestatis (as opposed to the *curiales*), et nullis per provincias functionibus obligatis, vel longae militiae labore vel proximis erga nos juvantibus codicillos senatorios reportaverint, nisi vitiis aut actae vitae opprobriis amplissimo ordine deprehendantur indigni, indepti semel clarissimatus dignitatem perpetuo manebunt in ordine senatorum.'

§ 3. *The Censorian Infamia in its connection with the 'equites.'*

The constitution of the next class, the *equites*, demands a more particular examination, in connection with the censorian revision to which it was subjected, than need be accorded to the two other classes of the voting populace and the Senate. The reason is that the word *eques* itself varied considerably in its applications during the period of the Republic, and perhaps even in the time of the Empire; and although it would be out of place to go minutely into the history of the Roman knights, some consideration of the various senses in which the word was used is necessary in order to guard against misconceptions as to the nature of the particular class which is mentioned as subject to this special scrutiny. The word *equites* was primarily applied to the citizen cavalry of 1,800 men, serving on horses supplied by the State. These formed the *centuriae equitum equo publico*, which remained unaltered in numbers at least until the time of Sulla, and in all essential respects unaltered in form to the close of the Republic. This body was the *ordo equester* in the strict sense of the words[1], but this title soon became extended beyond its proper bounds. Somewhere about the close of the fifth century B.C.—tradition puts the change at the time of the siege of Veii 403 B.C.—individuals not included in the eighteen centuries were admitted to serve as cavalry-men with their own horses (*equo privato*). A particular *census* was required from such individuals. They formed no

[1] The official terminology applicable to the order is known to us chiefly from inscriptions of the Empire. The full official title was *eques Romanus equo publico* (Wilmanns, 2178, 2182), which was shortened, sometimes into *eques Romanus*, sometimes into *equo publico* (Wilmanns, Index, p. 540), the latter expression being less usual and more technical than the former (Mommsen, Staatsr. iii. p. 480).

definite corps; but, after they had proved their monetary qualification before the censor[1], they were selected for service by the *imperator*. One of the consequences of this change may have been that the qualification required for these *equites equo privato*[2] was extended to the *equites equo publico*: although, since the latter had no doubt always been selected from the richer citizens, this was no great innovation. Another and far more important consequence was that the term *eques*, and even the expression *ordo equester*, were transferred from the possessors of public horses, not only to those who served *equo privato*, but to all who had proved, by reference to the *census*, their right to serve in the cavalry at all. The term *eques* thus came loosely to denote anyone possessed of a certain *census*, which was subsequently fixed at 400,000 sesterces, and who was therefore potentially a knight[3]. When we bear in mind this extension of the term, we are not surprised to find the designation *equites*

[1] Polyb. vi. 42, 9 πλουτίνδην αὐτῶν γεγενημένης ὑπὸ τοῦ τιμητοῦ τῆς ἐκλογῆς.

[2] There seems to be no direct authority for the expression *equites equo privato* as an official title. Yet that those who served *equo privato* were called *equites* is undoubted. Belot (Histoire des chev. rom.) employs these words to describe the moneyed class created by this extension of service. Marquardt employs the convenient, but hardly authorized, expression *equites censu* to describe this class (Hist. eq. Rom. iii. 2).

[3] There is no direct authority for this particular *census* earlier than the Principate: unless we accept as such the conjectural filling up of the *lacuna* in the qualifications for the *judices* under the *Lex Acilia Repetundarum* (C. I. L. i. 198, l. 16) 'facito utei CDL viros ita legat quei ha[ce *civitate HS $\overline{CCCC}$ n. plurisve census siet*].' That the 'knights' who sat on the juries were chosen by reference to a *census* is shown by Cicero (Phil. i. 8, 20 'census praefiniebatur—in judice enim spectari et fortuna debet et dignitas'). Mispoulet (Inst. Rom. ii. p. 200) concludes from a passage of Livy (xxiv. 2) that no *census* existed for the *equites* in 214 B.C. The passage may perhaps be taken as an indication that no strict *census* then existed for the *equites equo publico*; but it proves nothing in respect to the other 'knights,' who at that time had none of the characteristics of a corporate body, and would not therefore have been mentioned in an official enumeration such as this.

applied to the important political class created by the *Lex Judiciaria* of C. Gracchus in 123 B.C. The main qualifications of the Gracchan jurors, so far as they can be determined, were, that they should be possessed of the equestrian *census*, that they should not hold or have held certain public offices which were specified, that they should not be senators or men of senatorial family. These qualifications would, therefore, have excluded many of the *equites equo publico*, who were sons of senators: but the *judices* would all have been *equites* in the wider sense of the word: and hence the civil class of *equites* was given something of a corporate character, and because of itself something approaching to an *ordo*. Such is the history of the *equites* so far as it can be traced with any certainty. The history of the order after this period can only be a matter of conjecture[1]. The important point to be borne in mind throughout, with reference to the censorian revision, is—that the only corporate body which the censor specially examines is that of the old *centuriae equitum equo publico*. The other knights appear as individuals with the mass of the citizens; the censor's only business with them is to admit them as 'knights' by admitting that they possessed the requisite *census*. The censor, therefore, would not have revised specially such a class as that created by C. Gracchus; it is equally improbable that he would have revised specially such

[1] The history of the order from the time of Sulla to the close of the Republic, and its constitution during that period, must rest largely on conjecture. The only certain point is that some of the constituent elements of the *centuriae equitum* in the later years of the Republic can be made out with a fair degree of accuracy. Such elements were the sons of senators, the mounted officers of the army—at least the *tribuni militum*—and perhaps also the members of the vigintivirate, who belonged to the *laticlavii* of the Empire; these may have been enrolled as a matter of course in the equestrian centuries. A large portion of the body would have held this position simply as preparatory to a subsequent senatorial career.

equites as those to which later *leges judiciariae* gave wholly or partially the control of the law-courts.

If we imagine that the *equites* to whom the Gracchan and other laws gave the courts were selected exclusively from the *equites equo publico*, this fact would indeed have given additional importance to the censorian revision of the equestrian centuries. It must have ceased to become a purely military revision, and the consideration of the mode in which the duties of this order had been performed in the courts of law must have been specially taken into account[1]. But if, as is more probable, by *equites* were

[1] Mommsen considers that the *equites* included in the *album judicum* created by the *Lex Aurelia* of 70 B.C. were the *equites equo publico* (Staatsr. iii. p. 486); and he takes the same view of the *Lex Judiciaria* of C. Gracchus. But the account of the *Lex Aurelia* in Schol. Bob. ad Cic. pro Flacco, 2, 4 ('lex enim Aurelia judiciaria ita cavebat, ut ex parte tertia senatores judicarent, ex partibus duabus tribuni aerarii et equites, *ejusdem scilicet ordinis viri*'), compared with the passages of Cicero in which he identifies the *equites* and *tribuni aerarii* (pro Font. 12, 36; pro Cluent. 43, 121, 47, 130; pro Flacco, 38, 96) can best be understood if we imagine that by *equites* under this law were meant merely the possessors of the requisite monetary qualification. If we accept Belot's conjecture that the *tribuni aerarii* were the second class in the *census*, no sharp line could be drawn between them and the first class. To admit members of the highest *census* would be a political change, which would justify the importance attributed to the laws of Gracchus and Cotta by Cicero, and explain their known effects, especially in connection with provincial government. But this effect could scarcely have been produced by a mere admission from the *equites equo publico*, a body which was losing in importance at this period, and was largely composed of men under senatorial age. The whole history of the political contests that centred round the courts of law at this period prove that the contest was between the government, i. e. the senate, on the one hand, and the moneyed class on the other. It is true that in the letter of Q. Cicero, de Pet. Cons. (8, 33) the influence of the *ordo equester* (in the wider sense of the term) over the *centuriae equitum* is mentioned; but this was an influence that could not be guaranteed to be perpetually effective. The mode in which the latter are spoken of, as young men with no very definite political convictions, shows how inappropriate it would have been, from the standpoint of the anti-senatorial party, to entrust the courts of law to such hands.

simply meant all citizens of equestrian *census*—with certain restrictive conditions added by the Gracchan law, and perhaps by others—then the censorian supervision of the *judices*, the importance of which we learn from Cicero's appeal in the 'Divinatio,' must have been conducted only as a part of the general scrutiny of the mass of citizens.

We are met by precisely the same difficulty in connection with the organization of the early Principate. The question arises whether, under this *régime* as under that of the Republic, we have in the *ordo equester* a civil as well as a military class, or whether the only *equites* during the Empire were those serving *equo publico.* The balance of evidence is on the whole in favour of the existence of two orders during the reigns of the earliest emperors, and of the disappearance of one of these at a period corresponding to the close of Trajan's or the beginning of Hadrian's rule[1].

[1] Mommsen (Staatsr. iii. p. 489 ff.) thinks that all the *equites* under the Empire were *equites equo publico.* According to this view the definition of an *eques* would be 'a citizen whose monetary qualification had been admitted, and who had sent in a request for an *equus publicus* which the Emperor had granted.' Mispoulet (Inst. Rom. ii. p. 204) seems to minimise the importance of the imperial selection : but that the selection was of importance is clearly proved by such inscriptions as *equo publico honoratus* (Wilm. 244, 2208, 2246 *b*), *a divo Hadriano equo publico honoratus* (Wilm. 1825), *equo publico exornatus ab Impp. Severo et Antonino Augg.* (Wilm. 1575). The view of Mommsen has been combated by Willems (Le dr. publ. p. 385). To his arguments we may add that the usurpation of the gold ring by freedmen, which was repressed by Claudius (Suet. Cl. 25) and Domitian, and the inspection in the theatre instituted by the latter (Martial, v. 8), can refer only to a civil order of *equites* ; these pretenders could scarcely have claimed to be *equites equo publico* : and again that Dio Cassius, according to the probable interpretation of the passage which is given by Naudet (De la noblesse chez les Romains, p. 82) distinguishes the *equites equo publico* from 'the other' *equites* (Dio, lvi. 42, οἵ τε ἱππεῖς, οἵ τε ἐκ τοῦ τέλους καὶ οἱ ἄλλοι). On the whole we follow the view of Belot, who thinks that the *equites* were at the beginning of the Principate what they had been at the end of the Republic, i. e. the general class regulated by a *census* together with the close order of the *equites equo publico*, but believes that the order ended by becoming what it had been in origin, the corporation of the *equites equo publico* (Hist. des chev. rom.

The distinction, however, between the modes of revision of the two orders is of less importance under the Empire than under the Republic. The civil *equites* would no longer have been taken with the mass of the citizens. Even before the institution of the special imperial bureau *a censibus*, some commission with corresponding powers, such as those occasionally employed by Augustus, would no doubt have kept and constantly revised the list of both the *equites* and the *equites equo publico*, as long as these two classes existed side by side.

The review of the knights (*recognitio equitum*) was during the Republic an integral part of the *census*, and is sometimes spoken of as the *equitum census*[1]. It took place, however, not in the Campus Martius, where the *concio* of the citizens was summoned for assessment and scrutiny, but in the Forum[2], where most of the censorian business was transacted. The knights appear as a cor-

ii. pp. 334 and 365). This view is probable and may be supported by the following evidence; (1) the title *quadrigenarius* which appears in later inscriptions as expressing the qualification for a *judex* seems distinct from equestrian rank; compare (e. g.) *L. Lucceio—judici CCCC selecto* (Orelli 2357) and *quin. decur. judi(cum) (inter) quatringenarios* (Henzen, 6469) with *judex decuriarum V equo publico per Trajanum* (Wilm. 2294), *equo publico judex selectus ex V decuriis* (Wilm. 2110), *equum publicum habens adlectus in V decurias* (Wilm. 2203); (2) the gold ring became eventually a means of conferring, not equestrian rank, but *ingenuitas* merely (Dig. xxxviii. 2, 3; Justin. Novellae, 78); (3) the most probable interpretation of certain words of Gaius and Ulpian is that the monetary qualification was not alone sufficient to confer equestrian rank under the Antonine Emperors (Gaius in Dig. xxiv. 1, 42; Ulpian, Fragm. 7, 2). The change in the character of the *equites* may, therefore, be considered established, but there is no evidence to fix its date. It is not improbable, however, that it accompanied Hadrian's reorganization of the bureaucracy.

[1] Recognitio equitum (Suet. Claud. 16): so 'equitatum recognoscere (Liv. xxxix. 44; Val. Max. ii. 9, 7); 'equitum turmas recognoscere' (Suet. Aug. 38); 'equitum census' (Cic. pro Cluent. 48, 134; Liv. xxix. 37; Gell. iv. 20); so 'equites recensere (Liv. xxxviii. 28; xliii. 16; Suet. Vesp. 9).

[2] Plut. Pomp. 22.

porate body, and, while the censor reads the list of names[1] each member of the corps is summoned in turn by the herald's voice[2] before the tribunal. They appear, like the other citizens, in the order of their tribes, and each knight files past in turn, leading his horse by the bridle, and waits before the magistrates to hear the words of praise or blame. It was, in the first place, a military scrutiny; the attention of the censors was first directed to the question whether they could claim their discharge. In the earliest times of the Republic, when the knights were the active citizen cavalry at Rome, there was an evident incompatibility between the possession of a public horse and a seat in the senate:—later this incompatibility was not felt, and in the year 204 B.C. we find that both censors were themselves *equites*[3]. But again, towards the close of the second century, the rule was enforced by law that a man who entered the Senate must cease to be an *eques*[4], and to quit the centuries he had to 'enumerate each of the generals and commanders under whom he had served, to submit to an examination of his conduct, and thus be released from the service[5]'. When further we remember that, at least as late as the period of the Gracchi, military service, in the camp or the province, was a necessary qualification for a magistracy, and that this service, which for the cavalry was ten

[1] Suet. Calig. 16 'eorum, qui minore culpa tenerentur, nominibus modo in recitatione praeteritis.' Lange (Röm. Alt. i. 584) takes this of the *recitatio* of the *album equitum* which closed the procedure. The list, however, must have been read by the censors during the *recognitio*: and it is improbable that it was read a second time, especially in the time of the Empire when enormous numbers took part in the procession.

[2] Val. Max. ii. 9, 7; Varro ap. Non. p. 61.

[3] Liv. xxix. 37.

[4] Cic. de Repub. iv. 2 'nimis multis jam stulte hanc utilitatem tolli cupientibus, qui novam largitionem quaerunt aliquo plebiscito reddendorum equorum.'

[5] Plut. Pomp. 22.

years, had to be proved before the censors[1], we see how the military discharge granted by these officials became of political importance. No doubt, as a rule, this *missio honesta* had to be granted, if the *eques* proved his case: but the censors claimed and exercised the right of not allowing past service to count, and even, while taking away the public horse, of demanding renewed cavalry service at the rider's own expense[2]. It is one of the cases in which infamia almost becomes a penal measure.

More important, however, and more significant of the censorian power than this enforced retention in the service, is the ignominious dismissal from the centuries before the term of service was completed. As this was primarily a military revision, we find certain special grounds of censure such as the uncared-for condition of the horse (*impolitia*[3]), determining its rider's removal from the ranks, or at least prohibiting his receiving any further assistance from the State for its support[4]. But every ground of censure which could be based on any moral taint is as applicable to the knight as to the commoner, and even more so, since the standard of *existimatio* is in the former case higher than in the latter. To dismiss a knight from the centuries was often felt to be too slight a penalty, and it was often, perhaps usually, combined

[1] Plut. C. Gracch. 2. This qualification was abolished in the later Republic. The *stipendia*, which were one of the qualifications for municipal magistracies, might be served *in castris inve provincia* (*Lex Julia Municip.* l. 100).

[2] Liv. xxvii. 11 (209 B.C.). '(Censores) addiderunt acerbitati (i. e. the deprivation of the public horse) etiam tempus, ne praeterita stipendia prodereut iis, quae equo publico emeruerant, sed dena stipendia equis privatis facerent.' It resembles in principle the arbitrary increase of taxation of an *aerarius* (Liv. iv. 24) or of a *caelebs* (Val. Max. ii. 9, 1).

[3] Gell. iv. 12 'si quis eques Romanus equum habere gracilentum aut parum nitidum visus erat "impolitiae" notabatur.'

[4] Festus, p. 108, 'impolitias censores facere dicebantur, cum equiti aes abnegabant ob equum male curatum.'

with removal from the tribe or relegation to the *aerarii*. After the knight had appeared before the tribunal, if the censors desired him to remain in the centuries, they told him to lead his horse on (*traduc equum*[1]); when they judged him unworthy to remain, they bade him sell his horse (*vende equum*[2]). Removal from the ranks of the knights is generally expressed by reference to the deprivation of the public horse[3]. Since the main object of the revision was the military efficiency of the corps, bodily unfitness for further service was naturally a ground for dismissal. It was equally naturally not a ground for censure, and counted, with the retirement from service consequent on a completion of the requisite campaigns, as a *missio honesta*[4].

The final duty of the censors was the filling up of the places thus left vacant. Fresh knights were recruited from the ranks of the infantry (*pedites*), either at the censors' own discretion, or, if we suppose that at any period of the Republic a fixed *census* was required for members of the *centuriae equitum*, with reference to such monetary qualification.

The corps of the *equites equo publico* continued on into the Empire, and on a vastly extended scale. During the earlier Principate the censorship was occasionally resumed, yet even at this period the conferment of the public horse at the discretion of the *princeps* was probably not unknown[5],

[1] Cic. pro Cluent. 48, 134; Val. Max. iv. 1, 10.

[2] Liv. xxix. 37; xlv. 15.

[3] *Adimere equum*, Liv. xxiv. 18; xli. 27; xlii. 10, &c.

[4] Gell. vii. 22 'nimis pingui homini et corpulento censores equum adimere solitos—non enim poena id fuit, ut quidam existimant; sed munus sine ignominia remittebatur.' For 'ignominia' as applied to dismissal from the centuries, see Suet. Calig. 16; Claud. 16 ('sine ignominia dimisit'). The missio in the case mentioned by Gellius is parallel to the 'missio causaria, quae propter valetudinem laboribus militiae solvit' (Ulpian in Dig. iii. 2, 2).

[5] The passage in Suet. (Tib. 41) where it is stated that Tiberius became

and thus the centuries might be recruited even when there was no official *census*. But where censors are found, as under Augustus, or where Emperors themselves undertake this office, as Claudius and Vespasian, the selection and elimination of *equites* must have followed the same rules as those which characterised the Republican revision[1]. The old censorian principles of infamia were followed in these cases[2], and these principles were of greater importance now that the *corps d'élite* of the later Republic was rapidly becoming the civil service staff of the imperial administration. But the censorship was only an occasional office under the Empire, and the *equites equo publico*, already a large class under Augustus, became still larger when the principle was recognised that there was no other mode of attaining equestrian rank, and gaining admission to the official career which depended on it, than by receiving the gift of the public horse from the Emperor[3]. We are not therefore surprised to find a permanent bureau established which had the duties of admission to the ranks of this order as one of its special functions. This bureau, which was also concerned with the necessarily less frequent requests for admission into the Senate, appears to have been a branch of the department of petitions (*a libellis*[4]):

so careless 'ut postea non decurias equitum unquam supplerit,' cannot be taken as an evidence: since when the *equites* are spoken of as *judices* at this period, we do not know what knights are referred to.

[1] It has been thought that the revision of knights described in Suet. Claud. 16; Vesp. 9 refers to the censorships of these Emperors. It may, however, refer to the proceedings at the *pompa*.

[2] Suet. Claud. 16.

[3] When Strabo (iii. 5, 3, p. 169) says that as the result of a census 500 knights (πεντακοσίους ἄνδρας τιμηθέντας ἱππικούς) were recognised at Gades, and as many at Patavium in Italy, he is speaking of a time when there was more than one mode of admission to equestrian rank. We cannot assume, therefore, that this great number of municipal knights consisted all of *equites equo publico*.

[4] *A censibus a libellis Aug.* (Wilm. 1249 b), *a libellis et censibus* (Wilm. 1257),

H

and although the primary duties of its members were those of admission, yet they must also have kept a watch over the maintenance of the qualifications requisite for the retention of rank in an order. They would probably have pointed out to the *princeps* the cases in which either the money or the character qualification had ceased to exist, and many a knight would probably have found himself removed from the corps, without the open disgrace of being deprived of his public horse at the annual procession.

The revision at this annual procession can only be regarded as supplementary to that of the standing bureau, from the time that these two institutions existed side by side. This third mode of revision has, like the second, no parallel in the time of the Republic. It was then a simple pageant which was witnessed on the Ides of July, when the knights passed on horseback—

> 'From Castor in the Forum to Mars without the wall,'

to celebrate the help given by the Twin Brethren at the battle of the Lake Regillus. This pageant, which had fallen into disuse in the later Republic, was revived by Augustus: and the procession of the knights (*transvectio equitum*) became to some extent a revision of the order (*probatio equitum*)[1]. It differed from the *recognitio equitum* of the Republic in that the knights now passed

a censibus equitum romanorum (Wilm. 1275, C. I. L. x. 6657), which Wilmanns interprets as though it were *a censibus accipiendis equites romanos*, but it clearly refers to the department *a libellis*, and Mommsen is no doubt right in saying that this one mention of the knights is a proof that their requests for admission were the most frequent which the bureau had to consider. Greek equivalents ἐπὶ κῆνσον τοῦ Σεβαστοῦ (C. I. Gr. 3497), ἐπὶ κῆνσον (C. I. Gr. 3751).

[1] Suet. Aug. 38 'Equitum turmas frequenter recognovit, post longam intercapedinem reducto more transvectionis.' When Suetonius adds 'sed neque detrahi quemquam in transvehendo ab accusatore passus est (quod fieri solebat)' he seems to be confusing the *recognitio* with the *transvectio* of the Republic.

sitting on horseback, and in the far greater numbers which appeared in the procession; we are told that on one occasion as many as five thousand knights took part in the *pompa* before Augustus[1]. The *missio* which the censors had granted in the earlier period of the Republic was now no longer necessary—nor indeed attainable. The position of an *eques* was now one that was held for life: and except that the career ended for a member of the order with his entrance into the Senate (for the standing incompatibility of the positions of *eques* and *senator*, recognised in the later Republic, had now been emphasized by the still more divergent careers of the two orders), exemption from the formal duties of an *eques equo publico* was the exception rather than the rule. As a means of meeting demands for retirement from this tiresome official duty, Augustus, besides making unavoidable concessions to those whose physical infirmities prevented them from riding, finally permitted all members above the age of thirty-five to return their public horse and thus retire from the corps[2]. But the censure was directed nearly in the same manner as in the Republican *recognitio*; the knights were questioned one by one, and made to give an account of their conduct[3]; those whose answers were unsatisfactory were visited with *ignominia*, which in its severest form could hardly have gone further than the deprivation of the public horse[4]. This *probatio* of the *equites* was no doubt

[1] Dionys. vi. 13.

[2] Suet Aug. 38 '...et senio vel aliqua corporis labe insignibus permisit, praemisso in ordine equo, ad respondendum, quoties citarentur, pedibus venire; mox reddendi equi gratiam fecit eis, qui majores annorum quinque et triginta retinere eum nollent.'

[3] The words quoted from Suet. (Aug. 38, on the preced. page) seem to imply that the accusation by a third party, not unusual though not necessary in the time of the Republic, was dispensed with by Augustus.

[4] Suet. Aug. 39. 'Unumquemque equitum rationem vitae reddere coëgit; atque ex improbatis alios poena, alios ignominia notavit; plures

regarded by Augustus as a serious part of the duties of the State; it is shown by the fact that more than once he asked the Senate for committees, either of three members or of ten, to assist him in the work[1]. There can be little doubt, therefore, of the seriousness of the infamia thus publicly pronounced. The *pompa* is found recurring under subsequent Emperors, it is mentioned in connection with the reigns of Caligula, Nero, Vitellius, and Severus Alexander[2], and the existence of it can be traced as late as the fourth century A.D.[3] But its importance, as a means of producing infamia, must probably have diminished after the institution of the permanent bureau, which had as one of its duties the *census* of the knights[4].

With the close of the Principate we have come to an end of the history of the *equites*, as a great administrative order of the Empire. The knights disappear with the dyarchy. Under the monarchical rule of Constantine and his successors, which made the assignment of all functions and the title of each branch of nobility depend immediately on the sovereign, there was no motive for keeping the equestrian career entirely distinct from the

admonitione, sed variâ.' (The *poena* here must have been an increase of service or burdens parallel to those penalties inflicted by the censors of the Republic: see p. 95.) Suet. Calig. 16, 'palam adempto equo, quibus aut probri aliquid aut ignominiae inesset.' Cf. Ov. Trist. ii. 541.

[1] Suet. Aug. 37 'triumviratum legendi senatus, et alterum recognoscendi turmas equitum, quotiescunque opus esset.' Cap. 39, 'impetratisque a senatu decem adjutoribus.' These commissions are brought into relation with the *pompae* by Suetonius. It is possible, however, that they may have acted on other occasions.

[2] Caligula (Suet. Calig. 16); Nero (Dio Cass. lxiii. 13); Vitellius' regulations about the *equites* (Tac. Hist. ii. 62) probably have reference to the *transvectio*; a similar reference is perhaps implied in the words of Lampridius (Alex. Sev. 15) '(senatum et) equestrem ordinem purgavit.'

[3] Zosimus, ii. 29.

[4] With reference to purely military offences the penalty of loss of standing could of course be pronounced at once. Dig. xlix. 16 (*de re mil.*) 5, 1 'qui in pace deseruit, eques gradu pellendus est.'

senatorial. By a curious revolution of history the title *equites* is again restricted to a definite urban organisation. We have seen that the review of the knights still persists in the fourth century A.D., and a constitution of this period still calls that body the second order in the Empire[1]. They, therefore, still exist as a corporation, but a corporation found mainly in the two capitals, Rome and Constantinople[2], the members of which are registered, under Constantine, before the prefect of the watch. That a city prefect, not of the highest rank, should deal with the civil honour of members of this order shows the little distinction it enjoyed: and this is still further shown by an examination of the class, which still perpetuated to some extent the functions and dignities of the old equestrian order. In the third century two titles are borne by the *equites*, those of *egregius* and *perfectissimus*. The title *egregius* disappears during the later Empire; but a class of functionaries of inferior rank to the *clarissimi* is still designated by the title *perfectissimi*. Imperial constitutions show that *vir perfectissimus* is now quite distinct from *eques*[3]: and the *perfectissimatus* denotes a class composed of very different elements, connected only by a common title of nobility, and created by the Emperor, which bears a shadowy resemblance to the equestrian order, composed as this was in the later Principate of functionaries of different rank, connected only by the gift of the public horse. Like the list of the

[1] Cod. Theod. vi. 36, 1 (Valentinian and Valens 364 A.D) 'equites Romani, quos secundi gradus in urbe omnium obtinere volumus dignitatem ex indigenis Romanis et civibus eligantur, vel his peregrinis, quos corporatis non oportet annecti.'

[2] The title appears to have been occasionally given to provincial corporations, e.g. to the *navicularii*, supposed in this case to be those of Africa (Cod. Theod. xiii. 5, 16; Gratian, Valentinian and Theodosius A.D. 379).

[3] Cod. Theod. vi. 36 and 37 (the distinct titles dealing with the distinct orders): cf. the constitution cited in the next note.

equites, that of the *perfectissimi* is made out by an urban functionary, apparently by the vicar of one of the city prefects[1].

In concluding this review of the infamia, regarded as a branch of public law, some distinctions are suggested between its operation in the Republic and in the Empire. During the Republic the civic privileges possessed by the ordinary citizen, especially the right of voting, were of more importance, and were therefore carefully regulated by the State. In the Principate the *populus* had sunk into comparative unimportance, and the *cura morum* of the *princeps*, which is not so much a definite function attaching to his office as one arising naturally from the other administrative duties in which he is engaged, was concerned, more exclusively than in the Republic, in preserving the purity of the two higher orders, the Senate and the *equites*[2]. Once, indeed, during the later Principate we find the censorship restored. In the year 251 A.D., during the reign of Decius, an attempt was made to call the old institution into new life. The duty of election was entrusted to the Senate, and the acclamations of the fathers made Valerian guardian of their own morals and of those of the community. But the prudence of Valerian was proof against the committal of a blunder and an anachronism. 'Do not call me,' he said to the Emperor, 'to pronounce judgment on the people, the soldiers, the Senate, the world; it is for this task that you bear the name Augustus. With you the censorship rests, no mere citizen

[1] Cod. Theod. ii. 17, 2 (Constantine A. D. 321), 2 'ita ut senatores apud gravitatis tuae officium de suis moribus et honestate perdoceant, perfectissimi apud vicariam praefecturam' (? 'vicarius praefecturae urbis,' an office which we know existed under Constantine, C. I. L. vi. n. 1704; Mommsen, Mem. del Instit. ii. 309-311), 'equites Romani et ceteri apud praefectum vigilum, navicularii apud praefectum annonae.'

[2] So of Severus Alexander (A. D. 222-235) we are told 'senatum et equestrem ordinem purgavit' (Vit. Alex. 15).

can fill it[1].' The Empire which succeeded the Principate, showed equal anxiety, though in a less discriminating way, to maintain the dignity of the orders of nobility which it created. The definite infamia, developed from the praetor's Edict, came in time to involve exclusion from all honours and dignities. How early this result was reached we cannot say with certainty. In the time of Hadrian and the early Antonine Emperors infamia is often mentioned as debarring from special posts: but the references to exclusion at this period look rather as though it was based on special grounds applicable to special cases. Once indeed we find a regulation, dating from the reigns of Severus and Antoninus, unimportant in itself but of great interest as one of the earliest instances known of exclusion from office being based on the infamia of the praetor's Edict. A rescript of these Emperors declared that no one could be a *legatus*, or accredited representative of a municipal town, who had not the *jus postulandi*, that is, apparently, who belonged to the second class named by the praetor, the *in turpitudine notabiles*, who had no right of postulating for others[2]. The obvious necessity for such a regulation in the case of a *legatus*, and the very fact that a rescript was required to create or confirm the disability, show that legislation on this subject was occasional and dictated by the necessity of meeting particular contingencies as they arose. Again, the hesitating manner in which Marcian, writing probably under Antoninus (Caracalla), speaks of infamia as a bar to the exercise of

[1] Vita Valerianorum, 5 & 6.

[2] Marcian in Dig. l. 7, 5 (4), 1, 'sed et eos quibus jus postulandi non est legatione fungi non posse et ideo harena missum non jure legatum esse missum divi Severus et Antoninus rescripserunt.' The reference seems to be to the class in the second Edict 'de postulando' (Dig. iii. 1, 1, 5), although it is doubtful whether gladiators occurred, in the second Edict with *bestiarii*, or in the third Edict with actors (see p. 121).

the important office of *assessor*, or recognised legal assistant to a judge or provincial governor[1], shows that there was no definite rule of exclusion recognised at this period[2]. We have, in fact, no certain knowledge of the universal application of the infamia for this purpose earlier than the regulation of Constantine, which has been so frequently referred to in this work as marking an epoch in the history of Civil Honour.

The history of the *ordines*, which has here been sketched, is but another proof of the old lesson that the truest type of aristocracy is to be found in Republican governments. Caesar, the great iconoclast, knew that he was breaking the spirit of the Republic when he flooded the Senate with men of low and foreign birth, and caused admission to nobility to depend on the will of the *princeps* alone. In his reaction against this policy, as in his other institutions, Augustus restored the Republic. But Caesar's was the policy of the Empire, not of the Principate. As it was Caesar that designed the plan of crippling Roman law by codifying it in its infancy,—a consummation for which the world was only prepared six centuries later,—so it was he who first suggested the great distinction which we observe between the orders of nobility as they existed respectively under the Republic and under the Empire of Constantine. But nearly four centuries were required before the Roman world was fit for the realisation of even this portion of the plans of the over-hasty dictator: and meanwhile the conservatism of Augustus had given the

[1] Marcian in Dig. i. 22, 2 'liberti adsidere possunt. Infames autem licet non prohibeantur legibus adsidere, attamen arbitror, ut aliquo quoque decreto principali refertur constitutum, non posse officio adsessoris fungi.'

[2] One of the grounds of the praetor's infamia—ignominious dismissal from the army—excluded from *honores* in the Antonine period, Cod. xii. 35 (36), 3.

nations a dignified administration and their golden age of peace. Constantine and his successors created an artificial aristocracy: and one, therefore, that was based on personal standing rather than on birth. In the later Empire there were many rounds in the ladder of promotion, but the transition from the lowest to the highest ranks in the State was easier than it had been either in the Republic or in the Principate, because it depended more fully on the will of the Emperor. 'We have laid stress,' says a careful student of the Byzantine organisation[1] 'on the arbitrary nature of the imperial selection, in showing how deeply the Emperors dipped into the middle and lower classes; but then they attach almost all these new comers to the Senate; they ennoble them. One need not see in this the evil intention of drowning the ancient aristocracy in these foreign elements; it was rather an homage to, and a mark of confidence in, the Senate, which regains its legitimate place in the government and in the palace.' But it was a thoroughly artificial hierarchy, and the artificial mode of exclusion represented by the codified infamia was eminently suited to such a nobility.

§ 4. *Effects of the Censorian Infamia.*

The primary effect of the censorian infamia was always a disqualification for certain public rights. The nature of the disqualification depended partly on the rank of the person disqualified, but was always regulated to some degree by the gravity of the offence. The senator, guilty of an action that disgraced his position, was removed from the list[2], the knight was forced to give up his position in

[1] Lécrivain, op. cit. p. 57.
[2] Val. Max. ii. 9, 2.

the equestrian centuries[1], and the commoner was removed from the tribe (*tribu moveri*) or made an *aerarius* (*aerarius fieri, relinqui*). This final disqualification, the only one applicable to the whole citizen community, will require a more detailed examination, due not only to its importance, but to the fact that there are few more controverted points in the history of the infamia than the precise meaning of relegation to the *aerarii*. The theory as to the meaning of this word *aerarius* which seems to have gained most general acceptance in recent times is that of Mommsen; it is a theory which depends on the assumption that in the earliest times the tribes at Rome were strictly local, in the sense that possession of land was the only means of obtaining membership of a tribe. *Aerarius*, according to this view, is opposed to *tribulis*. The *tribulis* was the land-holder (*assiduus*), who was taxed on his holding and required to bear arms; the *aerarii* were the non-*assidui* who were taxed on their personal property. Originally, therefore, the word implied exclusion from the tribes: and if the censor, at this epoch, made a man an *aerarius*, he deprived him of his vote and of his right of service in the legions. But, according to Mommsen, a complete change in the word resulted, in the year 312 B.C., as a consequence of innovations which were then introduced in the structure of the tribes. Appius the censor divorced the tribes from land, and gave the landless citizens, the *aerarii*, a place in these divisions[2]. The censor henceforth assigned the tribe for each individual: and the necessary consequence of this change was that the *aerarii* as such vanished, and with it the censor's right of excluding individuals from the *comitia* and from the army. The final change occurred in 304 B.C., during the censorship of L. Fabius and P. Decius.

[1] Liv. xxix. 37, 9.

[2] Diodor. xx. 46; Liv. ix 46.

In this year a compromise was adopted between those who maintained landed and those who upheld personal rights. For the more aristocratic country tribes the principle of membership recognised before the time of the censor Appius continued in force. His innovation remained valid only for the four city tribes, into which the landless citizens were now distributed[1]; and, consequently, it is thought that the principle established by Appius continued to be recognised; that is, that the censor could no longer deprive a man wholly of his tribe, which meant deprivation of his vote[2]. From this time the freedman and the *notatus* had a tribe. But the censor could still strike out of the land tribes and relegate to the tribes of the landless citizens *using the old formula of relegation to the* aerarii *but in a different sense.* Relegation to the *aerarii* henceforth meant only relegation from a higher to a lower tribe, and in this sense brought with it no material disadvantages either as regards taxation or military service[3].

There are many serious objections to this theory, even if we admit that the slender evidence, on which the supposed great change of the year 312 B.C. rests, can bear this interpretation[4]. Firstly, it makes a curiously unmeaning pleonasm of the juxtaposition of words which we constantly

[1] Liv. l. c. [2] Liv. xlv. 15.

[3] Mommsen, Staatsr. ii. 392 sq.; 402 sq.

[4] The passages of Diodorus (xx. 46) (App. Claudius as censor 312 B. C.) *ἔδωκε τοῖς πολίταις ὅποι προαροῖντο τιμήσασθαι*, and of Livy (ix. 46) 'forensis factio App. Claudi censura vires nacta, qui . . . humilibus per omnes tribus divisis forum et campum corrupit,' need in themselves imply nothing more than the conception of people, who had already been in some tribes, being spread over others, as understood by Lange (Röm. Alt. p. 381). Similarly, the event of 304 (Liv. l. c.) 'aliud integer populus . . . aliud forensis factio tendebat . . . Fabius simul concordiae causa, simul ne humillimorum in manu comitia essent, omnem forensem turbam excretam in quattuor tribus conjecit urbanasque eas appellavit,' is interpreted by Lange (l. c.) as a replacement of the *forensis factio* in the *tribus urbanae*.

find in Livy when this censorian procedure is described; the expression *tribu movere et aerarium facere* ought to signify two distinct acts[1]. Secondly, the assertion that is made that after 312 B.C. the principle was strictly observed that the censor could not deprive a citizen of his vote is by no means borne out by the passage of Livy usually quoted to support it[2]. The mere assertion of a member of the Claudian house, which always furnished the radical leaders of Rome, that no one could be deprived of his vote without the consent of the people, is by no means worthy to be elevated into a principle of Roman constitutional law; and we know that in the case of one class, that of actors, the principle of exclusion from the tribe was consistently observed. As they were forbidden to serve in the legions there is little doubt that they were also deprived of their vote. Thirdly, there is the incident of the censor of 204 B.C. who remitted to the *aerarii* (*aerarios reliquit*) thirty-four out of the thirty-five tribes for an alleged misuse of their voting power[3]. This censor evidently meant to disfranchise the voting community in some way, and relegation to the urban tribes is here out of the question. Fourthly, the theory that we have discussed concerning the meaning of the word *aerarius* can only be framed by going off the direct line of evidence;

[1] Liv. xlv. 15 'omnes iidem ab utroque et tribu remoti et aerarii facti'; xliv. 16 'tribu quoque is motus et aerarius factus'; xxvii. 11; iv. 24; xxix. 37 'aerarios reliquit'; Cic. de Orat ii. 64, 260; pro Cluent. 45, 126. Gell. iv. 12 & 20 'in aerarios retulit,' 'relatusque in aerarios.' In one passage of Livy (xxiv. 18) the order is reversed, 'ea supra duo millia nominum in aerarios relata, tribuque omnes moti'; for the probable reason of this, see note 3 on next page. A similar reversal of the order is found in Liv. xlii. 10. To elevate from the *aerarii* is 'ex aerariis eximere' (Cic. de Orat. ii. 66, 268).

[2] Liv. xlv. 15. The passages quoted by Belot (i. p. 201) to support this view (Cic. pro Domo, 29 & 30, pro Balbo, 11; pro Caecina, 33, 35) are not to the point, since they refer to *caput*.

[3] Liv. xxix. 37.

the only definition of *aerarius* which we possess refers, not to the tribes but to the centuries[1]. It is to the organisation of the *comitia centuriata* that Belot[2] has rightly looked in his account of this disqualification, and we may accept his conclusions with some modifications. The *aerarii* were the *capite censi*; they were not included amongst the citizens of the five classes, but were *infra classem*. Thus, as Belot says, the action of the censor Livius in 204 B.C., since it occurred after the reformation of the *comitia centuriata*, would have reduced this assembly to the ten centuries (five *seniores* and five *juniores*) of the tribe Maecia, the only one exempted from relegation to the *aerarii*. This view is borne out by other passages in Livy, which are best understood by considering that *aerarius* refers only to the centuriate organisation[3]. What then, we may ask, was the full disability implied in the expression 'they were removed from the tribe and relegated to the *aerarii*'? We know that removal from the tribe was used to signify mere relegation by the censor from the higher rustic to the lower urban tribes[4]. But this would hardly be a penalty corresponding to removal from the centuries, unless we suppose that a century of *proletarii*, composed of the *capite censi* or *aerarii*, still voted in the

[1] Ps. Asc. in Divin. p. 103 (Orelli) 'regendis moribus civitatis censores quinto quoque anno creari solebant. Hi prorsus cives sic notabant; ut, qui senator esset, ejiceretur senatu; qui eques Romanus, equum publicum perderet; qui plebeius, in Caeritum tabulas referretur et aerarius fieret, ac per hoc non esset in albo centuriae suae, sed ad hoc [non] esset civis, tantummodo ut pro capite suo tributi nomine aera praeberet.'

[2] Hist. des chev. Rom. p. 200 sq.

[3] Thus in Liv. xxiv. 18, *in aerarios relata* is put first to bring it into closer connection with *ex juniorum tabulis excerpserunt* preceding. Belot remarks (l. c.) that, in the case of the man whom the censors 'octuplicato(que) censu aerarium fecerunt' (Liv. iv. 24), the census of this *aerarius* was made equal to that of a member of the first class (12,500 asses raised to 100,000 asses according to the figures given by Dionysius, iv. 17).

[4] Liv. xlv. 15; Dionys. xix. 18; Plin. H. N. xviii. 3, 13.

reformed *comitia centuriata*[1]. It is possible, therefore, that in the later Republic 'removal from the tribe' was used in two senses, and that when the expression *tribu movere et aerarium facere* is found, the first two words mean total exclusion from the tribe, the last two total exclusion from the centuries. This second disqualification would have entailed exclusion from the legions, as long as the soldiers were selected from the *classes*, and before Marius introduced the custom of enlistment from the *capite censi*[2].

The removal from the tribe, whether in the milder or in the severer form was usually the work of the censor: it seems, however, that it might be made the consequence of criminal laws, amongst the other disqualifications which such laws enjoined, even where loss of *caput* was not one of these consequences[3]. The censor's power of removal from the tribe might also be limited by a provision of statute law, as it is by the *Lex Acilia Repetundarum*[4]. It can hardly be doubted that by the removal mentioned in such documents the severer kind of disqualification, entailing loss of the suffrage, is meant.

The question has been raised whether a man who had been made an *aerarius*, and who was therefore presumably also *tribu motus* in the sense of total exclusion from the tribe, still possessed what is sometimes called the *jus*

[1] As is supposed by Willems, le Droit publ. rom. p. 90; a view that is supported by Cic. de Repub. ii. 22.

[2] Sall. Jug. 86.

[3] If the *Lex Acilia* is earlier than the *Lex Servilia* we do not know what penalty followed a conviction for *Repetundae* at the time the law was passed: but removal from the tribe appears to have been one of its consequences: l. 77. (Amongst the rewards given to successful prosecutors under this law) [*in quam tribum, quojus is nomen ex h. l. detolerit, sufragium tulerit, in eam tribum sufragiu*]m ferunto inque eam tribum censento.'

[4] *Lex Acilia Rep.* l. 28 '. . . *q*]uei pequniam ex [h. l.] capiet, eum ob eam rem, quod pequniam ex h. l. ceper[*it, nei . . . neive tribu mo*]veto, neive equom adimito, neive quid ei *ob* eam rem fraudei esto.'

honorum, and preserved the right to stand for a magistracy at Rome. Cicero tells us that the censorian *ignominia* was no bar, so far as statute-law was concerned, to standing for a magistracy[1]; but this statement, besides being rendered doubtful, like all Cicero's assertions about the censorship, by the context in which it occurs, is of little value on this point; the censorian *ignominia* is so wide a term, and could be used without the connotation of its severest form, total exclusion from the tribes and from the centuries. There are, however, many instances of those *notati* by the censors being elected to magistracies, and in fact it became the usual mode of regaining a lost seat in the Senate after the time of Sulla[2], although there is no certain instance known of a man's reaching office, when the *nota* had made him an *aerarius*, and while this *nota* lasted. But, strange as the theory seems which permits a man who had been deprived of his vote to stand for a magistracy, its possibility can hardly be doubted. It is one of the anomalies of Roman constitutional law which is most easily explained. It rests on the fact that the censor had control over admission to the tribes, but none over admission to the *honores*. The magistrate who presided at election to office might no doubt exercise the right of rejecting anyone suffering from the *censoria notatio*, but it was a right exercised at his own discretion.

We have dwelt at some length on this severest of all the disqualifications which the censor claimed the right to

[1] Cic. pro Cluent. 43, 120.

[2] See the instances collected by Mommsen (Staatsr. i. p. 521, n. 3); C. Hostilius Mancinus, cons. 137 B.C., took the praetorship for this purpose (Cic. de Orat. i. 40, 181; Dig. l. 7, 18); P. Lentulus Sura, praetor, 76; cons. 71; removed from senate, 70; assumed the praetorship again, 63 (Plut. Cic. 17; Vell. ii. 24; Dio, xxxvii. 30); Sallust, quaestor, then tribune, 52; removed from senate, 50; quaestor again to return to the senate (Decl. in Sall. 6; Dio, xl. 63, xlii. 52); in the latter passage of Dio στρατηγὸς is a mistake.

impose, because it probably gives us the key to the developed conception of infamia which we shall soon proceed to examine. We are not surprised to find this extreme disqualification spoken of, however improperly, as a *capitis minutio*, or to find that certain actions which were held by the censors necessarily to involve it, are described by Cicero as 'summae existimationis et paene dicam capitis[1].' The fact that certain actions could be spoken of as necessarily involving this extreme infamia shows that disqualification was not wholly regulated by rank. The magistrate who has misused his functions, and the *eques* who has disgraced himself in war, may not only lose their rank in the Senate, and in the equestrian centuries, but be relegated to the position of *aerarii*[2]. And it is extremely probable, as has already been stated, that certain offences, by whomsoever they were committed, came to be considered as necessarily involving this relegation, and in the case of such offences the principle may have been upheld that the relegation should be permanent; that is, that it should be sanctioned in turn by each succeeding censor. In this way a table of actions which involved infamia might be drawn up and applied in various ways. In the *Lex Julia Municipalis* it is applied for the exclusion of unworthy members from the local Senate of *conscripti* or *decuriones*. We shall soon see that it was applied to a far different purpose by the praetor in his Edict, and that this application attained a development which was destined to alter the whole character of the infamia.

[1] See p. 26.

[2] Lix. xliv. 16; Val. Max. ii. 9, 7.

CHAPTER IV.

THE PRAETORIAN INFAMIA AND ITS DEVELOPMENTS.

We now turn to the infamia as it is known to us in its final stage, that of its codification. It contains the disqualifications recognised in the processes of civil law, and is known to us from the excerpts which we have of the praetor's Edict in the Digest. Although the final form of this conception of infamia was assumed in the Empire—at the latest at the time of Julian's redaction of the Edict in the reign of Hadrian[1]—yet its beginnings stretch back into the Republic, how far back is one of the questions which we shall have to answer. It must not, however, be supposed that the categories of the Edict exhaust the infamia of the Empire. We shall find many cases which are not in the Edict as it has been preserved to us. It is not, however, fair to assume, as has been done by some modern jurists, that all such cases were created posterior to the redaction of the Edict. Such an assumption ignores the fact that more than one kind of infamia was in working during the Empire as during the Republic, and that exclusion from the Senate and from the equestrian order still went on, perhaps in a progressive spirit. Some of these cases never crept into the *Edictum perpetuum* at all. But on the whole, most

[1] Further developments, so far as the Edict was concerned, were in the way of elimination, not of addition.

cases that we find in the legal books of Justinian, which are not in the Edict, may be with probability held to have been created subsequently to its redaction and to have been due to juristic interpretation.

The earliest titles of the *Edictum perpetuum* as consolidated by Salvius Julianus, dealt with the preliminaries of legal procedure: amongst others with the forms of legal request made by parties to an action before the praetor. Such legal requests made *pro tribunali* were from early times called postulations (*postulationes*), perhaps, as Rudorff suggests, because they chiefly had their origin in the *judicis arbitrive postulatio* of the *legis actio*[1]. It was in connection with such postulation that infamia was treated by the praetor. The only object of the praetorian infamia was to preserve the dignity of the praetor's court[2], and to prevent the frequent appearance in it of unworthy members of the community. Indiscriminate postulation was, therefore, only permitted to an *integra persona*, who, as the technical phrase ran, 'was allowed by the Edict to postulate' (*cui per edictum postulare licet*)[3]. The question naturally arises 'What was the connection between this praetorian and the censorian infamia which has just been treated?' Two alternative suppositions are possible as to their connection: one that they were pursued independently of one another, the other that the praetorian was based on the censorian. The second alternative must be preferred on many grounds. (i) From the general nature

[1] Zeitschr. f. Rechtsgesch. iv. p. 45. Postulation is defined by Ulpian as 'desiderium suum vel amici sui in jure apud eum, qui jurisdictioni praeest, exponere: vel alterius desiderio contradicere.'

[2] 'dignitatis tuendae et decoris sui causa' (Dig. iii. 1, 1).

[3] Paulus in Dig. xlvii. 23, 4 'Popularis actio integrae personae permittitur, hoc est cui per edictum postulare licet.' Ulpian in Dig. i. 16, 9 (the proconsul ought) eosque solos pati postulare, quibus per edictum ejus postulare permittitur.'

of the case. Since the only object of the praetorian infamia was to preserve the dignity of the praetor's court, it seems inevitable that it should have been based on the censorian, which had the more important object of excluding from service to the State, from the army, the Senate, and the *comitia*, people who were disgraced by unworthy acts or occupations. As regards the cases specified, there is precisely the correspondence between the two lists which we should expect, if the praetor's had been borrowed from the censor's. It is shorter, it deals only with the most aggravated cases, it is wholly non-political. We have already attempted to show that the censor's infamia was much more largely concerned with civil actions than has generally been supposed. It is these civil actions that come most prominently before us in the Edict, as was natural in a court of civil law. (ii) Procuratory, or representation by others, was unknown in the system of the *legis actiones*[1] or only recognised in certain very exceptional cases[2]. Now the praetor's list of infamous persons is a list of persons who are limited in postulation for others. Postulation for others has little meaning apart from representation by a *cognitor* or *procurator*, so that it is difficult to see how a developed conception of the infamia, applicable to civil process, could have originated before the introduction of the formulary system, perhaps as late as the beginning of the second century B.C.[3] At this time there must have been a fully developed conception of the grounds of censorian disqualification, and that the praetor should not have availed himself of it is inconceivable. (iii) If any weight is to be attached to the language in which the praetorian infamia

[1] Gai. iv. 82.

[2] Under the system of procedure *per legis actiones* procuratory was allowed only *pro populo*, *pro libertate*, or *pro tutela* (Justin. Inst. iv. 10).

[3] The date of the *Lex Aebutia* is wholly uncertain. It seems generally to be placed between the dates 150 and 250 B.C.

is described, by the praetor himself[1], and by the commentators, it is at once manifest that it is borrowed from the censorian procedure—more especially is this the case with the words *nota, notare, notati.* To speak of a *nota* in connection with the censor, who affixes a mark to individual names is a strictly accurate mode of speaking; it is not strictly applicable to the praetor who only makes out a general list of cases: and is evidently an expression borrowed from the censorian infamia, when a portion of that conception was taken up by the praetor for his own uses. But (iv) we possess a very valuable connecting link between the censor's and the praetor's use of the conception in the *Lex Julia Municipalis*, which is a codification of the most permanent portion of the censorian infamia, the cases codified being employed as the basis for disqualification for the position of a senator in a municipal town. So similar are the grounds of disqualification in this law and in the Edict, that Rudorff has with some success used Caesar's Local Government Act as a means for reconstructing this portion of the Edict as it must have existed at the close of the Republic and in the early Empire, before some of its clauses became antiquated by changes in law and in social life introduced subsequently to its redaction by Julian[2]. This is possible enough, but that the clauses of Caesar's law were borrowed from the praetor's Edict of his day is highly improbable. It is a case of concurrence, not of adaptation[3]. We cannot go so far as Savigny and say

[1] Dig. iii. 2, 1 'Praetoris verba dicunt "Infamia notatur qui &c."' For the terminology employed to describe the infamia, see above, p. 4.

[2] Rudorff in Zeitschr. f. Rechtsgesch. iv. ('Die Prozesseröffnung nach dem Edict'), p. 45 ('Postulation und Advocatur').

[3] Similar regulations borrowed from the censorship were no doubt to be found in the *Lex Pompeia* of the Asiatic provinces; Plin. ad Traj. 113 (115) 'eadem lege sancitur quibus de causis e senatu a censoribus ejiciantur.'

that these cases, which disqualified from the municipal Senates, would at Rome always have disqualified from the right of voting as well, nor can we even say with Mommsen that they would invariably have disqualified for offices at Rome: for, so far as we can judge, their use in this respect would have depended on the discretion of officials, at least as far as the majority of the grounds of exclusion are concerned[1]. It is in fact the earliest codification—at least the earliest known to us—of the principles usually recognised by the censors. The censorian infamia was adapted to this purpose by Caesar, as it had been adapted to the purpose of civil process by the praetor.

With respect to postulation, the praetor framed three rules which were expressed in three edicts. These edicts had reference to three distinct classes of individuals. The first class was composed of those not able to postulate for themselves at all: this prohibition being directed with reference to age or physical infirmity of a certain kind. Boys under seventeen fell under it, and those who were so deaf as to be unable to hear the praetor's rulings. Advocacy was, therefore, necessary in these cases, and if the parties could not furnish a representative, the praetor gave one[2]. The second class was composed of those able to postulate only for themselves. This prohibition was directed with reference to sex, physical infirmity, and gross moral turpitude. Under it fell women, the blind, and those who were *in turpitudine notabiles*. From the instances given by Ulpian, which led to the adoption of the rule in the first two cases, it seems clear that the motive of it was the dignity of the praetor's court[3].

[1] The cases of special disqualifications pronounced by criminal laws must always be excepted.

[2] 'Ait praetor "Si non habebunt advocatum, ego dabo."'

[3] The rule was adopted somewhat late. The Carfania of the Digest who made herself so objectionable in the praetor's court and gave rise

But of course they were both sharply distinguished from the remaining category of *in turpitudine notabiles*, which furnished illustrations of the extreme limit of infamia[1]. The third class contained those who were able to postulate for themselves, and only in exceptional cases for others. In this third class were included *omnes qui edicto praetoris ut infames notantur*[2].

It is on this third Edict *de postulando* that we must fix our attention, if we would estimate rightly the connection between infamia and the working of the praetor's court. The mention of the *infames* comes before us mainly in three portions of the legal books of Justinian: first, in the title dealing with postulation (*de postulando*), where the mention of the limitation of postulation of the *infames* is made[3]: secondly in the title immediately following it, *de his qui notantur infamia*[4], where a detailed list of the *infames* is given; thirdly, in a supplementary title of the Codex of Justinian, *ex quibus causis infamia irrogatur*[5].

It is the first two of these passages that contain the verbal extracts from the praetor's Edict, on which any attempt to reconstruct the Edict must depend. It is very evident that the order of the Edict is not followed in the Digest, and this is probably due not to the compilers but to the commentators themselves. The most remarkable fact

to the principle Rudorff identifies with Gaia Afrania (died 49 or 48 B. C.), wife of the senator Licinius Bucco. Val. Max. viii. 3, 2; Juv. ii. 69 (Zeitschr. f. R. G. iv. p. 47). The incident of the exclusion of the blind belongs, he thinks, to Caesar's time (ib.). For the Roman sentiment about women appearing in court he compares Plutarch, comp. Lyc. c. Num. 4, *λέγεται γοῦν ποτε γυναικὸς εἰπούσης δίκην ἰδίαν ἐν ἀγορᾷ πέμψαι τὴν σύγκλητον εἰς θεοῦ, πυνθανομένην, τίνος ἄρα τῇ πόλει σημεῖον εἴη τὸ γεγενημένον.*

[1] This distinction is made in the language of Ulpian (Dig. iii. 1, 5) 'in quo edicto *excepit* praetor sexum et casum, item *notavit* personas in turpitudine notabiles.'

[2] Dig. iii. 1. 1, 8.

[3] Dig. iii. 1, 1.

[4] Dig. iii. 2.

[5] Cod. ii. 11 (12) 'de causis, ex quibus infamia alicui inrogatur.'

that strikes a reader of these titles, is that while most of the praetor's *tertium edictum* is excerpted from the commentators, mainly from the sixth book of Ulpian's commentary to the Edict, the list of the *infames* is not. It bears on it the strange superscription, *Julianus libro primo ad edictum*, a heading which must be wrong in any case, since Julian's redaction of the Edict was, so far as we know, not divided into books, but was only one short book divided into rubricated titles [1]. Still the fact of the list of the *infames* being taken from Julian shows that it was not excerpted, in the form in which it stood in the Edict, by the commentators, but only referred to generally by them. It was important, in the compilation, to have this detailed list, and consequently it was excerpted from the *edictum perpetuum* of Julian. This portion of the third Edict, therefore, ran as follows (the words of the commentators being in italics):

'*Ait praetor:* "Qui lege, plebis scito, senatus consulto, edicto (i.e. the praetor's Edict as referring to persons other

[1] It would be rash to follow Rudorff in reading 'Ulpianus libro vi ad edictum' for *Julianus libro I ad edictum*: since it is impossible to see why the error should have crept into this one paragraph of the title. The view of Karlowa (Zeitschr. f. R. G. ix. p. 208) that the edictal list of the *infames* was not in the *tertium edictum de postulando*, but only a reference to it, contained in the words 'qui . . . edicto . . . nisi pro certis personis postulare prohibentur,' seems disproved by two facts: (i) that the list of the worst *infames* (the *in turpitudine notabiles*) was certainly in the second Edict, and summed up by Ulpian in the sixth book of his commentary: and (ii) there is no other possible place in the Edict where this list of *infames* could have come. The general conclusion reached above is practically that of Rudorff, but based on more general grounds, his detailed arguments being unconvincing. He bases it on the references by the commentators to the list of *infames* as being in this Edict. But these references can be explained, if there was a mere mention of the *infames*, as being (amongst others) limited in postulation, and not the detailed list of these persons. The view stated above differs from that of Rudorff in the belief that the compilers did not excerpt a detailed list of the *infames* from any of the commentators: probably because they could not find it there.

than the infames) decreto principum nisi pro certis personis postulare prohibentur: hi pro alio, quam pro quo licebit, in jure apud me ne postulent. Hoc edicto continentur etiam alii omnes qui edicto praetoris (i.e. the tralaticiary Edict) ut infames notantur."' (From the Sixth book of Ulpian's commentary to the Edict.)

[The last clause, 'Hoc edicto . . . ut infames notantur,' is taken by Mommsen, Karlowa, and Lenel, as a remark of Ulpian's, not as the words of the praetor. But they are probably words of the Edict; the first 'edicto' referring, not to the *infames*, but to persons similarly limited in postulation for other reasons.]

'*Praetoris verba dicunt:* "Infamia notatur qui,"' &c.; then follows the detailed list of the *infames* (taken from Julian's redaction).

'*Deinde adicit praetor:* "Qui ex his omnibus, qui supra scripti sunt, in integrum restitutus non erit."' (From the sixth book of Ulpian's commentary to the Edict.)

As will be seen from these words of the praetors, and from the commentators, the limitations on postulation mentioned in the third Edict affected persons other than the *infames*, just as the severer limitations in the second Edict were not confined to those *in turpitudine notabiles*. But with these other persons we have no concern, and we may fix our attention on the *infames* of two grades mentioned in these categories, and consider the grounds and the civil-law effects of this developed conception of infamia. The fact that the treatment of the grounds of this praetorian infamia will occupy a far larger space than the discussion devoted to the grounds of the censorian, must not be taken as a proof of the greater importance of the former in history. It is simply due to the accident of the greater wealth of evidence in the one case than in the other, and to the circumstance that it is only when we reach this stage of codification that intricate questions of civil law arise which require detailed treatment. The disproportionate nature of the evidence for the two stages of the infamia has been a misfortune as tending to give a false idea of their relative importance.

The cases of infamia, that are divided into two sections in the praetor's Edict, naturally fall all together in the *Lex Julia Municipalis*. Although they involved the same degree of political, they involved two degrees of civil, disqualification. The *edictum secundum*, in the list it gives of those who cannot postulate for others at all, contains the following instances of immediate infamia.

(i) 'Qui corpore suo muliebria passus est[1].'

(ii) Those who have hired out their services to fight with wild beasts. The *Lex Julia Municipalis* contains, as a parallel case, the acting as a training-master (*lanista*), and the hiring of one's self as a gladiator[2]. This case would naturally have disappeared from the Edict, after the abolition of gladiatorial shows; but Rudorff would add it to the Edict, as it existed in the time of Hadrian[3]. It is doubtful, however, whether it would have been contained in this second Edict or in the third[4].

As cases of mediate infamia it specifies—

(iii) Condemnation on a capital charge[5].

[1] This was repressed by a *Lex Scantinia* in the time of the Republic: but was a constantly growing evil in the time of the Empire. An attempt was made to repress it by an energetic Edict of Constantine (Cod. ix. 9, 30 (31)). It is paralleled in the *L. J. M.* by 'queive corpore quaestum fecit fecerit.'

[2] 'Queive lanistaturam . . . fecit fecerit, queive depugnandei caussa auctoratus est erit fuit fuerit.'

[3] Zeitschr. f. R. G. iv. p. 48.

[4] Lenel, Das Edictum perpetuum, p. 64. *Bestiarii* must always have been classed lower than *lanistae* or *gladiatores*.

[5] Edict—'qui capitali crimine damnatus est.' *L. J. M.* 'queive judicio publico Romae condemnatus est erit, quo circa eum in Italia esse non liceat, neque in integrum restitutus est erit.'

(iv) Apparently false accusation (*calumnia*) in an ordinary criminal court (*judicium publicum*). This case is peculiarly difficult in its occurrence under this head, since apparently the same case was specified in the third Edict[1]. There is, however, a difference of statement in the two cases: and it may answer to the two different kinds of criminal procedure by which *calumnia* was decided. *Calumnia*, we know, was taken cognisance of by a law, the *Lex Remmia*[2], which ordained a *poena legitima*; the trial in this case being one different from that in which the *calumnia* had taken place, although generally before the same judge[3]; in this case the *calumniator* might be said to be *calumniae damnatus*, and under these circumstances was entirely restricted from postulation. But, on the other hand, it is probable that *calumnia*, as assimilated to *praevaricatio*, might be decided *extra ordinem* in the course of the trial. This might be the case when the falsely accused brought no formal counter-charge of *calumnia*, but it had been decided on the motion of the judge during the trial (*in judicio publico*). In this case condemnation was followed only by a partial limitation of postulation[4].

[1] Ulpian says, with reference to the second Edict, 'item senatus consulto etiam apud judices pedaneos postulare prohibetur calumniae publici judicii damnatus (Dig. iii. 1, 6). In the third edict we find 'qui in judicio publico calumniae praevaricationisve causa quid fecisse judicatus erit' (Dig. iii. 2, 1).

[2] The punishment enjoined by the *Lex Remmia*—the branding with the letter K—became antiquated, perhaps as early as the time of Trajan (Rein, Criminalrecht, p. 811), the other provisions of the law seem to have been in force until a late period of the Empire (Dig. xlviii. 16, 1, 2 and 3; xxii. 5, 13).

[3] Dig. xlviii. l. c.

[4] This procedure *extra ordinem* was probably much more usual than that under the *Lex Remmia*. How closely connected *calumnia* and *praevaricatio* were is shown by the words in the third Edict, by the parallel passage in the *Lex Julia Municipalis* and by Macer in Dig. (xlvii. 15, 4) 'Si is, de cujus calumnia agi prohibetur, praevaricator in causa judicii publici pronuntiatus sit, infamis erit.'

The third Edict contained the following cases of immediate infamia.

(v) Ignominious dismissal of a soldier from the army[1]. Besides the actual punishments inflicted for breaches of military discipline, three subordinate penalties were recognised; these were change of service (*militiae mutatio*), degradation from one rank to another (*gradus dejectio*), and ignominious dismissal from the service (*ignominiosa missio*[2]). Such dismissal might be pronounced by the commander-in-chief—in later times the Emperor—or by any one to whom he had delegated his authority, and apparently at his own discretion, since no particular class of offences is mentioned as necessarily involving this degradation. Since there were many kinds of *missio*—the *honesta*, for instance, following the completion of military service or a fiction of this completion granted by the Emperor, and the *causaria* granted on grounds of ill-health—the assertion by the commander that it was ignominious (*ignominiae causa se mittere*) was necessary in order that it should entail infamia in accordance with the praetor's Edict (*ex edicto praetoris*)[3]. It is evident, therefore, that this case does not quite correspond to others of immediate infamia, since it does not follow on a course of action merely, but on one recognised by a judgment. The judgment, however, is not a legal sentence, and since the infamia is here recognised as the result of a matter of fact, it may be fairly brought under this category. The ignominious dismissal is here

[1] Edict: 'qui ab exercitu ignominiae causa ab imperatore eove, cui de ea re statuendi potestas fuerit, dismissus erit.' *L. J. M.* 'quoive aput exercitum ingnominiae caussa ordo ademptus est erit; quemve imperator ingnominiae caussa ab exercitu decedere jusit juserit.'

[2] Dig. xlix. 16 (*de re militari*), 3, 1.

[3] Ulpian in Dig. iii. 2, 2; Macer in Dig. xlix. 16, 13; the *exauctoratio* of the Empire, i. e. the deprivation of the *insignia militaria*, was accounted ignominious dismissal, and followed by infamia (Ulpian l. c.).

mentioned merely in connection with the purposes of the Edict. But throughout the history of Rome it involved other more serious disqualifications. In Caesar's municipal law it is made a bar to being a member of a local Senate; in the Empire such persons lost all the specific civil privileges of soldiers (*jus militiae*[1]) and were forbidden to live at Rome, and apparently in any place where the Emperor was residing[2].

(vi) Dishonourable trades or professions are next mentioned: and amongst these the profession of an actor; any one who has appeared on the stage (*scaena*), for the purpose of exhibiting himself, is declared *infamis* by the Edict[3]. The history of this disqualification has already been sketched, and it only remains to describe the legal interpretation put upon this prohibition by the classical jurists. As regards the main point, what constituted a stage, Ulpian quotes Labeo's definition, that it was any place to which the public was admitted, and where one exhibited one's self, in whatever manner, for their amusement[4]. But, with the growing taste for acting, a rule based on this rigorous definition could not possibly be permanent; and we find that even the rival schools of Proculians and Sabinians agreed that the question of payment was the crucial one in determining this infamia. This was the view even of the Proculians[5]. The Sabinians

[1] Dig. xxix. 1, 26.

[2] Dig. xlix. 16, 13, 3 'neque Romae neque in sacro comitatu agere potest'; hence excused from 'urbica tutela' (Dig. xxvii. 1, 8, 9): cf. Cod. xii. 35 (36), 3.

[3] Edict: 'qui artis ludicrae pronuntiandive causa in scaenam prodierit'; *L. J. M.* 'queive . . . artemve ludicram fecit fecerit.'

[4] 'Scaena est, ut Labeo definit, quae ludorum faciendorum causa quolibet loco, ubi quis consistat moveaturque spectaculum sui praebiturus, posita sit in publico privatoque vel in vico' (Dig. iii. 2. 2, 5).

[5] 'Eos enim, qui quaestus causa in certamina descendunt et omnes propter praemium in scaenam prodeuntes famosos esse Pegasus et Nerva filius responderunt' (Dig. l. c.).

went further, and exempted athletes, whose motive was honour (*virtus*) rather than money, from this category; and the exemption extended to other classes who occupied a dignified position at shows and games, which had been elevated by the abolition of gladiatorial combats. Ulpian mentions among such the musicians of the orchestra (*thymelici*), the athletes of the portico (*xystici*), the chariot-drivers (*agitatores*), and those who tended the horses after the race (*qui aquam equis spargunt*). All these, as well as the umpires at the games (*designatores*, βραβευταί)[1] were free from *ignominia*, as performing a service (*ministerium*) recognised by the *princeps*: and the spirit of this interpretation accords with the privileges conferred on athletes in later times by imperial rescript[2].

(vii) Immediate infamia also attached to one *qui lenocinium fecerit*[3], whether this trade was exercised directly or indirectly[4]; the stigma even attached to the freedman, who had exercised it during a condition of slavery.

(viii) The next case of infamia ensuing on a matter of fact is peculiarly interesting as being one of the latest survivals of the old pontifical law that for so long a period had the censorian notation as its sanction. It relates to the rules of mourning (*luctus*) at Rome. These rules had originally been very complicated: and the religious law

[1] In the *Lex Julia Municipalis* disqualification from local magistracies (*honores*) attaches to those 'quei praeconium dissignationem libitinamve faciet,' as long as they pursue these callings ('dum eorum quid faciet'). 'Designator' here may mean a man who shows people to their seats in the theatre (Plaut. Poen. prol. 19): it can hardly have its meaning of undertaker, as this is contained in the last words.

[2] As by that of Diocletian and Maximian (de athletis) Cod. x. 54 (53).

[3] *L. J. M.* 'queive lenocinium faciet.'

[4] Dig. iii. 2, 4, 2. In the case of the *lenocinium* created by the *Lex Julia de adulteriis* (Dig. xlviii. 5, 22) infamia in respect to the man 'qui de adulterio uxoris suae quid ceperit, item in eum, qui in adulterio deprehensam retinuerit,' was mediate, following on condemnation.

had prescribed the kind and the length of mourning to be observed for relatives, with reference both to the degree of kinship and the age at which they had died[1]. These rules had been gradually mitigated both by custom and by law: and it is probable that the Christian Empire abolished all the pontifical rules about the external signs of mourning, if indeed they had not sunk into desuetude earlier than the time of Constantine. The only rule of the kind which is found in the praetor's Edict, in the abbreviated form which it assumes in the Digest, relates to the year of mourning (*annus luctus*) prescribed for widows after the death of their husbands. There can be little doubt—even though it has been denied by the great authority of Savigny—that this 'year of mourning' had originally a religious or at least a moral significance. It was meant to satisfy the conventions of *mores*, meant also perhaps to appease the *manes* of the deceased husband. But from early times it had also a more practical significance, and was prescribed as a means of avoiding doubtfulness of paternity (*turbatio sanguinis*). It was possibly only in this form that it was taken cognizance of by the praetor, at the time of the redaction of the Edict: it was certainly the only meaning it had at the time of the legislation of Justinian when this excerpt from the Edict was introduced into the Pandects. The infamia following a breach of these rules would naturally be expected to attach primarily to the woman who violates them: and that such a one was *infamis* we shall see when we come to consider this conception in its connection with women. But the praetor's third Edict *de postulando* could take no cognisance of women, who only appear in the second, and are prohibited absolutely from postulation for others. In

[1] On this question—perhaps the one that has raised most controversy in the whole history of the Infamia—see Appendix, note 1.

this catalogue of the *infames*, therefore, the men only appear, who are in any degree directly responsible for the violation of the period of mourning. The infamia falls on (i) the father of the widow, if she is under his power, when he has given her in marriage within the given time, 'although he was aware that his former step-son had died at such and such a time, within which time the period of mourning should run[1]'. (ii) On a man *sui juris* who marries a widow during this period, in case that he acted with knowledge of the circumstances (*sciens*). He must know the fact, ignorance of the law being no excuse. If, however, he was not *sui juris*, and only acted on the commands of one, under whose power he was, he escaped infamia, and escaped it even when, on emancipation, he retained the wife so wedded. On the other hand the man, in whose power he stood, incurred it, if he had ordered or, with knowledge of the circumstances, tolerated the marriage[2]. To the question as to what should happen in the case of one who had not permitted this union, but had ratified it after it had been accomplished, Ulpian answers that he will not be marked with infamy, because the spirit of the Edict was only to look at the moment at which the marriage had been contracted[3].

(ix) The last case of immediate infamy mentioned in the Edict resembles the preceding in that it deals with marriage. A man was *infamis* who in his own name (*suo*

[1] 'Qui eam, quae in potestate ejus esset, genero mortuo, cum eum mortuum [*tum*] esse sciret, intra id tempus, quo elugere virum moris est, antequam virum elugeret, in matrimonium collocaverit.' The insertion of 'tum' in this passage, suggested by Karlowa, though not essential to the meaning, is rendered probable by the similar reading of the Fragmenta Vaticana (Zeitschr. f. R. G. ix. p. 235).

[2] 'Qui eum, quem in potestate haberet, eam, de qua supra comprehensum est, uxorem ducere passus fuerit.' See Dig. iii. 2, 11–13.

[3] Dig. ii. 3, 13 'praetor enim ad initium nuptiarum se rettulit.'

nomine) and not acting at the commands of another in whose power he was, committed bigamy, or entered into betrothal with two women at once. Infamia may also be imagined to have fallen on the woman guilty of the same offence, but it could not be mentioned in this Edict which dealt only with men. The same stigma attached to the individual, in whose power the man or the woman was, and who consciously forwarded such double marriage or double *sponsalia*[1]. Under the same category, according to the meaning of the Edict (*ex sententia edicti*), Ulpian tells us, was put the man, who, when betrothed to one woman, was married to another, or when married to one was betrothed to another. Bigamy was amply provided for by the criminal law of Rome, and it was not so much the effect in this case as the intention that was considered[2]. So much was this the case that legal disabilities to marriage were no bar to the infamia. If a man was improperly betrothed to a woman whom he could not marry he was none the less visited with the stigma.

(x) We now turn to the cases of *infamia mediata* mentioned in the Edict: foremost amongst them comes condemnation for *calumnia* and *praevaricatio* in the course of an ordinary trial[3] (*in judicio publico, in causa judicii publici*). *Calumnia* in this connection has been already discussed: it involved the disqualifications mentioned in the third Edict when the procedure dealing with it was assimilated to that usual in *praevaricatio*. As *calumnia*

[1] 'Quive suo nomine non jussu ejus in cujus potestate esset, ejusve nomine quem quamve in potestate haberet bina sponsalia binasve nuptias in eodem tempore constitutas habuerit.' 'Eodem tempore,' as Ulpian tells us, is to be understood as 'concurrently': cf. Cod. v. 5, 2.

[2] Cod. ix. 9, 18 'non juris effectus . . . sed animi destinatio cogitatur.'

[3] Edict 'qui in judicio publico calumniae praevaricationisve causa quid fecisse judicatus erit' (cf. Dig. xlvii. 15, 4 'in causa judicii publici'); *L. J. M.* 'quemve k(alumniae) praevaricationis caussa accussasse fecisseve quod judicatum est erit.'

consisted in bringing false charges (*falsa crimina intendere*), so *praevaricatio* consisted in concealing true charges (*vera crimina abscondere*)[1]. The large part these offences play in the history of Civil Honour at Rome is to be explained by the absence of public prosecution, which involved a greater necessity of guarding against malicious or negligent impeachment than would be necessary in a state where such an institution existed. *Praevaricatio* was declared to exist in cases 'where the accuser concealed or suppressed true evidence against the accused, or passed lightly over the main evidence, or did not call important witnesses, or so challenged the jury as to leave only the most corruptible[2].' There was never any separate law imposing penalties for prevarication nor any separate court in which it could be tried; it was always, therefore, a *cognitio extraordinaria*, and was punished by a *poena extraordinaria*[3], although by the *Senatus consultum Turpillianum* the penalty was so far fixed that it was assimilated to that of condemnation for *calumnia* in a *judicium publicum*[4]. The procedure remained throughout the same. When an accused had been acquitted through *praevaricatio*, he might be put on his trial again, but the new trial must commence by an accusation of the previous accuser for *praevaricatio*: after condemnation in this case, the original trial proceeded[5].

[1] Dig. xlviii. 16, 1, 1. In the praetor's Edict, and in the *Lex Julia Municipalis*, *praevaricatio* must be taken as covering what was afterwards called *tergiversatio*, the offence of 'in universum ab accusatione desistere' (Dig. l. c.). The *S. C. Turpillianum* covered both (Tac. Ann. xiv. 41; Dig. l. 2, 6, 3). *Tergiversatio* in the Empire was followed by infamia 'quam veteres jusserant sanctiones' (Cod. ix. 44, 1). It is doubtful whether this infamia was immediate, following merely on the abandonment of the trial, or whether this abandonment had to be noted by a *judex*.

[2] Rein, Criminalrecht, p. 801.

[3] Dig. xlvii. 15, 1 and 2.

[4] Tac. Ann. xiv. 41.

[5] Rein, Criminalrecht, p. 801.

This procedure was ratified by the *Lex Julia judiciorum publicorum*[1], and thus the offence of *praevaricatio* was always decided *in causa judicii publici*. The infamia could only follow condemnation in the regular form[2]; in all these cases of mediate infamia the sentence must be pronounced *causa cognita*. A mere remark of interrogatory addressed by the judge to the parties in the action, whatever belief it might express, was not sufficient to produce *infamia*[3].

(xi) The Edict next takes cognisance of certain private delicts: theft (*furtum*), robbery (*vi bona rapta*), injury (*injuriae*), and fraud (*dolus malus*); and much the same category is mentioned in the *Lex Julia Municipalis* as producing the disqualifications there in question[4]. It was only certain private delicts, in which a civil judgment adverse to the defendant necessarily involved disgrace; these are the *famosae actiones*. But the incidence of the infamia was not in these cases avoided by compromise (*pactio*). Compromise in the case of private delicts was tantamount to condemnation and entailed the same consequences[5]. To this rule, however, there were two limitations. The words of Ulpian show that the arrangement here meant must be a monetary one[6]: the defendant was, therefore, not marked, if the plaintiff gave up the action

[1] Dig. xlvii. 15, 3, 1 'Cavetur lege Julia publicorum, ut non prius accusetur, quam de prioris accusatoris praevaricatione constiterit et pronuntiatum fuerit.'

[2] Dig. iii. 2, 4, 4 'si fuerit... damnatus:' cf. *L. J. M.* 'judicatum est erit.'

[3] Ulpian in Dig. iii. 2, 13, 6: cf. Dig. xlviii. 1, 14. See p. 39.

[4] Edict 'Qui furti, vi bonorum raptorum, injuriarum, de dolo malo et fraude suo nomine damnatus pactusve erit'; *L. J. M.* 'Quei furtei quod ipse fecit fecerit condemnatus pactusve est erit; queive judicio... injuriarum sive d(olo) m(alo) condemnatus est erit.' For *furtum* cf. Collatio, 7, 5.

[5] Paulus in Dig. iii. 2, 5 'quoniam intellegitur confiteri crimen qui paciscitur.'

[6] Dig. l. c. 6 'Pactum sic accipimus, si cum pretio quantocumque pactus est.'

gratuitously: and secondly, even if the arrangement was monetary, but had been entered into at the bidding of the praetor, it did not produce infamia[1]. In contractual relations on the other hand, even though, as in those which will be discussed in the next section, condemnation was productive of infamia, arrangement was not followed by the same consequences, the idea apparently being that in these contractual relations a monetary arrangement did not involve the same admission of fraud.

(xii) In certain obligatory relations other than delicts an adverse judgment on the defendant produced infamia: this was the case with the contractual relations of partnership (*pro socio*), mandate and deposit, and the quasi-contract of *tutela*[2]. One of the limitations to the incidence of this infamia, as well as to that springing from the private delicts mentioned in the last section, is that the adverse verdict must be given against the defendant in his own name (*suo nomine*); those, therefore, who presented themselves in court and were condemned in the name of another (*alieno nomine*), such as procurators, tutors, curators, were not affected by infamia: nor could those in whose names they had presented themselves, if they had conducted the case throughout[3]. The first were not condemned themselves but in the name of another, while the second were not condemned in their own person[4]. On the same principle exemption from infamia is granted to the *heres*, if he simply represents

[1] Ulpian, l. c. § 3.

[2] Edict 'Qui pro socio, tutelae, mandati, depositi suo nomine non contrario judicio damnatus erit'; *L. J. M.* 'Queive judicio fiduciae, pro socio, tutelae, mandatei ... condemnatus est erit; queive lege Plaetoria ob eamve rem, quod adversus eam legem fecit, fecerit, condemnatus est erit': cf. Collatio, 10. 2, 4; 10. 6.

[3] Ulpian in Dig. iii. 2, 6, 2.

[4] In Cod. vii. 45 (*de sent. et interloc.*) 1, it is said of an individual represented by another, 'cujus persona in judicio non fuit.'

K 2

the testator, in any of these four actions, although he might be pursued *in solidum* in actions springing from contracts of the testator (even from the quasi-contract of *tutela*) and in actions springing from a delict[1]. With respect to the four contractual relations mentioned in the Edict, there was another condition requisite before infamia could result: and that was that the action springing from them must be direct (*non contrario judicio*), i.e. it must be an action meant to enforce the rights of the mandator, depositor, or ward. An *actio contraria*, on the other hand, that is, an action against the depositor or ward, to enforce the execution of obligations connected with the contract, but arising subsequently to it, such as indemnification for expenses, did not produce infamia[2]: since in those actions there was no question of bad faith (*perfidia*)[3]. This gives the reason why these obligations, and no others, are followed by infamia; they all involve breaches of trust. It is true that in a mandate non-fulfillment of the obligation might arise from negligence rather than fraud: but even negligence in such a matter seems to have been interpreted as fraud[4]; the rule was hardest in respect to

[1] For actions springing from contracts of the testator see Pomponius in Dig. xliv. 7, 12; for actions springing from delicts, Paulus, ib. 49. The *heres* might, however, be condemned in his own name, 'si in deposito vel in mandato male versatus sit,' and in this case became *infamis*. (Ulpian in Dig. iii. 2, 6, 6).

[2] The condition, *non contrario judicio*, though applicable to the last three contracts, is not applicable to partnership (*pro socio*); in this case the action on both sides is direct (Rabaud, De la note d'inf., p. 52). Yet the principle may have been extended to partnership, so far as mere indemnification was concerned.

[3] Ulpian in Dig. iii. 2, 6, 7 'in contrariis non de perfidia agitur, sed de calculo,' &c.; in Dig. xvi. 3, 5 'non ... de fide rupta agitur, sed de indemnitate ejus qui depositum suscepit.'

[4] Cic. pro Rosc. Amer. 39, 113: confirmed by a rescript of Constantine (Cod. iv. 35, 21): 'in re mandata non pecuniae solum ... verum etiam existimationis periculum est ... nec quicquam in eorum administratione neglectum ac declinatum culpa vacuum est.'

tutela; non-fulfilment of this obligation might arise from accidental circumstances; but even in this case the rigour of the law accounted it a *probrum* to be followed by infamia. It is explained by the jurists as due to the exigencies of society[1]: and this makes it impossible to agree with those modern writers who have considered that particular fraud (*dolus malus*) had to be proved in these cases[2]. They are assumed, in order to strengthen the feeling of obligation with respect to these trusts, necessarily to involve a breach of faith, however hard this interpretation might be in particular instances. It is one of the clearest survivals from the time when the censorship used its vast powers to enforce *bona fides*, as yet unsupported by any law.

This exhausts the cases of infamia mentioned in the *edictum perpetuum* in the mutilated form in which it has come down to us. It is quite certain that these do not exhaust the list framed by the praetor. Infamia necessarily changed to some extent, not only with the moral notions of the times, but with what to a certain extent expressed these: the recognition or non-recognition given by the positive law to certain courses of action[3]. Some of these sources of infamia became antiquated before the redaction of the Edict by Julian: others became antiquated between

[1] Ulpian in Dig. l. 16 (*de verb. signif.*) 42 (as opposed to *furtum* and *adulterium* which are *natura turpe*) 'Tutelae damnari hoc non natura probrum est sed more civitatis: nec enim natura probrum est quod potuit etiam in hominem idoneum incidere.' The chief passage quoted against the view that breach of *tutela* always involved infamia is Just. Inst. i. 26 (*de suspect. tut. et cur.*) 6 'suspectus autem remotus, si quidem ob dolum, famosus est; si ob culpam, non aeque.'

[2] Cf. Modestinus in Collatio, 10. 2, 5 'Depositi damnatus infamis est: qui vero commodati damnatur, non fit infamis: alter enim propter dolum, alter propter culpam condemnatur.'

[3] This was the case with usury. It does not appear to have been forbidden by positive law in the later Republic and early Empire. The infamia attaching to it was probably, at one time, in the Edict.

that period and the date of the codification of the law by Justinian. It is this latter process which the fortunate possession of the *Lex Julia Municipalis* enables us with some success to trace. There are few cases mentioned in it which may not have continued down to Hadrian's time, while all the cases (except perhaps one[1]) must certainly have appeared in the Edict at the close of the Republic.

The first case of the kind which we have to consider belongs to the class of causes of infamia which spring from actions, and refers to the legislation which was directed to the protection of minors. The *Lex Julia Municipalis* disqualifies anyone 'who has been condemned under the *Lex Plaetoria*, or on a ground arising from an offence against that law[2].' Condemnation under the *Lex Plaetoria* was condemnation in a *judicium publicum rei privatae* springing from this law; the latter portion of the ordinance, which refers to condemnation on a 'ground arising from the law' has been variously interpreted. Mommsen explains it of the *exceptio legis Plaetoriae* in a *privatum judicium*, having reference, e.g. to a loan (*pecunia credita*[3]). But, as Rudorff remarks, it is difficult to see how an *exceptio*, if held valid, could give rise to a condemnation; and it is best understood, as he explains it, of the *praejudicium*, or formal counter-action brought by the defendant in the original case in the form

[1] The clause in the *L. J. M.* against those who had taken part in a proscription ('Queive ob caput c(ivis) R(omanei) referundum pecuniam praemium aliudve quid cepit ceperit') is a political measure of Caesar's which could hardly have appeared in the Edict.

[2] 'Queive lege Plaetoria ob eamve rem, quod adversus eam legem fecit fecerit, condemnatus est erit.'

[3] Mommsen in C. I. L. I. p. 125, 'Lege Plaetoria condemnatur vocatus in judicium publicum rei privatae, quod ex hac lege descendit (Cic. De N. D. iii. 30, 74); ob eam rem, quod adversus legem Plaetoriam fecit, condemnatur qui in judicio privato sive pecuniae creditae sive alio ideo non obtinuit, quia reus exceptionem legis Plaetoriae (Dig. xliv. 1, 7, 1) a praetore impetraverat judicique probaverat.'

of the *sponsio*[1]. If his cause were established by the plaintiff, the defendant was condemned in the small amount of the *sponsio*. But at the same time it was decided that he had offended against the *Lex Plaetoria*: and either as a result of condemnation in this *praejudicium*, or in the *judicium publicum rei privatae* by which it was followed, he was declared *infamis*. It was really a condemnation for fraud, proved in the *praejudicium*, and was therefore in any case included in the praetor's list, as we possess it, under the words *dolus malus*.

(xiii) The next case that comes before us in the *Lex Julia Municipalis*, and which was certainly contained in the praetor's Edict, was that of bankruptcy. It is strange that it should have been cut out of the Edict even by the Justinianian compilers: for, quite apart from the mitigation of the law of debtor and creditor, effected during the Empire and completed by Justinian, the case of fraudulent bankruptcy must still have remained, and we should have expected it to deserve special consideration. When bankruptcy first made its appearance as a ground for the praetorian infamia it is impossible to say: but there is abundant evidence that, at the close of the Republic, it was frequently, though not invariably, made a ground for exclusion from honours by the censor[2]. The peculiar severity of the old Roman bankruptcy law makes it natural to believe that political disabilities were from early times attached to an act which seems to have been regarded as a failure in civic duty. The nexal debtor of early times, although in bonds, was still a citizen and could serve in the Roman legions when necessity required it. But we have no direct evidence to show whether his political status was seriously affected, if he emerged from

[1] Zeitschr. f. R. G. iv. p. 51.

[2] See p. 27.

being a *nexus*, or whether a similar disability attached to the jural debtor who had been incarcerated. The very early practice, however, of instituting a slave as an heir to a bankrupt estate (*damnosa hereditas*), in order to spare the memory of the testator, shows the sentiment on the subject, and sentiment of this kind is apt to be reflected in the law [1].

It is after imprisonment for debt had practically, although not legally, disappeared, and been replaced by the enforced sale by the creditor of the debtor's goods (*bonorum venditio*) introduced by the praetor in the last century of the Republic, that we first find infamia connected with bankruptcy. The seizure and sale of the debtor's goods (*bonorum possessio, proscriptio*) in accordance with the Edict (*ex edicto praetoris*) seriously affected *existimatio*: and this is just such a case as the praetor would most readily have taken up from the censors' lists, since it was so intimately connected with the working of his own court. The disqualifications of the *Lex Julia Municipalis* affect the man [2] 'who has sworn before the court that he has no means of meeting his engagements, or has sworn that he has some means of meeting his engagements, either in giving notice to his securities or creditors that he is not solvent, or by coming to an arrangement with his creditors on the ground of

[1] Just. Inst. i. 6, 1 'valde enim prospiciendum erat, ut egentes homines ... vel servum suum necessarium heredem habeant, qui satisfacturus esset creditoribus, aut hoc eo non faciente creditores res hereditarias servi nomine vendant, *ne injuria defunctus afficiatur*': cf. Gai. ii. 154.

[2] 'Queive in jure [*bonam copiam abjuravit*] abjuraverit, bonamve copiam juravit juraverit; quei (omit *ve*) sponsoribus creditoribusve sueis renuntiavit renuntiaverit se soldum solvere non posse, aut cum eis pactus est erit se soldum solvere non posse; prove quo datum depensum est erit; quojusve bona ex edicto ejus, qu(ei) j(ure) d(eicundo) praefuit praefuerit,—praeterquam sei quojus, quom pupillus esset reive publicae caussa abesset neque d(olo) m(alo) fecit fecerit quo magis r(ei) p(ublicae) c(aussa) a(besset) [*possessa proscriptave sunt erunt*]—possessa proscriptave sunt erunt.'

insolvency; or one who has caused his securities to pay for him; or one whose goods have been seized and put up for public sale, in accordance with the Edict of the judicial magistrate, except he be a ward or absent *bona fide* on the service of the State[1].' The cases of bankruptcy which are here mentioned as producing infamia fall therefore under two heads, (1) the case of ordinary bankruptcy, whether accompanied or not by a compromise affected by the creditors, (2) the case where a creditor has entrusted to his securities (*sponsores*) the duty of paying for him, and has not reimbursed them—a proceeding which was technically a breach of *mandatum*, and therefore of itself infamous, though not involving specific fraud (*dolus malus*). Lastly comes the provision referring to the enforced sale of goods (*bonorum venditio*), which was at this period possible in any case of bankruptcy, whether fraudulent or not, except of course in the contingencies mentioned of arrangement with creditors or settlement by securities. It is impossible to see in either of the cases here mentioned, as has been done by some modern writers[2], a reference to fraudulent bankruptcy: and the extreme severity of the Roman law in this respect, so consistent with the rigorous instincts of mercantile honesty that distinguished the nation, continued unabated until the early Empire. The change came with the *cessio bonorum* introduced by the *Lex Julia*; this gave the debtor the power of securing freedom from personal arrest by the surrender of his property, although it did not amount to a discharge;

[1] A conclusive proof that regulations such as these figured in the Edict of Julian is furnished by Rudorff (Zeitschr. f. R. G. iv. p. 52), who notices that the expressions *solidum non solvere* (Dig. xlvi. 3, 85, 1), *reipublicae causa abesse* (Dig. xlix. 16, 1) were found in the Edict as commented on by Ulpian and Callistratus. If so, they must have appeared in the provisions respecting infamia in Julian's Edict.

[2] E.g. Huschke and Rudorff, see Appendix, note 2.

and the principle was finally observed that the cession of goods, even though followed by their sale *en masse*, did not produce infamia[1]. The *cessio bonorum* was, however, essentially a *beneficium*[2], and could not have applied to fraudulent bankrupts. The *bonorum venditio* had disappeared as a whole with the *judicia ordinaria* by the time of Justinian[3]. It was this that infamia had followed: and the absence of any mention of bankruptcy in the list of *infames* as cut down by the compilers of the Digest shows that it could not have affected civil honour in the final stage of the Roman law.

Such are the cases by which the Edict may be supplemented by this law of Caesar's. There is one case remaining which was certainly in the Edict; for it was, perhaps more than any other, a source of infamia directly created by the praetor, and the absence of any specific mention of it in the form in which the Edict has come down to us is not easily explained, since it was a point of law which never became antiquated.

(xiv) It had reference to the removal of a *tutor*, and in later times a *curator* as well, who was under the suspicion of maladministering the affairs of his ward (*suspecti crimen*). This removal might be based on various grounds; some produced infamia, others did not. A distinction was drawn between actual fraud (*dolus*) and mere fault or negligence (*culpa, negligentia*)[4]. The former ground produced infamia

[1] Cod. ii. 11 (12), 11 (Severus Alexander, A. D. 223), 'Debitores qui bonis cesserint, licet ex ea causa bona eorum venierint, infames non fiunt.'

[2] Cod. vii. 71, 1 'in eo enim (i.e. 'cessio bonorum') tantum hoc beneficium eis prodest, ne judicati detrahantur in carcerem.'

[3] Inst. iii. 12 'cum extraordinariis judiciis posteritas usa est, ideo cum ipsis ordinariis judiciis etiam bonorum venditiones exspiraverunt.'

[4] Inst. i. 26 (*de susp. tut. et cur.*), 6; 'suspectus autem remotus, si quidem ob dolum, famosus est: si ob culpam, *non aeque*.' This has been explained by reference to Dig. xxxvii. 15, 12 'licet enim verbis edicti non habeantur infames ita condemnati, re tamen ipsa et opinione hominum non effugiunt

in the legal sense, the latter did not; and naturally, when the ground of removal by the magistrate was mere lack of ability, energy, or force of character, *existimatio* remained intact[1]. It was thus extremely important that the praetor should state the ground of removal[2]. Where by any chance the magistrate had omitted to state the ground of the removal, the verdict of Papinian was accepted, that this removal did not produce infamia[3].

(xv) Closely connected with the foregoing, as having reference to *tutela*, is a case of infamia which may be posterior to the redaction of the Edict. It was created by a *senatus consultum*, of unknown date, but earlier than the reign of M. Aurelius[4], which forbade tutors or curators to marry their wards or to give them in marriage to their sons. In the former case the guardian, in the latter both he and his son were *infames*, and this was the case even though the son were under power at the time of his marriage[5]. The marriage itself was in such case null; but the invalidity was removed and the infamia averted if the formal consent of the father of the ward had been

infamiae notam.' The same principle is affirmed in Cod. v. 43, 9 (Diocletian and Maximian, A. D. 294).

[1] Ulpian in Dig. xxvi. 10, 3, 18.

[2] Ulpian in Dig. xxvi. 10, 4, 1 'decreto igitur debebit causa removendi significari, ut appareat de existimatione.'

[3] Mentioned by Callistratus (Dig. xxiii. 2, 64), Tryphoninus (ib. 67), and in a constitution of Diocletian and Maximian (Cod. v. 6, 7).

[4] Paulus in Dig. xxiii. 2, 66 'Non est matrimonium, si tutor vel curator pupillam suam intra vicesimum et sextum annum ... ducat uxorem vel eam filio suo jungat: quo facto *uterque infamatur* ... nec interest filius sui juris an in patris potestate sit'; 'uterque' must refer to father and son: not as Marezoll takes it (Bürg. Ehr. p. 159) to *tutor (et) curator*, in spite of its apparent contradiction to the principle laid down with respect to the rules of mourning (qui jussu patris duxit ... non notatur,' Dig. iii. 2, 12). The constitution of Diocletian and Maximian (Cod. v. 6, 7) has only reference to the case of the father, and cannot be adduced as evidence against the principle laid down by Paulus, as it is by Hepp (De la note d'Inf. p. 47).

obtained either during his lifetime or through his testament, or else by a grace of the Emperor [1].

The reason given for this singular provision was that such a marriage was assumed to be tantamount to a confession of maladministration, and to be a cloak to cover irregularities committed during guardianship [2]. The part played by tutory in the history of infamia—the three modes by which civil honour was affected, condemnation in an action, removal on suspicion, and this supposedly fraudulent marriage—is a good instance of the manner in which *fides* was protected, throughout the history of Roman law, by this form of sanction [3].

Immediate infamia was also produced in the time of the Empire by

(xvi) an accusation to the *fiscus* which was not proved by the accuser [4]; a mode of checking rash delation, which resembles the penalties imposed by the Senate on its members in the early Principate, and the stigma attached to *delatores* in the later Empire; and

(xvii) to usury [5]. This, as has been remarked, may once have figured in the praetor's Edict, as it was doubtless a ground for the *nota* of the censor at the time when usury was forbidden by law, and even, perhaps, when it was discountenanced, though not forbidden. It may, therefore, be treated as one of the sources of infamia

[1] Dig. xxiii. 2, 66; Cod. v. 6, 7.

[2] 'velut confessum de tutela' (Cod. v. 6, 7): cf. Dig. xxiii. 2, 67.

[3] As regards the formal classification of these two cases of infamia resulting from tutela, the latter appears to be immediate, the former mediate; for the removal on suspicion may be assimilated to a sentence, and the infamia does not follow here on a course of action but on its recognition by a magistrate.

[4] Dig. xlix. 14 (*de jure fisci*), 2, and 18, § 7.

[5] Cod. ii. 11 (12), 20 (Diocletian and Maximian, A.D. 290) 'Improbum foenus exercentibus et usuras usurarum illicite exigentibus infamiae macula irroganda est.'

that had a long, if interrupted, recognition in Roman law; although it is only known to us as producing this effect from a constitution of Diocletian and Maximian of the year 290 A.D. How this infamia was pronounced is not quite clear: it was immediate, since it followed on the fact of the exaction of an illicit rate of interest; but this fact could hardly have become apparent otherwise than in an action for recovery [1].

Turning now to cases of *infamia mediata* other than those mentioned in the Edict, we find the penalty attached to two extraordinary delicts. These were the violation of a sepulchre, and robbery of an inheritance.

(xviii) Violation of a sepulchre was an extraordinary delict, in which a money-penalty could be recovered by means of an *actio*; and this action produced infamia [2]. It was also an extraordinary crime punished by a *poena* [3], and in one particular form could actually be made the subject of a *judicium publicum* [4], as technically falling under one of the clauses of the *Lex Julia de vi publica*. In this case also it would produce the infamia which followed condemnation in these courts. The very nature of this offence shows that it must have had a long history in Roman law as a means of derogating from civil honour. The Emperor Julian, when in the year 363 he made it sacrilege, goes back in memory to the spirit of the older religion which had treated it as such, and mentions the form of expiation (*piaculum*) to which it led [5]. It belonged, in fact, to the old pontifical law of Rome, the offences against which, when its own peculiar sanctions had been

[1] Rabaud, Sur l'infamie à Rome, p. 50.

[2] Dig. xlvii. 12, 1 and 9.

[3] Paulus in Dig. ib. 11.

[4] Macer in Dig. ib. 8.

[5] Cod. ix. 19, 5 (Julian, A.D. 363), 'Lapidem hinc movere et terram sollicitare et cespitem vellere proximum sacrilegio majores semper habuerunt—ne in piaculum incidant contaminata religione bustorum, hoc fieri prohibemus poena sacrilegii cohibentes.'

rendered invalid, were taken up and punished by the censors. It formed part of their care of the *sacra gentilicia*; and it is a mere accident that this kind of infamia is known to us only in its latest stage, as the result of a formal delict or a formal crime.

(xix) The *actio expilatae hereditatis* belongs to that class of extraordinary delicts which approximated to *furtum*, but were not technically included under that head. It naturally led therefore to the same consequences as the main offence to which it approximated, and produced infamia [1]. The Emperor M. Aurelius organised for it a special procedure in criminal law [2], and Ulpian classes it with *stellionatus* as a *crimen extraordinarium* [3]. In this case it must have been followed by a *poena extraordinaria*: and probably the same disabilities resulted from the imposition of this penalty as were consequent on the *actio*. It seems fair to conclude that all the other offences approximating to *furtum* which were punished *extra ordinem* [4] must have produced infamia, although this is not mentioned in connection with them.

With respect to criminal law in its developed form, infamia might follow as a consequence of condemnation both in the ordinary courts and in the *judicia extraordinaria*. With respect to the former, the final assertion of the principle, that condemnation in any *judicium publicum* produced infamia, has already been noticed. With respect to the *cognitiones extraordinariae*, *calumnia*, *praevaricatio*, *tergiversatio*—all of which followed this form—have already been treated in connection with the praetor's Edict. But one great extension was necessary in order to make infamia co-extensive with almost the whole circle

[1] Ulpian in Dig. xlvii. 19, 2; Cod. ii. 11 (12), 12.

[2] Dig. xlvii. 19, 1.

[3] Ib. 11, 3.

[4] As those mentioned in Dig. xlvii. titles 16 to 18.

of the criminal law; and this was effected by making it the invariable accompaniment of the crime of *stellionatus*.

(xx) *Stellionatus* is sometimes treated as a delict: more often as a crime, to which an extraordinary penalty was attached[1]. It was more properly the latter and the widest of charges, covering the whole field of criminality not usurped by special courts; it was, in fact, in criminal matters what fraud (*dolus malus*) was in civil actions[2], and as such naturally produced infamia[3].

[1] Papinian in Dig. xlvii. 20, 1, '*Actio stellionatus* neque publicis judiciis neque privatis actionibus continetur.' Cf. Ulpian in Dig. ib. 3. Cod. ix. 34, 3 (Gordian, A.D. 242), 'Stellionatus accusatio inter crimina publica non habetur.'

[2] Ulpian in Dig. xlvii. 20, 3, 'quod enim in privatis judiciis est de dolo actio, hoc in criminibus stellionatus prosecutio—et ut generaliter dixerim, deficiente titulo criminis hoc crimen locum habet. . . . . Poena autem stellionatus nulla legitima est, cum nec legitimum crimen sit.'

[3] Ulpian in Dig. iii. 2, 13, 8, says, 'Crimen stellionatus infamiam irrogat damnato, quamvis publicum non est judicium': in Dig. xlvii. 20, 2 he says, 'Stellionatus judicium famosum quidem [non] est, sed coercitionem extraordinariam habet.' We must follow Favre and Krueger in omitting the 'non' in this latter passage. This would be an unjustifiable mode of cutting the knot if it were only done to reconcile the conflict between the two extracts; but it is necessary in order to give a tolerable sense to the second passage standing by itself.

CHAPTER V.

LATER HISTORY OF THE INFAMIA.

We now reach the last stage in the history of the infamia. The praetorian conception had swallowed up the censorian, and it was natural that the codified form should prevail. But the notion, inherent in the censorian procedure, of exclusion from public honours, now again became the dominant idea. When it became so cannot be stated with certainty; we know of no general principle which made infamia a ground of exclusion from *all* public honours before the time of Constantine. But, already in the second century of the Empire, infamia seems to be extended as a fixed conception to new cases. It was employed to meet one of the growing evils of the times—that of *delatio*.

(xxi) False *delatores* were punished with 'the *nota*' by M. Aurelius; even those who proved their case were made *infames* by Macrinus[1].

But it was chiefly after the conception had been fixed by Constantine that we find a change in the character of the infamia. It was a change that naturally accompanied the transference of law-making from the judges

[1] Vit. M. Anton. 11, 'Calumniis quadruplatorum intercessit, adposita falsis delatoribus nota': Vit. Macrini, 12, 'Delatores, si non probarent, capite adfecit, si probarent, delato pecuniae praemio infames dimisit.' Already in the early Principate it had been made a ground of exclusion from the Senate (Tac. Ann. iv. 31, 8; xii. 59).

and the interpreting jurisconsults to the sole person of the Emperor. The infamia has no longer a natural growth: it almost loses its moral significance. It is employed merely as a very powerful weapon in the hands of the Emperor to check evils of administration as they arose. The added cases of infamia form only a disconnected list. They are chiefly valuable as throwing light on some of the evils which threatened the administration even of the 'divine' and 'hallowed' rule of the later Caesars. They may be conveniently divided into judicial and administrative.

1. In judicial matters the judge was *infamis*

(xxii) Who, in a case which he had sent on appeal to the Emperor, had not forwarded all the documents which had been produced by the parties in the case, and were necessary to the full solution of the question at issue. The reason given for this threat was the necessity of obviating the delay, which would ensue if the Emperor had to refer back to the lower court for information which should have been supplied from the first[1]. But the wisdom of this *nota* can still better be defended if we think of the power that suppression of documentary evidence might give to an unjust or corrupt judge. (Constantine, A. D. 319.)

(xxiii) Who has tolerated the harsh treatment of prisoners and who has not executed summary punishment on the guardians of prisons (*stratores*) guilty of such treatment. (Constantine, A. D. 320[2].)

(xxiv) A judge or provincial governor who has submitted to torture a *principalis* or senator of a municipal town. (Gratian, Valentinian II, and Theodosius I, A. D. 381[3].)

[1] Cod. vii. 62, 15 'ne causas, quae in nostram venerint scientiam rursus transferri ad judicia necesse sit, instructiones necessarias plene actis inseri praecipimus,' &c.

[2] Cod. ix. 4, 1, 5.

[3] Cod. x. 32 (31), 33: for the principle that decurions might not be tortured, see Dig. l. 2, 14.

(xxv) The judge who has made a *praefectianus* or *palatinus* or ordinary soldier, or anyone who has filled these posts, *intercessor* or *executor*, in any case whether public or private. (Valentinian II, Theodosius I, and Arcadius, A. D. 386[1]).

(xxvi) Who has shelved, left unpunished, or visited with a lighter penalty than that ordained by law, a crime of breach of the peace (*violentia*) which has been proved before him. (Valentinian II, Theodosius I, and Arcadius, A.D. 390[2].)

(xxvii) After the Court the Bar deserved attention: and we find the Emperors taking precautions against a form of civilised barbarism peculiarly difficult to deal with—the unmeasured license of invective and insinuation which not unfrequently marks the pleadings of advocates. Probably lawyers of the free Republic, having no privileged position, were always open to a charge of slander, although the pleadings which have been preserved show that it could not have been effectual. At a time when the jury-system had disappeared such forms of oratory must have been less usual, since they are only effective before popular courts. The Emperors Valentinian and Valens treated such invectives as *injuria* and visited them with infamia (A.D. 368)[3].

Other employments of the *nota* were made to check the abuse of the right of appeal to the Emperor and to the higher courts of appeal which he had established, particularly to that of the *praefectus praetorio*.

(xxviii) The first regulation refers to the case of an appeal which has not been allowed by a subordinate

[1] Cod. i. 40, 8.

[2] Ib. ix. 12, 8, 3.

[3] Cod. ii. 6, 6 'agant (advocati) quod causa desiderat; temperent ab injuria. Nam si quis adeo procax fuerit, ut non ratione, sed probris putet esse certandum, opinionis suae imminutione quatietur.'

Judge of Appeal, but which has then been brought to the highest court, that of the *praefectus praetorio*, to be heard afresh[1]. If, in this final stage, the appellant lost his case he was *infamis* (Constantine, A.D. 331).

(xxix) Infamia also visited the appellant who, instead of employing the normal course of appeal, addressed a special supplication to the sovereign (*petere per supplicationem*), (Constantine, A.D. 331)[2]. By a constitution of Valentinian II, Theodosius I and Arcadius, issued in the year 384 A.D., this procedure was treated as *ambitus*, and possibly the infamia in this case was mediate, arising from a condemnation on this charge[3].

(xxx) Before this period the appellant guilty of contempt of court by insulting the judge had been visited with infamia[4].

(xxxi) In civil matters, the only new regulation—if indeed it was a new one and not the restatement of an old principle—that comes before us during this period, recalls the early working of the infamia in its connection with private law; for it refers to the violation of verbal compacts. By a constitution of Arcadius and Honorius, of the year 395 A.D., any one over age who has violated a pact or transaction by not fulfilling the promises contained in it, or has attempted to evade it by a request made to the judge, or a supplication addressed to the sovereign, is declared *infamis*[5].

(xxxii) In criminal matters we also meet with new applications of infamia, answering to changes in procedure

[1] 'ut apud eos de integra litiget tamquam appellatione suscepta' (Cod. vii. 62, 19). There was no appeal to the Emperor from the *praef. praet.* (ib.)

[2] Cod. i. 21, 3.

[3] Cod. i. 16 'ut, si quisquam speciali supplicatione eliciendum aliquod rescriptum temptaverit . . . damnatus ambitus crimine maneat infamis.'

[4] Dig. xlvii. 10, 42 (Paulus, lib. v. sent. [4. 18]).

[5] Cod. ii. 4, 41.

or to the increased disapprobation with which certain special crimes were viewed.

The first regulation refers to the change in procedure adopted in the case of contumacious *rei* who refused to appear before the court. The Emperors Severus and Antoninus, while maintaining by a rescript the old principle that no one could be condemned in his absence, yet ordained that in such cases the individual should be posted up as wanted by the court (*absens requirendus adnotatus*), and that the governors of provinces should issue Edicts to demand their presence[1]. These Edicts, called *programmata*, did not in any way prejudge the guilt of the *requirendus adnotatus*[2]: but, while in civil actions (*pecuniariae causae*) such an Edict produced no effect on character, it was enacted by a constitution of Honorius and Theodosius II in 421 A.D. that the individual against whom a *programma criminale* had been issued in consequence of a *crimen publicum* which he had committed should be *infamis*[3]. This was in reality only a more general application of an older principle which had prevailed in the time of the classical jurists. Trajan's principle that no one should be condemned in absence was upheld. Punishments, however, were imposed on *contumaces*, but the rule was adopted that these punishments on the absent should be only such as affected *existimatio*, never such as affected *caput*[4]. By this later constitution of the fifth century all the *requirendi*, who were presumably contumacious, were immediately rendered *infames* without the necessity of awaiting the special sentence of a criminal court.

(xxxiii) The only other criminal ordinance which requires mention in connection with the infamia marks the

[1] Dig. xlviii. 17, 1.
[2] Cod. vii. 57, 6.
[3] Cod. ix. 40, 3.
[4] Dig. xlviii. 19, 5 (Ulpian).

climax of the law of treason, ever the curse of the Roman Empire. In the matter of abstract injustice it goes far beyond any other use to which the Romans put their conception of Civil Honour. By a constitution of Arcadius and Honorius in 397 A.D. it was enacted that the sons of those who had entered into a dangerous conspiracy against the Emperor or the imperial councils—i.e. members of the Consistory and the Senate—should be *infames*, excluded from all honours and from the army, and should be further debarred from receiving any direct or indirect inheritance. It was a remarkable abuse of the conception in both these respects: as transmitting the stigma from father to son, contrary to the principle that the infamia was not hereditary; and as attaching a civic disability to the *nota* which did not usually accompany it[1]. To this ordinance a rider was added, that any one who interceded for those, on whom the disabilities were imposed, should be also *infamis*.

II. The other regulations made by the Emperors, from Diocletian and Constantine onwards, were concerned with questions of general administration.

(xxxiv) To the beginning of this period belongs the amplification of a rule respecting freedmen. The *Lex Visellia* of 23 B.C. had imposed penalties on men of this class who ventured to usurp the offices and honours (*honores et dignitates*)

[1] Cod. ix. 8, 5. 'Filii vero ejus . . . a materna vel avita, omnium etiam proximorum hereditate ac successione habeantur alieni, testamentis extraneorum nihil capiant, sint perpetuo egentes et pauperes, infamia eos paterna semper comitetur, ad nullos umquam honores, nulla prorsus sacramenta perveniant.' To daughters the Falcidian fourth was allowed; the dowries of the mothers that would have gone to the sons were to fall to the *fiscus*: but the fourth of these also was allowed to daughters. The offender himself, if convicted after death (*convicto mortuo*), was punished by *damnatio memoriae*. On the relation of this ordinance to the general theory of punishment and to the law of treason in particular, see Appendix, Note III.

reserved for men of free birth (*ingenui*)—amongst these offices being that of a senator in a municipal town. The rule only affected freedmen who had not had the fiction of free-birth bestowed on them by the right of the gold ring (*jus aureorum anulorum*), or, later, by the restoration to the birth-right (*natalibus restitutio*)—both in the gift of the Emperor. By a constitution of Diocletian and Maximian, issued about 300 A.D., freedmen guilty of such conduct were not only punished but declared *infames.* As they were already debarred from office, infamia in this case must have been felt chiefly in its civil consequences. It is not likely that such a man would ever have attained the fiction of *ingenuitas* from the Emperor: but, if this ever happened, we must assume that the infamia would have been withdrawn at the same time by an imperial decree[1]. This ground of infamia naturally disappeared when Justinian abolished the distinction between *libertini* and *ingenui*, by enacting that the conferment of *ingenuitas* should follow as a matter of course all cases of formal manumission[2].

(xxxv) A further employment of infamia had reference to forbidden marriage. Unions had been prohibited between senators and men of high position, and a class of women described as *humiles abjectaeque*, in consequence of birth or occupation[3]. By a regulation of Constantine issued in 336 A.D. dignitaries of the State—*senatores*, *perfectissimi*, *duumviri* of the municipal towns, and the members of the

[1] Cod. ix. 21 'Lex Visellia libertinae condicionis homines persequitur, si ea quae ingenuorum sunt circa honores et dignitates ausi fuerint attemptare vel decurionatum adripere, nisi jure aureorum anulorum impetrato a principe sustentantur . . . in curiam autem se immiscens damno quidem cum infamia adficitur.' Cf. Cod. x. 33 (32), 1 (Diocletian and Maximian) 'si libertus vel jus aureorum anulorum adeptus non est vel natalibus suis non restitutus,' &c.

[2] Nov. 78, 1.

[3] Cod. v. 5, 7.

religious colleges of Phoeniciarchs and Syriarchs are given in the enumeration—are marked with infamy, if they pass as legitimate children born of such women as those with whom marriage was interdicted[1]. This ground of infamia again was removed by Justinian, when he repealed the prohibitions of marriage ordained by his predecessors[2].

(xxxvi) The next regulation is an attempt to meet an evil which appeared at the very outset of the Roman imperial system as organised under a single rule, and which grew with its growth. This was the extreme unwillingness of citizens of the municipal towns to fill the offices of their native places. The life of a senator (*decurio*) came in course of time to be one of burden, expense, and even of danger: and concealment of the unlucky people who were qualified for the local senates was not unusual. A constitution of Valentinian I, Valens and Gratian, of 371 A.D., punishes any one guilty of such concealment with infamia[3].

(xxxvii) An incidental case of infamia originated with the regulations of Theodosius II and Valentinian III as regards imperial rescripts. While in 426 A.D. laying down rules for, and in some respects limiting, the validity of such rescripts, they enacted that any one who gave a bad or distorted interpretation, or impugned the validity of an imperial answer which he had elicited, should be *infamis*[4].

(xxxviii) The next employment of this disability which we meet with is interesting and important as having reference to education. It proceeded from Theodosius II and Valentinian III in 425 A.D., but the principle on which it

[1] Cod v. 27, 1.

[2] Nov. 89, 15, the Constitution of Constantine is mentioned as having sunk into desuetude ('non utendo perempta est'), and is formally repealed ('quam videlicet constitutionem etiam omnino perimimus'). Cf. Nov. 117, 4.

[3] Cod. x. 32 (31), 31.

[4] Cod. i. 14, 2.

depended was established by the Emperor Julian in 362 A.D. Julian created a state-sanction for education by requiring that all teachers and professors (*magistros studiorum doctoresque*) should show special qualifications, both moral and intellectual, and that this should be recognised by a diploma granted, in the States of the Roman world generally, by a decree of the local Senate[1]. Whether Julian meant to stamp out private and unauthorised instruction or not, the constitution of Theodosius and Valentinian only punished unqualified professors with infamia, who lectured in the public halls and lecture rooms (*in publicis magistrationibus cellulisque*) and did not affect private tutors[2].

(xxxix) The last instance of infamia that we have to chronicle was an inevitable consequence of the recognition of a canon of orthodoxy by the State. By an Edict of Gratian, Valentinian II, and Theodosius I, published in 380 A.D., all heretics are declared *infames*[3]. Special disabilities were from time to time inflicted both on heretics and pagans. Theodosius I declared the Eunomians *intestabiles*; a similar threat was pronounced by the same Emperor against Christians who had gone over to heathendom[4]. But it was on heretics rather than on pagans that disabilities were most frequently imposed; and by this infamia was finally meant exclusion from all honours and dignities. In the times of turmoil and confusion that intervened between Theodosius I and Justinian such a regulation could not always be enforced. Catholic Emperors were often at the mercy of their Arian supporters, and Gothic princes could set at defiance the rules

[1] Cod. x. 53 (52), 7. [2] Cod. xi. 19 (18).

[3] Cod. i. 1 (*de summa trinitate et de fide catholica*), 1. (*Impp. Gratianus, Valentinianus, et Theodosius A. A. A. ad populum urbis Constantinopolitanae*).

[4] Cod. Theod. xvi. 5, 6–23; xvi. 7, 1, 2.

of the orthodox Empire. Yet, so far as the internal administration of peaceful provinces was concerned, we may perhaps suppose these disabilities to have been really enforced from the time of Theodosius onwards. The definitions of heresy depend on the decisions of the successive councils. By Justinian orthodoxy was defined in accordance with the decisions of the Councils of Nicaea, Constantinople, Ephesus and Chalcedon[1].

[1] Cod. i. 1. 2 (*Nicaena fides* recognised by Gratian, Valentinian II, and Theodosius I 381 A.D.), 3 (Nicaea and Ephesus by Theodosius II and Valentinian III, A.D. 448), 4 (Chalcedon by Marcian, A.D. 452), 6, § 11 (Nicaea, Constantinople, Ephesus, and Chalcedon by Justinian, A.D. 533).

In this list of the imperial applications of infamia two cases have been omitted as being unauthentic.

The first is a constitution of Constantine, A.D. 319 in Cod. vii. 49, 2: 'De eo, qui pretio depravatus aut gratia perperam judicaverit ei vindicta quem laeserit non solum existimationis dispendiis, sed etiam litis discrimine praebeatur.' In spite of the many curious expressions used to describe the infamia in imperial constitutions, *existimationis dispendia* is almost too singular to stand, and the right reading is perhaps that of Godefroy, *aestimationis*. Cf. Dig. v. 1, 15 'judex tunc litem suam facere intellegitur, cum dolo malo in fraudem legis sententiam dixerit . . . ut veram aestimationem litis praestare cogatur.'

The other is the pretended Edict of Justinian's appended to Cod. ii. 58 (59): 'Pateat omnibus nostram rem publicam procurantibus conventiculam seu conspirationem jurisjurandi religione vel quoquo modo compositam a nostra majestate prohiberi et detestari: unde hujus rei fautores et socios ab omni publico honore sibi commisso infamiae nota privamus, non habentibus autem ad ullum publici honoris gradum accedendi licentiam penitus amputamus.' It is generally regarded as an apocryphal addition of the twelfth century.

CHAPTER VI.

EFFECTS OF THE DEVELOPED CONCEPTION OF INFAMIA.

IT has now been sufficiently demonstrated that infamia was always primarily a matter of public law; it was only secondarily, and in accordance with the use to which the praetor put the conception in order to guard the dignity of his own court, a matter of private law. This justifies us in treating the consequences of infamia as a whole under the main divisions of its primary and its secondary effects.

The most important amongst the primary effects of infamia were those which touched the *honores*, or individual magistracies of the State. With respect to these we have seen that there was no universal regulation in the time of the Republic. Criminal laws had occasionally as one of their sanctions exclusion from *honores*, and the magistrates who presided over the admission to office might have been bound to respect them. At the same time the censors, acting independently of any decree of the State, took it upon themselves to exclude from all functions, over which they had control, certain classes of individuals which developed into something like a fixed category in consequence of the rulings of successive holders of the office. But to create a perpetual exclusion of *infames* as such from office two things were necessary: one was the fixing of the conception of infamia through the persistence of the praetorian list, and the commentaries of the jurists to which it gave rise; the other was the decree of an

Emperor. Both were realised: and after Constantine a definite category of persons called *infames* were for ever excluded from the *dignitates* of the State.

There are two political capacities, however, which deserve further consideration in connection with the *infames*. These are the judicial bench and the army.

As regards *judices*, we know that special laws which prescribed the mode of selection for the *album judicum* excluded certain people on moral grounds, and pronounced them *infames* for this limited purpose. And these grounds are, as we should expect, in touch with the wider category of the praetorian *infames*. Thus the *Lex Acilia Repetundarum* of 122 B.C. excludes anyone who has hired himself out to fight as a gladiator, or whose condemnation in a criminal court has entailed exclusion from the Senate[1]. Again certain criminal laws had appended as one of their formal penalties that a man condemned under them should for ever be prohibited from being a *judex*. This was one of the provisions of the *Lex Julia de vi privata* and also of the *Lex Julia repetundarum*[2]; and we may notice that the juristic interpretation of this latter law put exclusion from the Senate and exclusion from the judicial bench on the same level[3]. Such principles were sure to develope: and were helped out by the very free hand which the praetor had in the selection of his *judices*. The 'urban praetors,' says Cicero, 'are bound on oath to select the best men[4].' It is, therefore, in the highest degree improbable

[1] *Lex Acil. Rep.* l. 13.

[2] For *Lex Julia de vi privata* see Marcian in Dig. xlviii. 7, 1 (p. 22), *Lex Julia Repetundarum*, Dig. xlviii. 11, 6.

[3] Marcellus in Dig. i. 9, 2. 'Cassius Longinus non putat ei permittendum, qui propter turpitudinem senatu motus nec restitutus est, judicare vel testimonium dicere, quia lex Julia repetundarum hoc fieri vetat.' Cf. Cod. xii. 1, 12.

[4] Cic. pro Cluent. 43, 121 'praetores urbani, qui jurati debent optimum quemque in selectos judices referre.'

that the praetor would ever have selected as *judices* those whom his own Edict had declared *infames* for the much less important purpose of postulation. The praetor, like the censor, was partly limited by law, partly followed his own discretion. He was not bound to follow the line taken by the censors, in their pronouncements of *ignominia*; but that he systematically disregarded the censorian rulings is, as we have seen, in spite of Cicero's apparent statement to that effect, extremely improbable. It was, in fact, rendered almost impossible by the circumstance that the censors had the first chance of excluding from lists (the Senate and to a less degree the *equites*) from which the *judices* were afterwards selected by the praetor. The praetor's scrutiny must in fact have been more severe than that of the censors: and it may be taken as certain that none of the individuals whom the praetor's Edict pronounced *infames* could appear on the judicial bench. Since this was the category utilised and developed by the later Empire, a similar exclusion may safely be assumed as having been perpetuated under that *régime*, so far as there yet remained any room for *judices* proper under the *cognitiones extraordinariae* by which the *judicia ordinaria* had been replaced. We shall have occasion to examine later on the cases in which either laws or certain observed principles of procedure prohibited certain classes of individuals from appearing as witnesses in courts of law. In these cases again we may argue *a fortiori* that the individuals in question would have been excluded from the position of *judices*[1].

[1] The mode in which these special prohibitions about evidence were extended as cases of infamia may be illustrated by a comparison of Dig. xxii. 5, 3, 5 (the list of persons whom the *Lex Julia de vi* prohibited from giving evidence) with Cod. viii. 12, 8 'quod si illi (i.e. servi) metu atque exhortatione dominorum violentiam admiserint, palam est secundum

The question 'Did the developed conception of infamia, as it existed under the Empire, exclude from service in the army?' we may answer in the affirmative: but only with confidence so far as the most extreme grounds of this disqualification were concerned[1]. Service in the legions was regarded as a *honor* rather than a *munus*, and the law here follows the analogy of the regulations about *dignitates*. We find for instance that, if a soldier had been 'relegated,' and after fulfilling the term of his exile, sought enlistment, the reason for his condemnation (*causa damnationis*) was the essential point in the decision. If it was such as to involve perpetual infamia it also involved perpetual exclusion from the ranks. Again the *requirendus adnotatus* was excluded from the ranks, and a man in this position was, as we have seen, made *infamis* by a constitution of Honorius and Theodosius of the fifth century A.D. Admission was also denied to those condemned for *adulterium*, or in any *judicium publicum*, and these were amongst the *infames*[2]. Lastly, an imperial constitution which we possess, while providing for restoration of exiles through a grace of the Emperor (*generalis indulgentia*), denies that restoration to the ranks can be one of its consequences, and puts military functions on the same level as *integra existimatio*[3]: and the sons of traitors who, by the constitution of Arcadius and Honorius, are debarred *honores*, are also forbidden the *sacramenta*[4].

legem Juliam dominum infamem pronuntiatum loci aut originis propriae dignitate non uti.

[1] The list of grounds on which enlistment was forbidden given in the Dig. (xlix. 16, 4, 1-9) includes only certain cases of infamia; but it is possible that this list is not exhaustive, so far as the rules of service of the later Empire are concerned.

[2] Dig. xlix. 16 (*de re militari*), 4, §§ 4, 6, and 7.

[3] Cod. ix. 51 (*de sententiam passis et restitutis*), 7.

[4] Cod. ix. 8, 5, see p. 149.

If we turn now to the secondary, or civil law effects of infamia, we find that these were naturally connected with the working of the praetor's court, and with the purpose for which he framed the Edict including the list of *infames*. What was spoken of as the second Edict contained a list of those who were allowed to postulate only for themselves: and amongst this class were the *in turpitudine notabiles*. Improper attempts at advocacy on the part of such persons were not merely repulsed by the magistrate, but were punished *extra ordinem* with a fine. The third Edict contained the list of those able to postulate for themselves, and only in exceptional cases for others[1]. In this third class were included *omnes qui edicto praetoris ut infames notantur*. This limited capacity for postulation was followed by some important consequences. One of its results was that an infamous person could not, as a rule, act as a *cognitor*, nor as a *procurator*[2]. The consequence of this was that the assignment of an action to an infamous person was impossible, because all such assignments took the form of commissions to a *cognitor* or *procurator*. This effect of infamia was,

[1] The exceptional cases were enumerated by the praetor as follows: 'Pro alio ne postulent praeterquam pro parente, patrono patrona, liberis parentibusque patroni patronae . . . liberisve suis, fratre sorore, uxore, socero socru, genero nuru, vitrico noverca, privigno privigna, pupillo pupilla, furioso furiosa.' ['fatuo, fatua,' added by Gaius, but probably not in the Edict (Lenel, p. 63)], cui eorum a parente aut de majoris partis *tribunorum* (Lenel) sententia aut ab eo, cujus de ea re jurisdictio fuit, ea tutela curatiove data erit.'

[2] Fragm. Vat. §§ 322-324 'verba autem edicti haec sunt: "alieno," inquit, "nomine, item per alios agendi potestatem non faciam in his causis, in quibus ne dent cognitorem neve dentur, edictum comprehendit." quod ait "alieno nomine item per alios" breviter repetit duo edicta cognitoria, unum quod pertinet ad eos qui dantur *cognitores, alterum ad eos qui dant* (Suppl. Hollweg); ut qui prohibentur vel dare vel dari cognitores, idem et procuratores dare darive arceantur. Ob turpitudinem et famositatem prohibentur quidam cognituram suscipere, ad sectionem (i. e. postulation as an 'adsector in libertatem') non nisi suspecti praetori.'

however, counteracted in time by the form of assignment known as *utiles actiones*. These did not require the nomination of a *cognitor* or *procurator*: and since the person to whom the assignment was made in this form prosecuted the claim in his own name[1], an infamous person to whom postulation in his own interest was never forbidden could not be excluded. Another result of the limitation of the power of postulation by an infamous person was that no such person could undertake a *popularis actio*, that is, a case in which a money penalty was enforced on behalf of the State, because the sustainer of such an action was a procurator of the State[2]. In all these cases in which *infames* were prohibited from postulating the consent of the adversary was not sufficient to establish their claim to appear in this character. Even had they gained such consent, the prohibition was still upheld by the praetor, in his own interest and in that of his court[3].

So far we have been considering the disabilities which affected an infamous person in consequence of his incapacity to be a *cognitor* or *procurator*: a result which in itself follows from the limitation on the right of postulation, which was the main object of the praetorian infamia. Another and much less accountable consequence of infamia was that a person so affected could not give a *cognitor* or *procurator*. It is difficult to connect this disability at all closely with the fact of limitation in postulation: and various theories have been framed to account for it. It has been held that it was done in the interest of the opposite party, that the defendant could with more success

[1] Cod. iv. 39, 9 'utiliter eam movere suo nomine conceditur.'

[2] Dig. xlvii. 23, 4.

[3] Gaius in Dig. iii. 1. 7 'quos prohibet praetor apud se postulare, omnimodo prohibet, etiamsi adversarius eos patiatur postulare.'

take exception to the acts of an *infamis* when the latter appeared in person: or that the capacity of being represented would have given the *infames* the opportunity of avoiding open disgrace and reprehension. Whatever the immediate motive may have been, it must be taken as in some sort a penalising measure, representation being regarded as a privilege not to be extended to unworthy persons[1]. It is only very distantly connected with the limitation in postulation, and Karlowa is no doubt right in holding that the list of those who could not give was by no means necessarily coincident with the list of those who could not be cognitors and procurators[2]. We know from the Vatican Fragments that the *edictum cognitorium* contained two parts, or, as it is expressed, that there were two *edicta cognitoria.* The first referred to those who could not be *cognitores*, the second to those who could not present *cognitores.* It is in this second list that the persons labouring under the disability we are considering must have come: but this second list may have been wider than the first; for women, although they cannot be cognitors, since they are unable to postulate for others at all, may yet give cognitors; and Karlowa is no doubt right in thinking that this is the origin of the list of *mulieres famosae*, fragments of which have come down to us.

These limitations in the matter of representation, by which the *infames* were affected, were maintained chiefly

[1] We may agree with Karlowa (Zeitschr. f. R. G. ix. p. 223) that it is an anachronism to base this disability on such a principle as that stated in Nov. 71 praef. ('fertur enim quibusdam constitutionibus, ut nulli clarissimorum liceat per se litem exercere, sed per procuratorem omnino'); but yet representation may always have been regarded in the abstract as a privilege, the exception and not the rule. How much this privilege depended on the discretion of the magistrate is shown by Papinian in Dig. iii. 1, 9.

[2] Zeitschr. f. R. G. l. c.

by the judicial power, but in part also by the adversary. The latter could not be compelled to contest an action with a procurator who was *infamis*, or with a procurator appointed by an *infamis*. He could put forward an *exceptio*, which the praetor was bound to grant. These *exceptiones*, partly on account of their infrequent use, partly on account of their dilatory nature and the fruitless controversies to which they gave rise, were finally abolished by Justinian[1]. As we know that the limitations in postulation were still upheld in the law sanctioned by Justinian, this removal can only mean that the motion for rejection of the *infames* was taken out of the hands of the adversary, and entrusted entirely to those of the presiding judge.

When we turn from these disabilities in the matter of procedure to consider whether any special disabilities as regards civil rights in general were imposed on the *infames*, we find ourselves again confronted by the difficulty that met us in the early history of the infamia. We shall find many civil disabilities imposed on individuals in consequence of some stain on their moral character or some defect in their social standing; but how far the persons so enumerated are coincident with the list made out by the praetor and developed by the imperial legislation is in most cases a matter of doubt. We shall have to consider the probability of their identity in each particular case. But it is clear that a civic disability,

[1] Inst. iv. 13, 11 'eas vero exceptiones, quae olim procuratoribus propter infamiam, *vel dantis vel ipsius procuratoris*, opponebantur: cum in judiciis *frequentari nullo modo perspeximus*, conquiescere sancimus; ne dum de his altercatur, ipsius negotii disceptatio proteletur.' The words 'frequentari ... perspeximus' have been variously interpreted; but the meaning given by Savigny (Syst. ii. p. 218, note h), 'since they are seldom resorted to (and therefore there is no practical need for their maintenance)' is probably correct.

recognised by the State, and resting on moral grounds, is an integral part of the history of Civil Honour, and as such these cases require discussion, whether we believe that, in treating them, we are dealing with the *infames* proper or not.

We find in the title of the Digest that deals with punishments the statement that the traditions of the Roman law had been to inflict a heavier penalty on *famosi* than on those whose reputation was untouched. This was a natural provision, whether stated in each given case by the laws or left to the discretion of the judge. It is simply the usually recognised principle that the past record of a condemned man must be considered before punishment can justly be meted out. If it refers to a definite class of *infames*, the provision is certainly not limited to these, but may be taken as also embracing those whom the Roman law summed up vaguely as *turpes*[1].

But in this connection we may notice a peculiar suspension of the ordinary guarantees of legal protection which did affect certain of the *infames*. The Roman law of adultery recognised the right of private vengeance for the maintenance of family honour; it tended, however, to limit the exercise of this right to the father of the household. But the right even of the husband to slay the adulterer was recognised, if the latter was a gladiator, a *bestiarius* or condemned in a *judicium publicum*, or one of those *qui corpore quaestum faciunt*[2]. The *Lex Julia de adulteriis* contained, therefore, a particular enumeration of persons, most of these belonging to the class called by

[1] Callistratus in Dig. xlviii. 19, 28, 16, 'majores nostri in omni supplicio severius . . . famosos quam integrae famae homines punierunt.'

[2] Collatio 4. 3, 1; 4. 12, 13; it was a question whether a *libertus* could slay his *patronus* if the latter was one of these *infames* (Dig. xlviii. 5, 39, 9).

the praetor *in turpitudine notabiles.* This is one of the instances in which we find a list, created with a special purpose, and narrower than that fixed by the praetor.

Another instance of the framing of such a list introduces us to a disability of considerable importance in the public law of Rome. The right to bring criminal accusations was universal, except where it was restricted by special limitations. Such were those created by status, sex, or age, which do not concern us here. But amongst them is one which is in touch with the infamia; prosecution is forbidden to a class of individuals *propter delictum proprium ut infames.* This class was a fixed one: and the enumeration of its members is given by Ulpian: it is simply a list of some of the worst cases of the praetor's Edict, including *bestiarii*, actors and *lenones*, those found guilty of *calumnia*, or those who have been pronounced guilty of *calumnia* and *praevaricatio* in a criminal court[1]: to which were added those who have accepted money for their functions as prosecutors. An important point to notice in connection with this list of Ulpian's is that the extract in which it occurs is taken from his work *de adulteriis.* It seems probable, therefore, that the list was first framed by the *Lex Julia de adulteriis*, with special application to that law, but was afterwards made universal. If this is the case it is another illustration of an interesting point in the history of the infamia: the influence namely of the Julian legislation (whether of Caesar or Augustus) in fixing the conception of infamia by employing a list, sometimes as wide as, sometimes

[1] Dig. xlviii. 2, 4. The distinction between 'calumnia notati' and 'qui praevaricationis calumniaeve causa quid fecisse judicio publico pronuntiatus erit' appears to be the same as that in the praetor's Edict (p. 122); to this Macer and Paulus add (ib. ll. 8 and 9) conduct resembling *calumnia.*

narrower than, that of the praetor, for the purpose of very various kinds of disqualification.

In the title of the Digest (*de accusationibus et inscriptionibus*), in which this list is found, the disability is stated as being universal. Sometimes, however, it is met with in a modified form. Thus, in a prosecution for adultery, in the case of a concurrent accusation of a woman by her husband and her father, the husband was preferred: but he lost this prior right of prosecution if the father could point out that the husband was *infamis* or likely to be guilty of collusion[1]. The estimate as to what constituted this infamia may have been based on the provisions of the law, but may conceivably have depended to some extent on the discretionary power of the judge. Occasionally, when the public interest was supposed to require it, we find this bar to prosecution removed altogether. An *infamis* could accuse in cases of treason, or in questions connected with the corn-supply[2].

But, if the list of *infames* was in this case a comparatively narrow one, the extension of the terminology applicable to this conception is the point specially noticeable in the next civic disability which we have to consider. Ulpian states a principle which seems to have been observed very early in Roman law: namely, that a person of disreputable character could not bring an action for *dolus malus* against a person of honourable character and position, 'since it produced infamia' (*cum sit famosa*). If by this is meant that no *actiones famosae* could be brought under such circumstances, it certainly was a serious disability, when we consider the extent of such actions. But the disability, whatever its extent may

[1] Dig. xlviii. 5 (*ad leg. Jul. de adult.*), 3.

[2] Treason (Dig. xlviii. 4, 7); 'propter publicam utilitatem ad annonam pertinentem' (Dig. xlviii. 2, 13).

have been, did not fall on the *infames* of the Edict alone; they are found, or rather their existence is implied, in a mixed company of *luxuriosi*, *prodigi*, and *viles*[1].

It was the same with respect to a curious provision as regards inheritance by which individuals of bad reputation, including the *infames*, were affected. The formal complaint that might be lodged against a will which violated family obligations without due cause (*querela inofficiosi testamenti*) was always at the disposal of ascendants and descendants. By two anomalous constitutions of Constantine it was open to consanguineous brothers and sisters, if the *scripti heredes* were tainted by infamia, low moral character or even low social standing[2]. We must agree with Savigny that this is not a consequence following on any fixed conception of infamia: but that the decision in each particular case as to whether the testament was *inofficiosum* must have been left to the decision of the judge[3].

We now turn to a civic disability which had a long history throughout the whole period of Roman law, and which, in one of its aspects, is the oldest disability of the kind known to us. It is the incapacity to be a witness: and this incapacity may be treated from three points of view: according as it was concerned with evidence in public courts of law, with evidence in formal acts of private law, and with evidence connected with testamentary dispositions. We shall see that there was the tendency, which we should expect, to make the limitations of evidence in these three cases coincide. Theoretically they were summed up in one general principle: it is

[1] Dig. iv. 3 (*de dolo malo*), 11 'et quibusdam personis non dabitur... vel luxurioso atque prodigo aut alias vili adversus hominem vitae emendatioris. Et ita Labeo.'

[2] Cod. iii. 28, 7 'si scripti heredes infamiae vel turpitudinis vel levis notae macula adsparguntur.' More fully in Cod. Theod. ii. 19, 1 and 3.

[3] Syst. ii. p. 223.

only from the point of view of their history that they can be distinguished.

The great general principle was that anyone could give evidence, both in criminal and in civil cases, according to the demands of circumstances, except where testimony was legally interdicted or excused [1]. Limitation of the capacity for evidence based on character was therefore fully recognised, and from the nature of the limitation, it is one that demands a place in the history of Civil Honour at Rome.

(i) The incapacity to give evidence in the public courts was, like most such incapacities, created by the special criminal laws of Rome, and was sometimes one of the provisions of procedure created under the law, sometimes one of the formal penalties which it inflicted. As an instance of the first kind of provision we may take the clause of the *Lex Julia de vi*, which mentioned a class of individuals, closely resembling those of the *Lex Julia Municipalis* and the praetor's Edict, who were forbidden to give evidence under this law. The prohibition affected anyone who had been condemned in a *judicium publicum*, and had not been reinstated, who was in bonds or custody of the State, who had hired himself out to fight with beasts, who had been convicted of taking money for the purpose of giving or refusing to give evidence, and the woman *quae palam quaestum faciet feceritve* [2]. There was no mention of the *infames* here, and there probably was none in any of the criminal laws of Rome. Where special

[1] Dig. xxii. 5 (*de testibus*), 1, 1 'adhiberi quoque testes possunt non solum in criminalibus causis, sed etiam in pecuniariis litibus, sicubi res postulat, ex his quibus non interdicitur testimonium nec ulla lege a dicendo testimonio excusantur.' Cf. Justinian (Nov. 90 praef.) 'licere autem omnibus etiam valde vilissimis testimonium perhibere et ante nos prohibuerunt legislatores: scilicet multas exceptiones facientes et plurimos excludentes etiam ipso testium nomine vel schemate.'

[2] Dig. xxii. 5, 3, 5.

laws did not make provisions such as those contained in the *Lex Julia*, the principle followed was the natural one of estimating evidence according to character and position[1]; and the application of this principle rested with the judge. He was limited, however, by the provisions of some of the other criminal laws: those, namely, which enacted that anyone condemned under them should lose the capacity for being a witness. The *Lex Julia repetundarum* enacted that anyone condemned under this law should lose the power *testimonium publice dicere*[2]; and the prohibition of testimony was also a consequence of condemnation under the *Lex Julia de adulteriis*[3]. The prohibition here probably applied in the first instance only to courts of law; but there was clearly the capacity for extension to testamentary evidence, which stood on quite a different footing[4]. There was equally clearly room for disagreement amongst the jurists on this point. Ulpian says that one condemned for *repetundae* can be a witness to a testament; Paulus says that he cannot[5]. Papinian rules that a man condemned for *adulterium* could not be a valid witness to a testament, and that, by the interpretation of the law, he was in every sense of the word *intestabilis*[6]. We see from these instances how very partial was the legal application of this disability for evidence based on character and on the fact of condemnation; nowhere is it stated that a

[1] Dig. xxii. 5, 2 and 3.

[2] Dig. xlviii. 11, 6; i. 9, 2; xxviii. 1, 20; xxii. 5, 15.

[3] Dig. xxviii. 1, 20, 6; xxii. 5, 14.

[4] E.g. women could be witnesses in *judicia publica*, but not to a testament.

[5] Ulpian in Dig. xxviii. 1, 20; Paulus in Dig. xxii. 5, 15.

[6] Papinian in Dig. xxii. 5, 14 'scio quidem tractatum esse, an ad testamentum faciendum adhiberi possit adulterii damnatus; et sane juste testimonii officio ei interdicetur. Existimo ergo neque jure civili testamentum valere, ad quod hujusmodi testis processit, neque jure praetorio, quod jus civile subsequitur, *ut neque hereditas adiri neque bonorum possessio dari possit.*'

definite list of *infames* was ever excluded, as a whole, from testimony.

(ii) In certain formal acts of private law a similar stress (and one naturally still more important in this connection) was laid on the fact that the witnesses must be of good character and position. A *depositum* in money claimed by an heir could only be opened in the presence of honourable persons (*honestae personae*)[1], the opening of a will in the absence of the witnesses ought only to be performed before men of the best reputation (*intervenientibus optimae opinionis viris*[2]), and a *pignus* or *hypotheca* drawn up as a written instrument between friends was not so valid as those *publice confecta*, unless the signatures of three or more witnesses of proved and sound opinion (*probatae atque integrae opinionis*) were appended to it[3]. The evidence of the *infames* proper would almost certainly not have been allowed on such occasions; but they are not the only persons referred to in the prohibitions.

(iii) When we turn to the third category—that of incapacity to be a witness to a testament—we find ourselves dealing with a conception which was one of the earliest in Roman law and one of the strangest in its later developments. This was the conception of a man being *intestabilis*. A provision of the Twelve Tables enacted that 'anyone who had consented to be a witness or *libripens* (to a testament transacted *per aes et libram*) and had subsequently refused to give evidence when required to do so, should be *improbus* and *intestabilis*[4].' The *primary* meaning of *intestabilis* here was clearly 'incapable of

[1] Dig. xvi. 3, 1, 36.

[2] Ib. xxix. 3, 7.

[3] Cod. viii. 17 (18), 11, 1.

[4] 'Qui se sierit testarier, libripensve fuerit, ni testimonium fariatur (*MS.* fatiatur, *Schoell*), improbus intestabilisque esto' (Gell. xv. 13). *Improbus* has been interpreted in this passage as *qui probare non potest*.

being a witness to a will'; the man who had broken faith on one occasion was not to be allowed another chance of exhibiting the same tendencies; but, when we consider the excessive importance of personal evidence in this formal act of testament-making, the sanction seems too light, and it is conceivable that even at this time *intestabilis* had the sense of 'incapable of having evidence given for him in turn'; that is, 'incapable of making a will.' That it acquired this meaning in later law is undoubted. Gaius indeed tells us[1] that 'when a man is created *intestabilis* by law, it means that his testimony is not to be received, and further, as some think, that he shall not have testimony given for him.' But later jurists have no doubt as to this second meaning being an integral part of the conception. Ulpian, in fact, and the Institutes of Justinian, treat it as primary[2]. It has already been noticed that, although the rules of evidence in courts of law and those for testaments had no necessary connection with each other, yet prohibitions originating with the former were extended to the latter. From an interpretation to the *Lex Julia de adulteriis* given by Papinian it even appears that *intestabilis* had reached the point of being understood as 'incapable of receiving under a testament[3].'

The *origin* of the conception is natural. It was limited capacity for giving evidence (or benefiting by evidence) based on bad moral character. It was rendered definite, however, by being made part of the formal sanction of

[1] Dig. xxviii. 1, 26.

[2] Ulpian in Dig. xxviii. 1, 18 'si quis ob carmen famosum damnetur, senatus consulto expressum est, ut intestabilis sit; ergo nec testamentum facere poterit nec ad testamentum adhiberi.' Inst. ii. 10, 6 'testes autem adhiberi possunt ii, cum quibus testamenti factio est... nec is, quem leges jubent improbum intestabilemque esse, possunt in numero testium adhiberi.'

[3] Dig. xxii. 5, 14, quoted p. 167, note 6.

positive law. Thus anyone condemned for a *carmen famosum* was *intestabilis* in the fullest sense of the word [1]. But, though we are here dealing with a derogation of Civil Honour, we are not dealing with the *infames* proper; there is not the least trace of their having been *intestabiles*.

As regards evidence in general, Justinian, by one of his *Novellae*, formulated the rule that witnesses must be either of good station or good character. From the extremely loose wording of the ordinance it is doubtful whether it intended to exclude the *infames* proper from evidence. It seems rather a general rule meant for the guidance of the judge and leaving much to his discretion [2].

We find a special disability, the ground of which approximates to infamia, imposed on certain freedmen under the *Lex Julia et Papia Poppaea*. A clause of that law enacted that a freedman, who had two or more children in his power, should be freed from their customary duties and engagements to their *patronus* and his children, except they had been actors or had hired out their services to fight with beasts [3].'

[1] Dig. xxviii, 1, 18, quoted on preceding page, note 2.

[2] Nov. 90, 1 'sancimus autem ... bonae opinionis esse oportere testes et aut carentes hujusmodi derogatione per dignitatis aut militiae aut divitiarum aut officii causam, aut si non tales consistunt, ex utroque tamen quia sunt fide digni testimonium perhibere (Greek, ὑφ' ἑτέρων γοῦν ὅτι καθεστᾶσιν ἀξιόπιστοι μαρτυρούμενοι), et non quosdam artifices ignobiles neque vilissimos nec nimis obscenos ad testimonium procedere, sed ut si qua de his dubitatio fuerit, possit facile demonstrari testium vita, quia inculpabilis atque moderata est.'

[3] Dig. xxxviii. 1, 37 (Paulus, *lib. ii. ad legem Juliam et Papiam*).

CHAPTER VII.

INFAMIA IN ITS APPLICATION TO WOMEN.

WOMEN were altogether exempt from the censorian infamia of the Republic, since it was concerned wholly with civic honours, in which women had no share. Neither could they be mentioned in the third Edict which contained the list of the praetorian *infames*, since this was a list of those who could postulate only in certain cases for others, and women were mentioned in the second Edict amongst those who could not postulate for others at all.

And yet there are several mentions in the texts of women being *infames*, e.g. in a passage of the Vatican Fragments taken from the Edict the woman who violates the rules of mourning is declared *infamis*. How they came to be such is a matter of much controversy: and more than one explanation of the fact has been adduced. According to Savigny's theory, which has been usually followed, it originated with the Julian marriage laws. By the *Lex Julia*, as it has been preserved to us by Ulpian[1],

[1] We must here accept Mommsen's transposition of the clause *corpore quaestum facientem* to its proper place; which has obviated so much difficulty. With this emendation the words of Ulpian (Fragm. tit. xiii.) run 'lege Julia prohibentur uxores ducere senatores quidem liberique eorum libertinas et quae ipsae quarumve pater materve artem ludicram fecerit; iidem et ceteri autem ingenui prohibentur uxorem ducere palam corpore quaestum facientem, et lenam, et a lenone lenave manumissam, et in adulterio deprehensam, et judicio publico damnatam, et quae artem ludicram fecerit: adicit Mauricianum senatus consultum a senatu damnatam.'

senators and their descendants are forbidden to marry freedwomen, actresses, and the daughters of actors or actresses. Other freeborn Romans (*ingenui*) were forbidden to marry prostitutes, *lenae*, a woman manumitted by a *leno* or *lena*, one caught in adultery or condemned in a *judicium publicum*, actresses; and, in accordance with a *senatus consultum*, a woman condemned by the Senate. According to Savigny's theory, it was first through this *Lex Julia* and its interpreters that the conception of infamia, hitherto applicable only to men, was extended to women as well; and this by a twofold process. The cases of illegal marriage mentioned in that law were for the future treated also as cases of true infamia, and conversely the cases of infamia mentioned in the Edict, so far as they could be thought of in relation to women (as they could be, for instance, in the violation of the rules of mourning) were taken up under the prohibitions of marriage in the *Lex Julia*. To the question, 'Why should these cases have been introduced into the praetorian Edict about the *infames*, where they were entirely out of place?' Savigny's answer is that it was done because the praetorian Edict about the *infames* was the only place where a list of the *infames* clothed with a legal aspect was found. The condition which the Edict assumed by these additions is presented by the text of the Vatican fragments; and the reason why the cases of infamia applicable to women, which are found here, do not appear in the Edict as embodied in the Digest, is that Justinian abrogated the *Lex Julia*; hence infamia as applied to women naturally disappeared.

The one fatal objection to this brilliant theory is that there could have been no motive or excuse whatever for introducing a list of infamous women into the Edict connected with the title *de postulando*, which referred only to procedure, and to a procedure in this case applicable only to men. The origin of infamia as attaching to women must certainly be praetorian, since it could have had no place in public law. The reason of this infamia can only be satisfactorily explained if it can be proved that there was a place in the praetor's Edict where a list of infamous women would naturally have come in. Such a place has been satisfactorily pointed out by Karlowa [1]. He connects the infamia of women with the second of the restrictions in postulation which have already been treated; that is, with the prohibition to give a *cognitor* or *procurator*. As women have the capacity to give cognitors, it is in that one of the two *edicta cognitoria* of which the Vatican Fragments speak, which treated of those who could not give *cognitores*, that a list of *mulieres famosae* may have come. Since such a list must have been far older than the Julian law, the cases mentioned in this law may have been in part suggested by the praetor's category—those prohibitions, e.g. which are based on character and standing rather than on birth; and this may account for the fact that *famosae* is used of the women debarred from marriage on certain grounds [2], and that, as Savigny has remarked [3], the phraseology of the infamia and especially the word *notare*, is applied to the women mentioned in the Julian marriage law. It was indeed inevitable that many of the cases should have been mentioned both in the law and in the Edict; prostitutes [4], *lenae*, the woman condemned in a

[1] Zeitschr. f. R. G. ix. p. 224 sq.

[2] Ulpian, Frag. tit. xvi. 2 'aliquando nihil inter se capiunt; id est, si contra legem Juliam Papiamque Poppaeam contraxerint matrimonium, verbi gratia si famosam ingenuus uxorem duxerit, aut libertinam senator.'

[3] Syst. ii. p. 519.

[4] Dig. iii. 2, 24 'Imperator Severus rescripsit non offuisse mulieris famae quaestum ejus in servitute factum' (from Ulpian's commentary to the Edict).

judicium publicum, the woman caught in adultery, must have appeared in both. Two other cases of infamia in its application to women, which appeared in the *edictum cognitorium*, have been preserved. The first is a case of *calumnia* in civil law: and refers to the woman who has been put into possession of the goods of her late husband by a false representation that she is *enceinte*[1]; she incurred infamia as deceiving the praetor, but only when she was *suae potestatis*. If she was under power, and therefore represented by her father, he incurred the *nota*. The second refers to the woman who violates the rules of mourning. The *edictum cognitorium*, as represented by the Vatican Fragments, makes the woman *infamis* (i) who has not fulfilled the rules of mourning for her husband, father, or children; (ii) who, being a widow, and not under her father's power, has married again within the prescribed period of mourning[2]. The first of these regulations, connected as it was with the old pagan rites of mourning, disappeared at least as early as the Christian Empire; the second continued in force, in consequence of its importance in preventing doubtfulness of paternity.

The effects of the praetorian infamia attaching to women, besides its immediate object, which was to limit the power of putting forward legal representatives in court, may have been similar to the civil-law consequences which affected men who were *infames*, so far as these could be thought of in relation to women. Such would have been the suspicion of their evidence in court, the *querela inofficiosi testamenti*, the aggravation of punishment. We have seen that many of the women, with whom marriage was forbidden by the

[1] Dig. iii. 2, 15 (Ulpian) 'notatur quae per calumniam ventris nomine in possessionem missa est, dum se adseverat praegnatem (16, Paulus) cum non praegnas esset vel ex alio concepisset.'

[2] Fragm. Vat. § 320.

Lex Julia et Papia Poppaea, were in the strict sense *famosae*, as being also included in the praetor's Edict. But the consequences of this marriage law do not belong to the history of Civil Honour, because, so far as we know, the incapacities imposed by this law were reciprocal, and attached as well to the husband who was not *infamis* as to the wife who was *famosa*. There is one regulation, however, that grew out of the Julian laws, which did apply to certain members of the class of infamous women. It was due to a curious mode adopted by certain women for the purpose of avoiding the penalties of the Julian criminal legislation. Suetonius tells us that in the reign of Tiberius women of bad character, in order to avoid the penalties of the laws, threw off the rights and the dignity of matrons by openly professing the trade of *lenae*[1]. The immediate object of this ruse was to avoid the penalties for adultery: and the abuse had to be met by a decree of the Senate[2]. But it also had, as Savigny has pointed out, another consequence: and that was, that such women, whatever their original position, could no longer be affected by the penalties imposed on voluntary celibacy, since they were now *lenae*, and as such were, by the Julian law, forbidden marriage even with freeborn citizens (*ingenui*)[3]. Their celibacy was now, legally speaking, involuntary. To meet this consequence they were, in the reign of Domitian, placed on a level with voluntary celibates, and debarred from receiving inheritances and legacies[4].

[1] Suet. Tib. 35 'feminae famosae, ut, ad evitandas legum poenas, jure ac dignitate matronali exsolverentur, lenocinium profiteri coeperant.'

[2] Papinian in Dig. xlviii. 5, 11 (10), 2 'mulier, quae evitandae poenae adulterii gratia lenocinium fecerit aut operas suas in scaenam locarit, adulterii accusari damnarique ex senatus consulto potest.'

[3] Syst. ii. p. 557.

[4] Suet. Dom. 8 'probrosis feminis lecticae usum ademit, jusque capiendi legata haereditatesque.'

But besides this exceptional regulation, which has, strictly speaking, no connection with the infamia, we do meet with special disabilities in private law imposed on one class of infamous women, in addition to the general disabilities which they might share with men. Two constitutions of Gratian, Valentinian, and Theodosius, given in the years 380 and 381 A.D., limit the rights of women, who have violated the rules of the 'year of mourning' to share in intestate inheritances, prohibit their acceptance of other bequests, and forbid them to retain the property settled on, or bequeathed to, them by their former husbands[1]. This is one of those peculiar disabilities, commoner in the earlier history of the infamia, rarer in the later, by which a special penalty was created to suit a special offence, even after universal disqualifications had been made a consequence of the general category of infamous actions, in which that offence was classed.

[1] Cod. v. 9, 1 & 2; the first constitution also limits the amount of dowry which such a woman might bring, or of property which she might bequeath, to her second husband.

CHAPTER VIII.

MODES OF EXTINGUISHING INFAMIA.

OF the theory of the censorian infamia, so far as its permanence was concerned, two possible views may be taken. One is that it was in theory perpetual, while subject to reversal by each succeeding censor: but that the power of the censor to rescind his predecessor's acts was treated as legally the exception and not the rule. The other view is that the disqualifications pronounced by the censor were considered as valid only for the lustral period of five years which intervened between his ordinances and the appointment of his successor[1]: that the reinstatement of the persons so disqualified was regarded as the rule, and the perpetuity of the infamia as the exception. Whichever of these two views we accept (and there is no direct literary evidence to decide our preference for either), there is little doubt that the actual procedure of the censorship, so far as the mass of cases that came before it was concerned, corresponded rather to the latter than to the former. There must have been comparatively few offences that came before the censorship which deserved a punishment of more than five years' duration. The exceptional cases, in which perpetuity of disqualification was enjoined by succeeding colleges of censors, tended,

[1] This second view is the one taken by Mommsen, Staatsrecht, ii. p. 387.

as we saw, to develope into the conception of the later definite and permanent infamia.

The praetorian infamia in its origin may possibly have been subject to variations similar to those of the censorian. The rules of procedure laid down by the praetor were theoretically valid only during his year of office, and might be modified by his successor. It was not inevitable that every praetor should take precisely the same view of the dignity of his court, or of the modes in which this dignity might be infringed. But, when we remember certain facts connected with the praetorian infamia, that the Edict in which it found a place had even a more tralaticiary character than the Edict of any other magistrate in Rome, that the class of *infames* which the praetors dealt with was less wide and more specific than that of the censors, and remember also the remarkable correspondence between the praetor's list and that of the *Lex Julia Municipalis* and other laws, there is a strong presumption that it became defined at a comparatively early period, and that fully two centuries before the redaction of the Julian Edict the praetor's list of the *infames* was fully formulated.

Starting from the assumption that the praetor adhered to a definite list of *infames* in the *edictum perpetuum*, the question presents itself 'Was there any mode of extinguishing infamia in any given instance?' Was it possible, for instance, to restore a man who had been condemned in a *judicium publicum*, or for *furtum*, to his old position of an *integra persona*? and was this restoration possible in the still more difficult case of a man who had incurred immediate infamy in any of the modes mentioned in the Edict? The question became still more important when the stage was reached at which the praetorian infamia was taken up by the State and became the ground of disqualification for office. It is from this double point of view, from the point of view both of the praetor's court and of the other consequences which came to attach to the praetorian infamia, that the classical jurists and the imperial constitutions give us answers to these questions.

The possibility of a remission of infamia was contemplated in the praetor's Edict. After speaking of the limitation in postulation which he enjoined, the praetor in his Edict concluded with the words 'so far as any of the above mentioned persons have not been restored to their original position[1].' The 'above mentioned persons,' to whom the praetor referred, might consist of either of the two classes, whom he had limited in postulation on moral or judicial grounds: that is, the *in turpitudine notabiles* of the second Edict and the *infames* of the third: but Ulpian tells us that *restitutio in integrum* could hardly be thought of, or was at least extremely difficult, in connection with the first of these two classes[2]: so that the praetor was thinking mainly of his list of *infames* proper when he spoke of a possible restitution.

It is also clear, from the use of the words *restitutio in integrum*, that the praetor is speaking mainly of one kind of infamia: that is, of the mediate infamia consequent on a judicial sentence, and which might be removed by the quashing of the sentence. The expression has no strict application to immediate infamy: although, as we shall see, there was in the later Empire a mode of abolishing even this: and, when it was removed, there can be no doubt that at that period the limitations in postulation were removed also.

[1] 'Deinde adicit praetor: "Qui ex his omnibus, qui supra scripti sunt, in integrum restitutus non erit"' (Ulpian in Dig. iii. 1, 1, 9).

[2] Ulpian in Dig. ib. 'ceterum si ex superioribus (fuerit), difficile in integrum restitutio impetrabitur.'

There can be no doubt that, when the praetor in the Republic used the words (as there is every reason to believe he did) 'Qui ex his omnibus . . . restitutus non erit,' he was thinking mainly of his own power of *in integrum restitutio.* But to the classical jurists commenting on the Julian Edict it was natural to raise the question what kind of *restitutio* was here meant. Pomponius answered the question by saying that the restitution meant was that granted by an indulgence of the Senate and *princeps*, as High Courts of Justice: it was an inevitable answer, because the complete rescinding of a sentence rested only with these high courts, and came, as time went on, to be vested more and more in the hands of the Emperor. This is not the place to trace the growth of the prerogative of the Emperor in his power of reversing or altering a sentence: but, how completely it was taken out of the hands of judges, whether at Rome or in the provinces, and how entirely transferred to those of the Emperor, we learn from many passages of the Digest[1]. It is natural therefore that, as regards the power of the praetor in this respect, the opinion of the jurists was that his restitution was only valid in the case of the *infames*, if it followed the ordinary rules which directed the praetorian restitution in other respects: in other words, if the praetor, following his ordinary rules, procured by *in integrum restitutio* the acquittal of one who had been

[1] Dig. xlii. 1, 45, 1, in increasing or diminishing a penalty 'sine principali auctoritate nihil est statuendum'; cf. Consultatio, 7, 2. Dig. xlviii. 18, 1, 27; the *praeses provinciae* has not the power *restituere*. Cf. xlviii. 19, 9, 11; Dig. l. c. 27 'nonnulla exstant principalia rescripta, quibus vel poena eorum minuta est vel in integrum restitutio concessa.' Dig. xlvii. 2, 64 (63) 'non poterit praeses provinciae efficere, ut furti damnatum non sequatur infamia' (i. e. probably in the case of a *pecuniaria damnatio* as mentioned in Dig. xlviii. 19, 10, 2); the passage no doubt means to imply that the *princeps* can do so.

condemned in a *famosum judicium*, such a man was not *infamis*, according to the opinion of Pomponius[1]

The legal principle underlying this extinction of mediate infamia is that *restitutio in integrum* quashes a sentence: for infamia does not depend either on a crime or on the infliction of a punishment, but only on a sentence. This accounts for the fact that remission of a penalty granted by the Emperor through a *generalis indulgentia* or *generalis abolitio* does not have the effect of averting the infamy which followed the sentence inflicting that punishment[2]. But such an indulgence might no doubt contain a clause specially remitting the infamia.

The final form which the remission of infamia assumed was, therefore, as follows. Mediate infamia could be extinguished by a *restitutio in integrum* granted by the Emperor, and probably also by an *abolitio infamiae* appended as a special grace to an indulgence remitting a penalty. Immediate infamia, on the other hand, which did not depend on a sentence, could only be removed by a special benefit (*beneficium*) of the Emperor. This was known as *abolitio infamiae*, and is often referred to in the legal texts[3]. It might sometimes be conditioned. For instance, if a woman had concluded an over-hasty marriage, and had male or female children by her first husband, the infamia that followed her violation of the rules of mourning could only be remitted if she made over half the property she possessed at the time of her second marriage to the children of the first[4].

[1] Dig. iii. 1, 1, 10.

[2] Cod. ix. 43 (*de generali abolitione*), 3 (Valentinian, Valens, and Gratian, 371 A.D.) 'Indulgentia, patres conscripti, quos liberat notat nec infamiam criminis tollit, sed poenae gratiam facit.' Cf. Cod. ix. 51, 7.

[3] Cod. x. 32 (31), 33, 'perpetua infamia inustus nec speciali quidem rescripto notam eluere mereatur'; Cod. ix. 8, 5. In Cod. vi. 56, 4 it is spoken of as *infamiae abolitio*, and is conferred by an *imperiale beneficium*.

[4] Cod. vi. 56, 4, 1.

We have seen that the judge has no power to avert the infamia following on a sentence which he has pronounced. This rule is absolute. But it was felt to be inexpedient and unwise to take wholly from the judge, who alone could know all the merits of a case, the power of remitting this terrible disqualification. Hence the curious principle was developed that the judge could remit the infamia which followed the ordinary sentence imposed in a given case, by pronouncing a heavier penalty than that recognised by custom or by law[1]. The principle was recognised both in civil actions (at least where these were concerned with delicts) and in criminal cases. The procedure was spoken of as a *transactio*, and was thus regarded as an agreement between the judge and the offender, the latter choosing between the lighter sentence with infamia and the heavier sentence without it. Some modern writers have stood aghast at this very anomalous procedure: and have declared it to be in direct conflict with the principle of Roman law that the judge has no discretionary power in imposing a sentence, to be in antagonism with the principle clearly stated by Papinian that 'the judge decides the fact and not the law[2].'

[1] Ulpian in Dig. iii. 2, 13, 7 'poena gravior ultra legem imposita existimationem conservat.'

[2] Dig. l. 1, 15 'cum facti quidem quaestio sit in potestate judicantium, juris autem auctoritas non sit,' quoted also by Marcian in Dig. xlviii. 16, 1, 4. The statement of Macer in Dig. xlvii. 10, 4, which has been quoted as expressing the same principle, is not to the point; it refers to the *error* of a judge by which infamia has been improperly averted. Equally little can be concluded from Macer's words in Dig. xlvii. 2, 64 (63) 'non poterit praeses provinciae efficere, ut furti damnatum non sequatur infamia.' We do not know the context here; it may refer to a *pecuniaria damnatio*, such as that mentioned in Dig. xlviii. 19, 10, 2, which is also from the second book of Macer *de publicis judiciis*. Now an increase in a money-penalty never remitted infamia; see on this Ulpian in Dig. iii. 2, 13, 7 (if in the case of *furtum* a heavier money-penalty has been exacted, e.g. four times for double the amount, 'hanc rem existimationem ei non conservasse, quamvis, *si in poena non pecuniaria eum onerasset, transactum cum eo videtur*').

But the jurists Ulpian, Macer, and Papinian himself state the principle with perfect clearness. It is represented as being applicable to all classes alike[1]; the remission of infamia thus effected may restore a decurion to his order[2] or a soldier to the ranks[3], when the sentence had been completed: although the offence for which they had been condemned would, if the ordinary penalty had been imposed, have involved perpetual disqualification for these functions. One illustration given us is the *actio famosa* of theft; if a corporal punishment had been imposed in place of the usual pecuniary compensation, the man so condemned was not *infamis*[4]. On the other hand, the principle is equally clearly stated, that a diminution of the penalty fixed by law cannot be employed as a means of averting infamia. From the words of Papinian alone[5] we can draw the conclusion, to which in any case we should be forced, that while the increase of the penalty, for the purpose of averting infamia, was not regarded as an instance of the judge's failing to carry out the sentence fixed by law, the diminution of the penalty was regarded in this light[6]. The meaning of the anomaly (if it be one)

[1] Macer in Dig. xlviii. 19, 10, 2 'in personis tam plebeiorum quam decurionum illud constitutum est, ut qui majori poena adficitur, quam legibus statuta est, infamis non fiat.'

[2] Papinian in Dig. l. 1, 15 and 2, 5.

[3] Dig. xlix. 16, 4, 4.

[4] Dig. xlviii. 19, 10, 2.

[5] The above quoted dictum of Papinian (Dig. l. 1, 15) comes immediately after the words 'minoribus vero, quam leges permittunt subjectos nihilo minus inter infames haberi,' and clearly only refers to the case of the lesser penalty.

[6] An instance of the application of this mode of averting infamia is known to us from a very obscure constitution of Severus and Antoninus, A.D. 198 (Cod. ii. 11 (12), 4) 'si Posidonium in tempus anni relegatum secundum sententiam non excessisse proconsulis probaveris, quinque annis exilio temporario damnandum inter infames haberi non oportet, quando sententiae severitas cum ceteris damnis transigere videatur.' The correction which has been suggested, 'relegandum' for 'relegatum,' and

is not very far to seek. The incidence of the infamia was largely due to historical causes, and in certain cases may have seemed hardly equivalent to the offence which incurred it: while the suitability of its application must have depended largely on the circumstances of the person and on the facts of the case. It was convenient, therefore, to leave some discretionary power to the judge: but this could not be given in the form of a power to remit infamia, which had come to be a prerogative of the Emperor. The exceptional and perhaps not very perfect system of imposing an equivalent sentence was, therefore, substituted in its stead.

This attempt to restrict the incidence of the permanent disqualification of infamia prepares us for the revival of the theory of temporary disqualification, which reappears again in the second century of the Empire. The earliest ordinances on the subject appear to be those of Hadrian, and the practice was continued by his successors. This temporary disqualification is known to us in connection with the disabilities imposed on *advocati* and on the senators of municipal towns (*decuriones*). It is treated in relation to both of the aspects of the developed conception of infamia, the praetorian rules of postulation and disqualification from office. Thus, by a rescript of Antoninus Pius, the advocate who had been forbidden the exercise of his functions for a period of five years, recovered, after this interval had elapsed, the unrestricted right of postulation[1]; by a rescript of Hadrian the same right was restored to a man who had returned from exile[2]: but in this latter case we must suppose that the exile had followed as a consequence of an extraordinary sentence,

'damnatum' for 'damnandum,' seems to be the only reading which can restore meaning to this passage.

[1] Papinian in Dig. iii. 1, 8.

[2] Ib.

which did not of itself involve infamia[1]. There is nothing exceptional in the assertion of this principle. It only shows, what has already been abundantly demonstrated from other sources, that the conception of infamia was becoming a fixed and definite one, and it was necessary to distinguish it from other kinds of merely temporary disqualification. This distinction is specially marked in the case of exclusion from the *ordo decurionum*. Temporary removal from the order was recognised as a consequence of many kinds of conviction; but it made the greatest difference whether this conviction in itself involved the definite infamia or not. Removal in consequence of a reason which in itself involved infamia, was regarded as necessarily permanent in its character; unless the infamia had been averted by the form of *transactio* already discussed[2]: on the other hand, if the ground of the removal was not of this character, we find indeed that the temporary exclusion did produce the effects of a temporary infamia, in the sense that the person so affected could not obtain other offices (*honores*) while the exclusion lasted[3]; but that, when this period of enforced retirement had elapsed, he could both re-enter his order and fill other offices of state[4].

[1] This follows as a consequence from the principle quoted from Papinian in the next note.

[2] Papinian in Dig. l. 2, 5 'ad tempus ordine motos ex crimine, quod ignominiam importat, in perpetuum moveri placuit. Ad tempus autem exulare jussos ex crimine leviore velut transacto negotio non esse inter infames habendos.'

[3] Cod. x. 61 (59), 2 (Gordian) 'ad tempus exsulare decurio jussus et impleto tempore regressus pristinam quidem dignitatem recipit, ad novos vero honores non admittitur, nisi tanto tempore his abstinuerit quanto per fugam afuit.' Cf. Papinian in Dig. l. 1, 15.

[4] Cod. ib. 1 (*pars edicti imperatoris Antonini*) 'quibus posthac ordine suo vel advocationibus ad tempus interdicetur, post impletum temporis spatium non prorogabitur infamia.' Cf. Dig. l. 2, 3.

CHAPTER IX.

MODIFIED FORMS OF DISQUALIFICATION BASED ON CHARACTER AND STANDING.

A DESCRIPTION of the developed conception of infamia, its causes and its consequences, by no means exhausts the subject with which the history of Civil Honour has to deal in the later stages of Roman public and private law. This has already been made apparent in the fact that many of the disabilities which we have discussed as falling on the *infames*, were also imposed on many who were not strictly included in this category, but were assimilated to it on moral grounds. Two forms of disqualification yet remain to be treated: the first are those which were based on general defects of moral character, and which affected a vaguely defined class of individuals, in which the *infames* were not necessarily included; the second consist of those which were based, not on character, but on occupation and social standing.

§ 1. *Disqualifications based on character.*

It is hardly necessary to point out how very familiar the idea was to Roman law of disqualifications based on the estimate formed of a man's character by a magistrate in authority. It was the essence of the censorship; but it affected a department of state even more important than that which the censors controlled—the admission to *honores*. The rescript of Constantine by which the *infames* were forbidden admission to office includes in the list of the prohibited those *quos scelus aut vitae turpitudo inquinat*[1]. This was no innovation, but merely the renewal of a practice familiar to the Republic. It is clear that the application of such a principle, which involved a moral estimate not defined by law, must have rested wholly on the discretionary power of the magistrate who controlled the admission to *honores*, and was limited only by the respect for precedent and the moral necessity which the magistrate was under of consulting his *consilium* in all cases of special difficulty[2]. Cicero tells us that the *censoria notatio* was no legal bar to a man's standing for a magistracy; yet undoubtedly the presiding consul would feel himself justified in refusing to receive the name of a candidate who was labouring under the *nota*. The Republican magistrate claims the right not only of refusing to receive the candidate's name[3], but of refusing to return him as elected[4], even if he receives a majority of votes at the *comitia*. This mode in which the rejection was exercised remained the same throughout the whole of Roman history; that is, it must have rested wholly with the officials in authority whether, in each particular case, they

[1] Cod. xii. 1, 2. The legal texts distinguish between the infamia of opinion and that of the Edict; Dig. xxxvii. 15, 2: Cod. ix. 9, 24 (25).

[2] Ascon. in or. in tog. cand. p. 115. The candidate was accused on a criminal charge. The procedure of the consul shows that there could have been no law on the subject; although, that the *reus delatus* could not seek *honores* was a fixed principle of later municipal law (Dig. l. 4, 7; cf. l. 1, 17, 2 and ib. 21, 5).

[3] Vell. ii. 92 '(C. Sentius Saturninus) consul (19 B.C.) . . . quaesturam petentes, quos indignos judicavit, profiteri vetuit.'

[4] Val. Max. iii. 8, 3 'quum an Palicanum suffragio populi consulem creatum renuntiaturus esset interrogaretur (Piso consul 67 B.C.) "non renuntiabo," inquit.' We may contrast with this discretionary power of the presiding magistrate the prohibition of the *renuntiatio* of legally disqualified candidates in the *Lex Julia Municipalis*, l. 132.

thought there were sufficient grounds to justify it. There is reason to believe that at Rome itself, the magistrate, in the Republic and early Principate, exercised a freer right of rejection than the officials who admitted to honours in the municipal towns: since offices were here regarded rather more in the light of burdens than of honours, and the tendency might have been to limit the moral disqualifications to those contained in laws, such as the *Lex Julia Municipalis.* In the later Empire it becomes a duty imposed alike on all officials who have control over the admission to *honores.*

Another disqualification which affected those distinguished for *turpitudo*, which is the usual expression for moral depravity employed in our texts, was exclusion from the position of a *judex.* We have not here to deal with specific disqualifications from the bench, such as those discussed above in connection with the *infames*[1], but with disqualifications based on a more general estimate of character. The praetor in the Republic could, as has been already remarked, exercise a very free choice in the selection of his panels, and might reject those whom he thought unworthy of the post. In the Principate such a supervision was exercised by the Emperor as well as by the praetor[2]. In the later Empire there is but little question of the choice of *judices* by a special magistrate. We are, therefore, not surprised to find, at a time when the word had almost changed its meaning, a specific regulation emanating from the Emperors Gratian, Valentinian, and Theodosius in 380 A.D., enacting that those judges who had proved themselves unworthy of their position should be stripped of their dignity[3]. The question as to the limitation of the right to give evidence in courts of law has

[1] P. 156, cf. Dig. i. 9, 2.

[2] Bethmann-Hollweg, Civilprozess, § 65.

[3] Cod. xii. 1, 12 'judices, qui se furtis et sceleribus fuerint maculasse convicti . . . honore exuti inter pessimos quosque et plebeios habeantur.'

already been sufficiently discussed in connection with the *infames*. It was seen that in all cases the admissibility of evidence, so far as not provided for by positive laws, depended wholly on the estimate of the judge[1].

Hitherto we have been considering the conception of *turpitudo* from the point of view of public law. But it played quite as large, if not a larger, part in the private law of Rome. There was ample room for the creation of such a conception in the free working of the praetor's court; it was inevitable that, in framing rules which were meant to facilitate the exercise of rights, he should make the application of them depend in certain instances upon character. This conception, which has been sometimes called *infamia facti* by modern jurists to distinguish it from the more definite and codified infamia (*infamia juris*), was taken up and applied by the classical jurists and played its part in the legislation of the later Empire. The principle of its application was precisely the same in private as in public law. The existence of *turpitudo* in each particular case was based on the estimate of character formed by the judge. Thus to the singular question that has been raised, whether *turpitudo*, like infamia, was permanent, no simple answer can be returned. It rested entirely with the judge to decide whether a bad record in the past had permanently affected a man's character, or whether a reform had taken place: although this estimate of the judge could hardly be employed in the particular cases in which members of this category corresponded to the *in turpitudine notabiles* of the Edict. In other cases, in which this conception assumed a more definite form through being followed by fixed legal disabilities, *turpitudo* was sometimes regarded as ineradicable; for the purposes of the *Lex Julia et Papia Poppaea*

[1] Pp. 167 and 170.

a prostitute's character could not be re-established by her subsequently resorting to a more honest mode of life[1].

The legal texts furnish abundant illustrations of the application of this conception of *turpitudo*, which is at once so real and so vague, by praetors, jurists, and emperors. We are not surprised to find it intimately connected with the law of guardianship (*tutela*), which played so large a part in the history of the infamia proper. Although in the case of a testamentary *tutela* guardians were not compelled to give security for the safety of the property they administered; yet the praetor under these conditions preferred to appoint as *tutores* those who were willing to offer security. But the advantages of this guarantee might be outweighed by blemishes of character: and the rule was not maintained in the case of a man of bad antecedents, who might be able to offer sureties, but whom it would be exceedingly dangerous to appoint as sole administrator[2]. The judge has here to decide between moral and material advantages as a guarantee for just dealing. In another and more remarkable regulation connected with the administration of goods, the rights of the father are themselves suspended on grounds of character. In an interpretation given by Constantine, in 321 A.D.[3] we find the principle restated, that a father who had been deported and restored recovered the *patria potestas* and the administration of the goods of his son; but the property was not to be entrusted to his absolute direction if, from prodigal or dissolute habits, he was considered likely to squander it. Another illustration of similar regulations made for the protection of children was connected with the

[1] Ulpian, *libro primo ad legem Juliam et Papiam* in Dig. xxiii. 2, 43, 4 'non solum autem ea quae facit, verum ea quoque quae fecit, etsi facere desiit, lege notatur; neque enim aboletur turpitudo, quae postea intermissa est.'

[2] Ulpian in Dig. xxvi. 2, 17, 1.

[3] Cod. ix. 51, 13, 2.

exhibitory interdicts of the praetor. In the case in which a writ *de liberis exhibendis* had been issued and obeyed, the child, if it was *impubes*, was entrusted to the custody of the professing father until the case was heard, but only on the condition that he was a man of good character[1]. To this category belong the many provisions for the interdiction of spendthrifts, which seem to have played a part in the very earliest Roman law, and are indeed based on the ancient theory that property belongs not so much to the head of the family as to the family itself[2]. Another special prohibition of a legal right, with reference to property which we meet with in our texts, is the refusal of an action for the recovery of a dowry to a father if his character leads to the presupposition that he would squander it when recovered[3].

We find the conception in a more extended form—sometimes approximating to the idea of lowness in social standing—influencing other points of procedure. An *actio injuriarum* pursued in the interest of a son under power was granted usually to the father, 'but sometimes it is thought that, even if the father remit the action, it should be given to the son, as for instance, if the father be a low and abject being, the son honourable; for such a parent should not be allowed to measure an insult done to his son by the standard of his own low character[4].' Such a regulation as this applies perhaps to low social standing—the legal disabilities consequent on which we shall have to consider in the next section—as well as to character. The same is true of the conditions under which the *querela inofficiosi testamenti* might be lodged by consanguineous brothers and sisters[5]—conditions which have already been discussed in connection with the *infames*. We also find

[1] Ulpian in Dig. xliii. 30, 3, 4. [2] Muirhead, Roman Law, p. 32.
[3] Ulpian in Dig. xxiv. 3, 22, 6. [4] Ulpian in Dig. xlvii, 10, 17, 13.
[5] Cod. iii. 28, 27, see p. 165.

turpitudo made a valid ground for excluding a daughter from an inheritance[1].

In betrothal and marriage the conception played an important part, as it well deserved to do. Betrothal was based on consent; but the consent of the father was taken as the consent of the daughter. Her only power of dissent was based on her showing that the husband proposed by her father was a low and disreputable person[2]. By one of the Novellae of Justinian badness of character was recognised as a valid motive of divorce for a woman against her husband[3].

We have already seen that the rigorously scientific character of Roman law in its codified form, which left so little to the discretion of the judge, was modified in connection with the infamia, in the particular cases in which an exemption from this penalty seemed desirable[4]. The modification which has just been discussed, the theory that disabilities in private law should be based on an individual estimate of character, was a healthier one still. It did not proceed on the paternal theory of protecting the individual against himself, but aimed only at the protection of the weak, where wrong might ensue from a too rigorous application of the principles of law. Codification was necessary to the infamia at a time when political disabilities were imposed by a central despotism over a world-wide Empire. Where private interests were at stake it would have been injurious, and the vagueness of the Roman conception of *turpitudo* is its real strength; the vaguest was the fittest expression which this form of equity could assume.

[1] Cod. iii. 28, 19 (Diocletian and Maximian, A. D. 293).

[2] Ulpian in Dig. xxiii. 1, 12: another motive, difference of religious belief, was added in the Christian Empire (Cod. v. 1, 5, 3).

[3] Nov. 22, 15.

[4] P. 183.

§ 2. *Disqualifications based on standing.*

We have now to consider certain disqualifications in public and private law which the Roman State considered a necessary accompaniment of a low degree of social standing. Such disqualifications are certainly based on a supposed absence of *existimatio* or *dignitas*, although the absence here is rather the result of social prejudice than of moral censure. There is always, however, a quasi-moral significance in the Roman conception of *vilitas*, as in the Greek conception of *βαναυσία*. Husbandry, according to Roman notions the noblest mode of winning a livelihood[1], did not disqualify from office, on however small a scale it might be practised. But a profession for which pay was given was in the Republic a bar to all honours[2], and all trading on a small scale was under a social ban, although we cannot say that it was followed by the same political consequences. The notion underlying this Republican prejudice must have been the same as that which Aristotle puts into philosophical language when he says that the free man is he who lives for himself and not for others: the taking of pay was supposed to destroy that independence of character which became the citizen of a free state. Roscius almost ceased to be an actor in the eyes of the Roman world, because he would not sell his gifts, just as Polygnotus escaped the charge of *βαναυσία* in the Greek world, because he painted for the pure love of his art. And the pettier the gain, the pettier were the means which it was thought would be taken to secure it; 'lying,' says Cicero, 'is the essence of retail trade.' Some particular trades were looked on with special disfavour; the purveyors of the amenities of life (*ministri voluptatum*)

[1] Cic. de Off. i. 42, 150.

[2] See p. 12.

were considered a degraded class; the Roman connected unpleasant associations with the collectors of port dues and with money-lenders, and took a gloomy view of auctioneers and undertakers [1].

We have already seen that the exercise of a trade or profession debarred from office during the Republic: and this exclusion from office necessarily kept those who followed this mode of life out of the Senate at Rome [2]. This must have been the rule throughout the Principate, although the energetic rescripts of the later Emperors show that it must have been much neglected during the later portion of this period. By a constitution, similar to that by which Constantine had debarred the *infames* and all *quos vitae turpitudo inquinat* from office, Constantius excluded from dignities every one engaged in a small trade, and the members of other professions which he specified [3]. This may be taken as a principle which was theoretically recognised throughout the whole of Roman history, but only in application to the offices of the central government. It never applied to municipal offices, after the qualifications to these were controlled by Rome. Caesar's municipal law only excluded individuals exercising certain specified professions from the *honores* and

[1] Cicero (l. c.) after enumerating the 'quaestus, qui in odia hominum incurrunt,' accounts as *sordidi* those 'qui mercantur a mercatoribus, quod statim vendant. Nihil enim proficiant, nisi admodum mentiantur.' He then mentions the 'artes . . . quae ministrae sunt voluptatum.' To all these he opposes (1) the arts requiring *prudentia* or which are of great utility, such as medicine, architecture, philosophy, (2) merchandise on a large scale, and (3) the best of all modes of living, agriculture.

[2] A *Lex Claudia*—a *plebiscitum* of 218 B.C.—sought to prohibit senators from engaging in maritime trade; but the law was *antiqua et mortua* by the time of Cicero (in Verr. v. 18, 45).

[3] Cod. xii. 7, 6 'ne quis ex ultimis negotiatoribus vel monetariis (generally understood as 'minters,' 'coiners') abjectisque officiis vel deformis ministerii stationariis omnique officiorum faece diversisque pastis turpibus lucris aliqua frui dignitate pertemptet. Sed et si quis meruerit, repellatur.'

the local senates; and in the Empire small traders, although submitted to degrading punishments, were not debarred either the decurionate or the municipal *honores*. This was a necessary permission considering the extreme difficulty of getting municipal offices filled at all: and we are told by Callistratus that the standard of qualifications should vary according to the ease or difficulty with which candidates were found in the different states[1].

Disqualifications which were based on the exercise of a trade or profession were by their very nature not perpetual. They were removed as soon as the trade or profession was abandoned. This was the principle of Republican Rome and of Caesar's municipal law, and the same condition seems to have been recognised during the Empire[2].

There is as striking an absence of strictly technical terminology to express this disability as that which we have found in other departments of Civil Honour, which throughout its history may almost be called a conception without a name. The individuals disqualified seem never to have been called *infames*; sometimes they are spoken of as *viles*, sometimes as *humiles*, according as the disgraceful profession or the low standing is the idea specially prominent at the time: but these two words do not exclude a variety of other names, all equally vague but of somewhat kindred meaning[3].

[1] Dig. l. 2 (*de decur. et fil. eor.*), 12.

[2] Lex Jul. Munic. l. 105 'neve eum—dum eorum quid faciet—renuntiato'; cf. Cic. ad Fam. vi. 18, written in 46 B.C. (quoted by Savigny, Verm. Schr. iii. p. 338) 'simul accepi a Seleuco tuo literas; statim quaesivi e Balbo per codicillos, quid esset in lege. Rescripsit, "eos, qui facerent praeconium, vetari esse in decurionibus; qui fecissent non vetari."'

[3] Dig. l. 2, 12 'viles personas'; Dig. iv. 3, 11, 1 'humilis,' as opposed to one 'qui dignitate excellet,' as 'plebeius' to 'consularis.' Dig. xlviii. 19, 28 'tenuiores homines' as opposed to 'honestiores.' Cod. xii. 1, 12

To the class of disqualifications expressed by these words one more may be added, which belongs, at least conceivably, to the same category; it is the disqualification which might be based on illegitimacy. At first sight this may seem a question rather of *status* than of *existimatio*, but really it is one that lies on the borderland between legal and social standing. It is quite conceivable that a State might recognise most of the legal rights of the illegitimate and yet debar them from certain honours. As a matter of fact this theory was but slightly pressed at Rome. It is true that at Rome the *spurii filii*, or *sine patre filii*, as the abbreviation of these words came afterwards to be interpreted[1], were at one time debarred from Roman magistracies; but this disqualification rested rather on grounds of *status*, since at that time they were not accounted free-born (*ingenui*). Subsequently, perhaps as late as the year 189 B.C.[2], they were placed on a level with the *ingenui*, and this disability was removed. In the Principate, however, it appears that *spurii* were limited as a rule to the four city tribes[3]; they were subject, therefore, to a limitation of rights somewhat similar to that which affected actors and the sons of actresses[4].

When we turn to municipal offices we find no trace of this disqualification being observed. It is true that

'pessimi et plebeii'; Justin. Nov. 90, 1 'et non quosdam artifices ignobiles neque vilissimos nec nimis obscuros.'

[1] Mommsen (Staatsr. iii. p. 72, n. 4) thinks that the *s(ine) p(atre) filii* of Gaius (i. 64) and Plutarch (Qu. Rom. 103) was a mistaken conjecture of the later jurists based on the abbreviated form of *sp(urii) filii*. Later, when they were reckoned *ingenui*, the designation was read as *Sp(urii) filii*, sons of an imaginary father *Spurius* (Festus s. v. nothum).

[2] If with Mommsen (Staatsr. iii. pp. 422, 423) we believe it to have been an effect of the *Terentinum plebiscitum*.

[3] Mommsen, Staatsr. iii. p. 443.

[4] These appear to be found mainly in the one tribe *Esquilina* (Mommsen, l. c.).

separate *municipia* may have enjoined regulations of their own with reference to this class; but Caesar's municipal law did not disqualify the *spurii* from office or from the Senate, and such disqualification was not recognised in the Antonine period[1]. The tendency of imperial legislation, under the guidance of the *jus naturale*, was in fact to remove as far as possible the disabilities arising from illegitimacy[2].

The fact of *vilitas*, therefore, if we may use the term, was a bar to the offices of the central government, but not to municipal offices; and it could not be thought of as a ground of exclusion from the army, since the profession of a soldier was, in the Empire at least, legally inconsistent with the exercise of any other trade or business[3].

There is a disqualification in public law which we have already had occasion to notice as affecting both the *infames* and the *turpes*; namely the limitation of the right to prosecute. It cannot be said that this limitation was imposed on the *viles* or *humiles* in general; but the possession of a certain amount of wealth was considered a condition necessary for the exercise of this right. Poor men were, therefore, excluded from this political privilege, except in those cases in which their own interests were directly concerned[4]. Again the principle already noted

[1] Ulpian in Dig. l 2, 3 'spurios posse in ordinem allegi nulla dubitatio est. Sed si habeat competitorem legitime quaesitum, praeferri eum (oportet *del.*), divi fratres . . . rescripserunt.'

[2] As shown, e.g. by the Orphitian *senatus consultum*, which gave children, legitimate or illegitimate, a prior right of succession to their mother, and by the modes of legitimation of children born out of wedlock introduced by Constantine and his successors.

[3] Vita Maximinorum 8 (A.D. 235–238); Cod. xii. 35 (36), 15 (Leo, A.D. 458); soldiers are here forbidden agriculture or trade, but only on the ground that such occupations interfered with their military duties.

[4] Dig. xlviii. 2, 10 '(prohibentur accusare) nonnulli propter paupertatem, ut sunt qui minus quam quinquaginta aureos habent.' In all these

that certain persons could not bring an *actio doli*, or possibly any action involving infamia, against honourable persons, was applied to men of low social standing as well as to those of low character; and this was a principle early recognised in Roman law[1].

But the law of the Empire went further than this; it cannot be said that all men were equal in its eyes so far as its infliction of penalties was concerned: and the man of small estate might be submitted to degrading punishments from which the more honourable classes were exempt[2]. A more defensible provision was one concerned with the infamia itself. The imposition of infamia could have but little effect on a man practically debarred from all honours by his social station. A judge was, therefore, entitled to pronounce in certain cases a severer penalty in place of a sentence involving loss of *existimatio*[3].

Finally, the principles regulating the admissibility of evidence, and the provision connected with the *querela inofficiosi testamenti*, which have been already treated, applied to individuals of low social standing as well as to the *infames* and the *turpes*: and under the same conditions which we have before described; that is, it depended entirely on the discretion of the judge, and on the merits of the case, whether he should allow the testimony or admit the validity of the petition.

The conception here discussed was clearly not confined to men; in its private law effects, and in one at least of its consequences in public law—that which permitted degrading punishments—it was equally applicable to

excepted cases the principle is held (Dig. ib. 11) 'si suam injuriam exequantur mortemve propinquorum defendent, ab accusatione non excluduntur.'

[1] Ulpian in Dig. iv. 3, 11, 1; he adds 'et ita Labeo.'

[2] Callistratus in Dig. xlviii. 19, 28.

[3] Ulpian in Dig. xlvii. 10, 35; cf. Cod. ix. 44, 2.

women. But the chief form in which a class of women is presented to us as of low station or origin is in connection with the marriage laws of the later Empire. Poverty was not sufficient to constitute lowliness of station for this purpose; but a definite list of *abjectae mulieres* was drawn up, based partly on birth, partly on profession, with whom marriage was forbidden to senators and high officials[1]. One of the sanctions of this law was nullity of the marriage, and we have seen that an attempt on the part of the husband to make the children of such unions pass as legitimate was visited by infamia[2].

[1] Cod. v. 5, 7 (Valentinian III and Marcian, A.D. 454) 'humiles vero abjectasque personas eas tantum modo mulieres esse censemus: ancillam ancillae filiam, libertam libertae filiam, scaenicam vel scaenicae filiam, tabernariam vel tabernarii vel lenonis aut harenarii filiam, aut eam quae mercimoniis publice praefuit.'

[2] See p. 151 for this infamia, and for the repeal of these marriage laws by Justinian.

APPENDIX

NOTE I, p. 126.

THE evidences for the rules of mourning in Republican Rome, as fixed by the college of *Pontifices*, are very slight. Plutarch, in his life of Numa (c. 12), sums up the Pontifical law on the subject as follows :—

αὐτὸς δὲ καὶ τὰ πένθη καθ' ἡλικίας καὶ χρόνους ἔταξεν· οἷον παῖδα μὴ πενθεῖν νεώτερον τριετοῦς, μηδὲ πρεσβύτερον πλείονας μῆνας ὧν ἐβίωσεν ἐνιαυτῶν μέχρι τῶν δέκα, καὶ περαιτέρω μηδεμίαν ἡλικίαν, ἀλλὰ τοῦ μακροτάτου, πένθους χρόνον εἶναι δεκαμηνιαῖον (ἐφ' ὅσον καὶ χηρεύουσιν αἱ τῶν ἀποθανόντων γυναῖκες).

With the exception of the last sentence, which will demand further comment, the passage treats of the length of mourning, as determined by the age of the deceased. The rules given by Plutarch refer only to children; the parallel passage in the Fragm. Vat. (§ 321) includes parents as well, and seems to show that in no case did the period of mourning ever exceed a year in duration, and that this year was always reckoned as ten months. The passage runs :—

'Lugendi autem sunt parentes anno[1], liberi majores x annorum aeque anno. quem annum decem mensuum esse Pomponius ait; nec leve argumentum est annum x mensuum esse, cum minores liberi tot mensibus elugeantur, quot annorum decesserint usque ad trimatum; minor trimo non lugetur, sed sublugetur; minor anniculo neque lugetur neque sublugetur.'

This statement, which is probably taken from Ulpian's

[1] There is a lacuna after 'anno,' as though a word had dropped out.

commentary to the Edict, is contradicted in many particulars by a passage in Paulus (i. 21, 13), found in the Codex Vesontinus, which runs as follows:

'Parentes et filii majores *sex* annis *anno* lugeri possunt: minores *mense:* maritus decem mensibus: et *cognati* proximioris gradus octo.'

But the valuelessness of this passage is generally admitted. Savigny (System, ii, Beil. vii. 11) regards it as an interpolation: and this opinion is followed by Karlowa (Zeitschr. f. R. G. ix. p. 237).

Such, then, were the rules of mourning laid down by the Pontifical college, and enforced by the censors. That these rules, which were no doubt always embodied in the *edictum censorium*, found their way into the praetor's Edict, seems shown by the fact that some commentator, probably Ulpian, found it worth while to mention them in that portion of his commentary which dealt with the *edictum cognitorium*. It is a portion of this commentary which is found in the extract from the Fragmenta Vaticana quoted above. Women, who were included in this Edict with respect to their capacity to give cognitors or procurators, are regarded as *infames* for the purposes of the Edict, if they did not fulfil these conditions of mourning. Such formal rules had apparently ceased to be binding upon men by the time when this commentary on the Edict was written, at least so far as the duty of mourning parents was concerned[1]. It is with reference to this change that we must probably explain a passage of Ulpian which speaks of fixed rules of mourning as having been abolished:

Dig. iii. 2, 23 (Ulp. *libr. viii. ad Edict.*) 'parentes et liberi utriusque sexus nec non et ceteri adgnati vel cognati secundum pietatis rationem, et animi sui patientiam, *prout quisque voluerit*, lugendi sunt: qui autem eos non eluxit, non notatur infamia.'

[1] There was, however, some doubt on the point; Fragm. Vat. § 320; '"parentem," inquit (praetor). hic omnes parentes accipe utriusque sexus, nam lugendi eos *mulieribus moris est.* quamquam Papinianus libro ii. quaestionum etiam a liberis virilis sexus lugendos esse dicat; quod nescio ubi legerit.'

Ulpian could never have meant this to be a general rule, at a time when the violation of mourning did produce infamia on women, as shown by the Fragm. Vat. It must, as Karlowa suggests (op. cit. p. 237) have occurred in a context referring only to men. It is quoted (out of its context) as a general principle in the Digest, because by the time of Justinian the formal rules of mourning had been wholly abolished.

Can we point to a time when these rules wholly ceased to be binding? It is possible that the date is given by a passage in the Code, which runs as follows:

Cod. ii. 11, 12 (15) (Gordian 239 A.D.) 'decreto amplissimi ordinis luctu feminarum deminuto tristior habitus ceteraque hoc genus insignia mulieribus remittuntur.'

But this only furnishes an approximate date on the two suppositions (1) that the *S. C.* referred to was one passed in Gordian's time (about 239 A.D.), and so after the death of Ulpian, who was murdered 228 A.D., and (2) that it was not a mere temporary remission of mourning for a temporary purpose. If the *S. C.* was passed at a period much before the time of Gordian, as held by Savigny, then the explanation, given by the Scholiasts to the Basilica and by Cujacius, that it was merely a temporary remission, must be the right one. For it is certain that the rules of mourning were binding on *women* at the time at which the Edict was commented on by Ulpian.

It is possible that this second explanation is correct: the temporary regulation becomes an absolute rule, as quoted in Justinian's Code; and Christianity, which must have laid but little stress on the external signs of mourning, succeeded in abolishing these rules of the Pontifical law. The rescript of Gordian, as embodied by Justinian in his Code, becomes a recognition of their final abolition.

There is, however, one exception to this abolition which deserves special consideration. The obligation imposed by the Pontifical law on a widow to mourn her husband during the space of ten months, before contracting a second marriage, is found in the Edict even in the mutilated form in which it has been preserved to us by Justinian's compilers. With reference to this obligation two questions have been raised: (1) What was the original meaning of the rule? (2) What was the object with which the rule was maintained in the Pandects of Justinian, at a time when all the other regulations about mourning parents and children had been abolished?

The answer to the first question appears to be that the mourning for the husband had from the first a twofold significance, unlike the mourning for other relatives. It was enjoined, firstly, as an external sign of grief required by religious law; and, secondly, as a means of preventing doubtfulness of paternity in the case of a posthumous child being born; the ten months' *luctus* of the widow was, to use the expression of the later Roman law, a means of avoiding *turbatio sanguinis*. This, indeed, has been denied by Savigny (System ii., Beil. vii. 6), who believed that the second was at all times the only motive. The arguments which he adduces from the passages cited from jurists in the Digest must, however, at once be disallowed; for the excerpts have evidently been so made as to bring prominently before us only the motive which was the ruling one in Justinian's time, that is, the avoidance of *turbatio sanguinis*[1]. But the evidences from earlier literature are on the whole against Savigny's view. The passages collected by Cujas (Observ. vi. 32) show the double motive of the older Pontifical regulations. This double motive appears in the notice of Ovid (Fasti, i. 33):

> 'Quod satis est, utero matris dum prodeat infans
> Hoc anno statuit temporis esse satis,
> Per totidem menses a funere conjugis uxor
> Sustinet in vidua tristia signa domo,'

and the religious objection to a second marriage within the

[1] Dig. iii. 2, 11, 1 and 2. On these passages see Karlowa's criticism (op. cit. pp. 235, 236); he assigns these passages to their true context in Ulpian's commentary to the Edict.

prescribed period of mourning was perhaps based on many grounds of sentiment, not the least potent of which may have been that dwelt on by Apuleius (Metamorph. viii.), fear of vengeance from the *manes* of the deceased husband.

We do find modifications in the external signs of mourning occasionally permitted the widow, e.g. on the occasion of a betrothal [1]. But Savigny's view that a new marriage might be concluded 'in a perfectly sober spirit,' and was, therefore, in itself no violation of mourning, appears contrary to Roman religious sentiment.

Yet the fear of *turbatio sanguinis* must always have been a powerful motive from the secular point of view, and naturally survived when the purely religious objections had almost disappeared. For perhaps these never did quite disappear even in the Christian Empire. The Scholiast to the Basilica at least recognises the 'reverence due to the husband' as one of the bars to marriage (Nicaeus ad Basil. 22, tit. 2, p. 622, Fabr.), and this sentiment still survives in the language of some of the constitutions of the Christian Emperors, e.g.:

Cod. v. 9, 1 (Gratian, Valentinian II, and Theodosius I, A.D. 380) 'si qua mulier nequaquam *luctus religionem* priori viro nuptiarum festinatione praestiterit, ex jure quidem notissimo sit infamis' (cf. the language of the next constitution given by the same Emperors, A.D. 381).

But it is equally apparent that the chief motive for the retention of this form of the infamia of the Edict by the compilers of Justinian, was the purely civil ground of the avoidance of *turbatio sanguinis* (Rudorff, Zeitschr. f. R. G. iv. p. 55). This is shown by the arrangement of the extracts which are found in the title of the Dig. (iii. 2) dealing with the *infames*: and although we occasionally get a reminiscence

[1] The betrothal of the widow herself, according to Savigny, but this is by no means the necessary meaning of the words of Festus (p. 155 Muell. *minuebatur . . . luctus . . . privatis . . . quum puella desponsaretur*). On these occasions the mourning was not 'shortened,' as Savigny explains, but 'lessened,' i. e. half-mourning was adopted.

of the old religious rules[1], these would never have survived apart from the secular ground which dictated the prohibition of a hasty second marriage.

Note II, p. 137.

The interpretation of this clause, which is given in the text of the work, demands some justification, for it differs essentially from those given by Huschke and Rudorff. The chief ground on which I venture to disagree with their explanations is that the meaning which they attach to the three words of most importance in the clause ('bonam copiam jurare') seems to me inconsistent with the probable interpretation of those words in the context which, of all others, throws most light upon their meaning.

The sentence in question runs:—

'Queive in jure [bonam copiam abjuravit] (*suppl. Mommsen*) abjuraverit, bonamve copiam juravit juraverit, quei (omitting *ve*) sponsoribus creditoribusve sueis renuntiavit renuntiaverit, se soldum solvere non posse, aut cum eis pactus est erit, se soldum solvere non posse.'

The words, on the meaning of which the whole interpretation of this passage turns, are 'bonam copiam jurare.'

Huschke (*Das Recht des Nexum*, pp. 138, 139) understands the second case here mentioned (i. e. the case of the man 'qui bonam copiam *juravit*,' &c.) as a *single* case of *fraudulent* bankruptcy. It is the case of a man 'who has *first* declared his insolvency to his creditors, or has already obtained a remission from them ("quei sponsoribus . . . se soldum

[1] E.g. in the extract from Ulpian (Dig. iii. 2, 11, 1) 'etsi talis sit maritus, quem more majorum lugeri non oportet, non posse eam nuptum intra legitimum tempus collocari,' the ground of the praetor's ruling in this case being *turbatio sanguinis*. Husbands, whom widows were excused from mourning, were those who had been *hostes*, *perduellionis damnati*, *suspendiosi*, or those *qui manus sibi intulerant non taedio vitae, sed mala conscientia* (l. c. § 3).

solvere non posse") but who *afterwards*, perhaps with reference to another creditor, has sworn his solvency before the court, to gain certain privileges thereby, probably to secure freedom from personal arrest in accordance with the Edict.' *Bonam copiam jurare* is here taken to mean 'to swear that one is solvent.' But, even if we believe that this can be the meaning of the words, it certainly seems that this explanation would require 'queive bonam copiam,' &c.; that is, it would require a new clause extending down to the words *solvere non posse*, sharply severed from the preceding clause, which would refer to the ordinary bankrupt, who has simply sworn that he is insolvent ('quei . . . abjuraverit').

Rudorff (Zeitschr. f. R. G. iv. p. 51 seq.) understands the words as referring to *two* kinds of *fraudulent* bankruptcy. 'The first is maintaining solvency on oath (when it is only done to escape arrest and avoid insolvency), the second is the announcement of insolvency and arrangement (through which the creditor is cheated of a portion of his goods).' The passages of Rudorff's explanation which I have enclosed in brackets seem to me purely gratuitous additions to the words of the law. They rest on the assumption (which is a mere assumption so far as these particular words are concerned) that the case treated of in the law must be one of fraudulent bankruptcy. The important point of this explanation is, however, that Rudorff agrees with Huschke in thinking that 'bonam copiam jurare' means 'to swear to solvency.' And this is the meaning attached to the words by Forcellini (*s.v.* 'ejuro': 'jurare bonam copiam est jurejurando in judicio affirmare, esse sibi tantam copiam rei familiaris, qua creditoribus satisfieri omnimodo possit').

But this meaning of 'bonam copiam jurare' will not suit the most important passage in which the words occur. Varro (L. L. viii. 105) in describing the emancipation of the *nexi*, says:—

'Liber, qui suas operas in servitutem pro pecunia quam debet dat, dum solveret, nexus vocatur, ut ab aere obaeratus. Hoc C. Poetilio

Libone Visolo (*Lachmann* for C. popillio vocare sillo) dictatore sublatum ne fieret; et omnes, *qui bonam copiam jurarunt*, ne essent nexi dissoluti.'

This C. Poetilius was dictator in 313 B.C., but the change referred to is no doubt that mentioned by Livy (viii. 28) in connection with the year 326[1]:—

'Jussique consules ferre ad populum, ne quis, nisi qui noxam meruisset, donec poenam lueret, in compedibus aut in nervo teneretur: pecuniae creditae bona debitoris, non corpus obnoxium esset.'

Livy makes it a universal release of *nexi*, Varro only of those debtors 'qui bonam copiam jurarunt.' As no *nexus* could possibly be solvent, or be kept in servitude after he was solvent (Varro l. c. *dum solveret*), the words cannot mean 'swore to solvency.' They have been taken to mean 'who swore that they had done their best, or would do their best, to meet their debts and satisfy their creditors.' I should prefer the explanation 'who swore that they had reasonable hopes (literally "means") of ultimately satisfying their creditors.' This agrees best with the words of the *Lex Julia Municipalis* and with a passage in one of Cicero's letters to Paetus (ad Fam. ix. 16, 7):—

'Tu autem, quod mihi bonam copiam *ejures*, nihil est; tum enim, quum rem habebas, quaesticulis te faciebam attentiorem; nunc, quum tam aequo animo bona perdas, non eo sis consilio, ut, quum me hospitio recipias, aestimationem te aliquam putes accipere; etiam haec levior est plaga ab amico quam a debitore.'

Ejurare here is equivalent to the *abjurare* of the law. Paetus, who had represented his wealth as rapidly disappearing in consequence of his being obliged to accept *aestimationes*, in accordance with Caesar's law, had written to Cicero to say that he was hopelessly insolvent.

If we accept this meaning for the words, the clause in the *Lex* must refer to the debtor 'who has sworn that he has

[1] The other reading, adopted by Forcellini [*s.v.* 'ejuro'], 'C. Popilio rogante Sulla dictatore,' though perhaps closer to the MS., is rendered impossible by the fact that no such condition as that of the *nexus* could have existed in the time of Sulla.

reasonable means of meeting his engagements, and, as having such, has come to an arrangement with his creditors on the ground of incapacity to pay in full.' It would show, therefore, a case of ordinary bankruptcy, but accompanied by a compromise accepted by the creditors.

If we turn now to the case of the man 'quei bonam copiam abjuravit,' it cannot mean, according to this explanation, to 'swear insolvency' simply. It refers to a man 'who has taken an oath that he has no means of meeting his engagements.'

The four divisions of the clause, in fact, balance one another in the following way:—

(i) the man who has sworn that he has no means of meeting his engagements, (*a*) and has made a *renuntiatio* to this effect:

(ii) the man who has sworn that he has some means of meeting his engagements, (*b*) and has come to an arrangement with his creditors.

Note III, p. 149.

This Constitution, issued in the year 397 A.D. under the names of Arcadius and Honorius—for we may exempt these Emperors, one of whom was fourteen and the other thirteen years of age at this date, from any active share in its promulgation—is of some importance as a singular violation of the theory of infamia and of the theory of punishment in Roman law.

We have already seen that the infamia was not hereditary (pp. 7 and 38): and we know that the principle was upheld by the lawyers of the Empire, in the case of disqualifications consequent on criminal condemnation, or analogous circumstances, such as criminal accusation, that these disqualifications could not be transmitted from father to son. The most general statement of this principle is made by Callistratus (Dig. xlviii. 19, *De poenis*, 26):—

'Crimen vel poena paterna nullam maculam filio infligere potest: namque unusquisque ex suo admisso sorti subicitur nec alieni criminis successor constituitur, idque divi fratres Hierapolitanis rescripserunt.'

A similar statement, with reference to the qualifications for municipal offices, is made by Ulpian (Dig. l. 2, *De decur. et fil. eor.*, 2, 7):—

'Nullum patris delictum innocenti filio poenae est: ideoque nec ordine decurionum aut ceteris honoribus propter ejusmodi causam prohibetur.'

More particular applications of the principle, with reference to municipal offices, are to be found in Dig. l. 2, 13, 2 and 4, 3, 9.

The theory that civic disabilities could not be entailed on a son in consequence of the crime or punishment of his father was only a part of the more general theory that punishment itself could not be transmitted. This was a very early principle in the Roman criminal law. Dionysius tells us (viii. 80) that, on the execution of Sp. Cassius in 485 B.C., a proposal was made that his children should be put to death; but that this proposal was indignantly rejected by the Senate. He continues:—

Καὶ ἐξ ἐκείνου τὸ ἔθος τοῦτο Ῥωμαίοις ἐπιχώριον γέγονεν, ἕως τῆς καθ' ἡμᾶς διατηρούμενον ἡλικίας, ἀφεῖσθαι τιμωρίας ἁπάσης τοὺς παῖδας ὧν ἂν οἱ πατέρες ἀδικήσωσιν, ἐάν τε προδοτῶν, ὃ μέγιστόν ἐστι παρ' ἐκείνοις ἀδίκημα.

He remarks that this principle was broken down as the result of the civil wars at the end of the Republic, adducing the disabilities imposed by Sulla on the children of the proscribed as the most glaring instance of its violation (see p. 7, note 4); and he regards Caesar's clemency after his victory as a restoration of the older view. He draws an interesting parallel between Greek and Roman law in this respect:—

Παρ᾽ Ἕλλησι δὲ οὐχ οὕτως ἐνίοις ὁ νόμος ἔχει, ἀλλὰ τοὺς ἐκ τυράννων γενομένους οἱ μὲν συναποκτίννυσθαι τοῖς πατράσι δικαιοῦσιν, οἱ δὲ ἀειφυγίᾳ κολάζουσιν, ὥσπερ οὐκ ἐνδεχομένης τῆς φύσεως χρήστους παῖδας ἐκ πονηρῶν πατέρων ἢ κακοὺς ἐξ ἀγαθῶν γενέσθαι. (Cf. Cic. *De inv.* ii. 49, 144.)

Ammianus Marcellinus (xxiii. 6, 81) draws a similar contrast between Roman law and that of Oriental nations:—

'Leges apud eos . . . abominandae aliae, per quas ob noxam unius omnis propinquitas perit.'

The most striking circumstance connected with the maintenance of this principle in the later Empire is that the most vehement assertion of it proceeded from the Emperors Arcadius and Honorius in 399 A.D., only two years after the promulgation of their law about treason. It runs (Cod. ix. 47, 22):—

'Sancimus ibi esse poenam, ubi et noxa est. Propinquos notos familiares procul a calumnia submovemus, quos reos sceleris societas non facit: nec enim adfinitas vel amicitia nefarium crimen admittunt. Peccata igitur suos teneant auctores nec ulterius progrediatur metus, quam reperietur delictum. Hoc singulis quibusque judicibus intimetur.'

It is a significant fact that Dionysius, when treating of the maintenance of this principle in the Republic, adds that it was observed 'even in the case of traitors.' Treason, in fact, formed the exception to the rule even in the early Principate, as may be gathered from the following passages:—

Suet. Tib. 61 'accusati damnatique multi, cum liberis atque etiam uxoribus suis' (cf. Tac. Ann. v. 9 [vi. 4] 'placitum posthac ut in reliquos Sejani liberos adverteretur'); Suet. Nero, 36 'damnatorum liberi urbe pulsi, enectique veneno aut fame.'

The reason for the death penalty, or, if this was not imposed, for disqualifications being extended to children in consequence of the treason of their father, is no doubt to be found in the fear of their pursuing a similar career. Ammianus (xxviii. 2, 14) assigns a similar motive for the complete extirpation of a robber tribe in Syria in the year 369 A.D.:—

'Oppressi interiere omnes ad unum, eorumque suboles parva etiam tunc, ne ad parentum exempla subcresceret, pari sorte deleta est.'

P 2

And this motive no doubt underlies the new law of treason issued in the reigns of Arcadius and Honorius.

The passages quoted above, which show that, even during the early Principate, the punishment for treason was sometimes transmitted to children, prove that Rein is in a sense right in saying (Criminalrecht, p. 539 note) that this law is only a new one in so far as it recognised as legally valid and made universal disabilities similar to those formerly imposed at the will of the Emperors. For even when penalties were not inflicted on children in consequence of their fathers' condemnation for treason, yet so entire was the control over admission to office exercised by the Princeps or the Emperor that the sons of traitors must often have been subject to a practical infamia[1]. Yet as a definite class of *infames* was created by this law, it must be regarded as a new application and extension of the principle of infamia.

As regards the relation of these two laws of Arcadius and Honorius to one another, it is not likely that the law of 399 A.D., reasserting the principle that punishment should not be transmitted, was meant in any way to repeal the law of treason passed two years previously. The law of 399 treats of punishment, and although the infamia pronounced by the law of treason, accompanied as it was by clauses prohibiting the acceptance of legacies, approaches more closely to the character of a penal measure than other forms of this disability, yet infamia is not *necessarily* regarded as a *poena*. It might be so regarded; in Dig. xlviii. 19 (*De poenis*), the disabilities pronounced by provincial governors (*praesides*) on advocates, notaries and others in the form of suspension from their duties are treated as *poenae*: and in the general classification of punishments Ulpian includes 'dignitatis aliquam depositionem aut alicujus actus prohibitionem' (Dig. xlviii. 19, 8). We see, therefore, that disqualifications consequent on a misuse of functions and approximating to infamia might be used as punishments; and

[1] The *renuntiatio amicitiae* sent by the Princeps was alone sufficient to debar from *honores* (Tac. Ann. iii. 24).

it is indeed very difficult, at some stages of the history of infamia, to draw any distinction between disqualification and punishment (see p. 29); but the two were at least sufficiently distinct in theory to make it possible that a law regulating the incidence of punishments should not of itself be held to abrogate a law creating a new class of infamous persons.

INDEX

(The references are to the pages.)

THE END.

Clarendon Press, Oxford.

I. LITERATURE AND PHILOLOGY.

SECTION I.

DICTIONARIES, GRAMMARS, &c.

ANGLO-SAXON. An Anglo-Saxon Dictionary, based on the MS. Collections of the late JOSEPH BOSWORTH, D.D., Professor of Anglo-Saxon, Oxford. Edited and enlarged by Prof. T. N. TOLLER, M.A. Parts I–III. A—SAR. 4to, 15*s*. each. Part IV. Sect. I. SÁR–SWÍÐRIAN. 8*s*. 6*d*.

ARABIC. A Practical Arabic Grammar. Compiled by A. O. GREEN, Brigade Major, Royal Engineers.

Part I. *Third Edition. Enlarged.* Crown 8vo, 7*s*. 6*d*.

Part II. *Third Edition. Enlarged and Revised.* 10*s*. 6*d*.

BENGALI. Grammar of the Bengali Language; Literary and Colloquial. By JOHN BEAMES. Crown 8vo, cloth, 7*s*. 6*d*.

CELTIC. Ancient Cornish Drama. Edited and translated by E. NORRIS, with a Sketch of Cornish Grammar, an Ancient Cornish Vocabulary, &c. 2 vols. 8vo, 1*l*. 1*s*.

The Sketch of Cornish Grammar separately, stitched, 2*s*. 6*d*.

CHINESE. A Handbook of the Chinese Language. By JAMES SUMMERS. 8vo, half-bound, 1*l*. 8*s*.

ENGLISH. A New English Dictionary, on Historical Principles: founded mainly on the materials collected by the Philological Society. Vol. I. A and B, and Vol. II. C. Imperial 4to, half-morocco, *each* 2*l*. 12*s*. 6*d*.

Part VIII. Section I. CROUCHMAS—CZECH. End of Vol. II, 4*s*.

Edited by JAMES A. H. MURRAY, LL.D.

Vol. III. D and E.

D. Edited by Dr. MURRAY. [*In the Press.*]

E—EVERY. Edited by H. BRADLEY, M.A. 12*s*. 6*d*. [*Published.*]

ENGLISH (*continued*).

ENGLISH. An Etymological Dictionary of the English Language. By W. W. SKEAT, Litt.D. *Second Edition.* 4to, 2*l.* 4*s.*

—— A Concise Etymological Dictionary of the English Language. By W. W. SKEAT, Litt.D. *Fourth Edition.* Crown 8vo, 5*s.* 6*d.*

—— A Concise Dictionary of Middle English, from A.D. 1150 to 1580. By A. L. MAYHEW, M.A., and W. W. SKEAT, Litt. D. Crown 8vo, half-roan, 7*s.* 6*d.*

—— A Middle English Dictionary. By FRANCIS HENRY STRATMANN. *A New Edition*, Re-arranged, Revised, and Enlarged by HENRY BRADLEY, M.A. Small 4to, 1*l.* 11*s.* 6*d.*

—— A Primer of Spoken English. By HENRY SWEET, M.A., Ph.D. Extra fcap. 8vo, 3*s.* 6*d.*

—— A New English Grammar, Logical and Historical. By HENRY SWEET, M.A., Ph.D. Part I. Introduction, Phonology, and Accidence. Crown 8vo, 10*s.* 6*d.*

—— A Short Historical English Grammar. By HENRY SWEET, M.A., Ph.D. Extra fcap. 8vo, 4*s.* 6*d.*

—— A Primer of Historical English Grammar. Extra fcap. 8vo, 2*s.*

—— A Primer of Phonetics. By HENRY SWEET, M.A., Ph.D. Extra fcap. 8vo, 3*s.* 6*d.*

—— Elementarbuch des Gesprochenen Englisch. Grammatik, Texte und Glossar. By HENRY SWEET, M.A., Ph.D. *Third Edition.* Extra fcap. 8vo, stiff covers, 2*s.* 6*d.*

FINNISH. A Finnish Grammar. By C. N. E. ELIOT, M.A. Crown 8vo, roan, 10*s.* 6*d.*

GOTHIC. A Primer of the Gothic Language; with Grammar, Notes, and Glossary. By JOSEPH WRIGHT, Ph.D. Extra fcap. 8vo, cloth, 4*s.* 6*d.*

GREEK. A Greek-English Lexicon, by H. G. LIDDELL, D.D., and ROBERT SCOTT, D.D. *Seventh Edition, Revised and Augmented throughout.* 4to, 1*l.* 16*s.*

—— An Intermediate Greek-English Lexicon, founded upon the Seventh Edition of the above. Small 4to, 12*s.* 6*d.*

—— A Greek-English Lexicon, abridged from Liddell and Scott's 4to edition, chiefly for the use of Schools. *Twenty-fifth Edition.* Square 12mo, 7*s.* 6*d.*

GREEK. A Concordance to the Septuagint and the other Greek Versions of the Old Testament (including the Apocryphal Books). By the late EDWIN HATCH, M.A., and HENRY REDPATH, M.A. Parts I and II. A–ʹΕΠΑΙΝΟΣ. Imperial 4to, *each* 21s. Part III. *In the Press.*

☞ *To be completed in Six Parts, at* 1*l.* 1*s. per Part; or to Subscribers at* 4*l.* 4*s. for the whole work.*

—— A copious Greek-English Vocabulary, compiled from the best authorities. 24mo, 3*s.*

—— **Etymologicon Magnum.** Ad Codd. mss. recensuit et notis variorum instruxit T. GAISFORD, S.T.P. 1848. fol. 1*l.* 12*s.*

—— **Suidae Lexicon.** Ad Codd. mss. recensuit T. GAISFORD, S.T.P. Tomi III. 1834. fol. 2*l.* 2*s.*

HEBREW. A Hebrew and English Lexicon of the Old Testament, with an Appendix containing the Biblical Aramaic, based on the Thesaurus and Lexicon of GESENIUS, by FRANCIS BROWN, D.D., S. R. DRIVER, D.D., and C. A. BRIGGS, D.D. Parts I and II. Small 4to, 2*s.* 6*d. each.*

—— The Book of Hebrew Roots, by ABU 'L-WALÎD MARWÂN IBN JANÂH, otherwise called RABBÎ YÔNÂH. Now first edited, with an Appendix, by AD. NEUBAUER. 4to, 2*l.* 7*s.* 6*d.*

—— A Treatise on the use of the Tenses in Hebrew. By S. R. DRIVER, D.D. *Third Edition.* Crown 8vo, 7*s.* 6*d.*

ICELANDIC. An Icelandic-English Dictionary, based on the MS. collections of the late RICHARD CLEASBY. Enlarged and completed by G. VIGFÚSSON, M.A. 4to, 3*l.* 7*s.*

—— A List of English Words the Etymology of which is illustrated by comparison with Icelandic. Prepared in the form of an Appendix to the above. By W. W. SKEAT, Litt.D. Stitched, 2*s.*

—— An Icelandic Primer, with Grammar, Notes, and Glossary. BY HENRY SWEET, M.A., Ph.D. Extra fcap. 8vo, 3*s.* 6*d.*

——An Icelandic Prose Reader, with Notes, Grammar, and Glossary, by Dr. GUÐBRAND VIGFÚSSON and F. YORK POWELL, M.A. Extra fcap. 8vo, 10*s.* 6*d.*

LATIN. A Latin Dictionary, founded on Andrews' edition of Freund's Latin Dictionary, revised, enlarged, and in great part rewritten by CHARLTON T. LEWIS, Ph.D., and CHARLES SHORT, LL.D. 4to, 1*l.* 5*s.*

—— A School Latin Dictionary. By CHARLTON T. LEWIS, Ph.D. Small 4to, 18*s.*

—— An Elementary Latin Dictionary. By CHARLTON T. LEWIS, Ph.D. Square 8vo, 7*s.* 6*d.*

LATIN. Scheller's Dictionary of the Latin Language, revised and translated into English by J. E. RIDDLE, M.A. 1835. fol. *1l. 1s.*

—— Contributions to Latin Lexicography. By HENRY NETTLESHIP, M.A. 8vo, *21s.*

MELANESIAN. The Melanesian Languages. By ROBERT H. CODRINGTON, D.D., of the Melanesian Mission. 8vo, *18s.*

RUSSIAN. A Grammar of the Russian Language. By W. R. MORFILL, M.A. Crown 8vo, *6s.*

SANSKRIT. A Practical Grammar of the Sanskrit Language, arranged with reference to the Classical Languages of Europe, for the use of English Students, by Sir M. MONIER-WILLIAMS, D.C.L. *Fourth Edition.* 8vo, *15s.*

—— A Sanskrit-English Dictionary, Etymologically and Philologically arranged, with special reference to Greek, Latin, German, Anglo-Saxon, English, and other cognate Indo-European Languages. By Sir M. MONIER-WILLIAMS, D.C.L. 4to, *4l. 14s. 6d.*

—— Nalopákhyánam. Story of Nala, an Episode of the Mahá-Bhárata: the Sanskrit text, with a copious Vocabulary, and an improved version of Dean MILMAN'S Translation, by Sir M. MONIER-WILLIAMS, D.C.L. *Second Edition, Revised and Improved.* 8vo, *15s.*

—— Sakuntalā. A Sanskrit Drama, in Seven Acts. Edited by Sir M. MONIER-WILLIAMS, D.C.L. *Second Edition.* 8vo, *21s.*

SYRIAC. Thesaurus Syriacus: collegerunt Quatremère, Bernstein, Lorsbach, Arnoldi, Agrell, Field, Roediger: edidit R. PAYNE SMITH, S.T.P. Vol. I, containing Fasc. I–V, sm. fol. *5l. 5s.*

Fasc. VI, *1l. 1s.*; VII, *1l. 11s. 6d.*; VIII, *1l. 16s.*; IX, *1l. 5s.*

TAMIL. First Lessons in Tamil. By G. U. POPE, D.D. *Fifth Edition.* Crown 8vo, *7s. 6d.*

BIBLIOGRAPHICAL DICTIONARIES.

Cotton's Typographical Gazetteer. 1831. 8vo, *12s. 6d.*

—— Typographical Gazetteer. Second Series. 1866. 8vo, *12s. 6d.*

Dowling (J. G.). Notitia Scriptorum SS. Patrum aliorumque vet. Eccles. Mon. quae in Collectionibus Anecdotorum post annum Christi MDCC. in lucem editis continentur. 8vo, *4s. 6d.*

Ebert's Bibliographical Dictionary, translated from the German. 4 vols. 1837. 8vo, *1l. 10s.*

SECTION II.

ANGLO-SAXON AND ENGLISH.

HELPS TO THE STUDY OF THE LANGUAGE AND LITERATURE.

A NEW ENGLISH DICTIONARY on Historical Principles, founded mainly on the materials collected by the Philological Society. Vol. I. A and B, and Vol. II. C. Imperial 4to, half-morocco, *each* 2*l.* 12*s.* 6*d.*

Part VIII. Section I. CROUCHMAS—CZECH. End of Vol. II, 4*s.*

Edited by JAMES A. H. MURRAY, LL.D.

Vol. III. D and E.

D. Edited by Dr. MURRAY. [*In the Press.*]

E—EVERY. Edited by H. BRADLEY, M.A. 12*s.* 6*d.* [*Published.*]

Bosworth and Toller. An Anglo-Saxon Dictionary, based on the MS. collections of the late JOSEPH BOSWORTH, D.D. Edited and enlarged by Prof. T. N. TOLLER, M.A. Parts I–III. A—SAR. 4to, stiff covers, 15*s.* each. Part IV. Sect. I. SÁR–SWÍÐRIAN. 8*s.* 6*d.*

Earle. A Book for the Beginner in Anglo-Saxon. By JOHN EARLE, M.A. *Third Edition.* Extra fcap. 8vo, 2*s.* 6*d.*

—— The Philology of the English Tongue. *Fifth Edition, Newly Revised.* Extra fcap. 8vo, 8*s.* 6*d.*

Mayhew. Synopsis of Old English Phonology. By A. L. MAYHEW, M.A. Extra fcap. 8vo, bevelled boards, 8*s.* 6*d.*

Mayhew and Skeat. A Concise Dictionary of Middle English, from A.D. 1150 to 1580. By A. L. MAYHEW, M.A., and W. W. SKEAT, Litt.D. Crown 8vo, half-roan, 7*s.* 6*d.*

Skeat. An Etymological Dictionary of the English Language, arranged on an Historical Basis. By W. W. SKEAT, Litt.D. *Second Edition.* 4to, 2*l.* 4*s.*

A Supplement to the First Edition of the above. 4to, 2*s.* 6*d.*

—— A Concise Etymological Dictionary of the English Language. *Fourth Edition.* Crown 8vo, 5*s.* 6*d.*

—— Principles of English Etymology. First Series. *The Native Element. Second Edition.* Crown 8vo, 10*s.* 6*d.*

—— Principles of English Etymology. Second Series. *The Foreign Element.* Crown 8vo, 10*s.* 6*d.*

—— A Primer of English Etymology. Extra fcap. 8vo, stiff covers, 1*s.* 6*d.*

—— Twelve Facsimiles of Old English Manuscripts, with Transcriptions and an Introduction. 4to, paper covers, 7*s.* 6*d.*

Stratmann. A Middle English Dictionary, containing Words used by English Writers from the Twelfth to the Fifteenth Century. By FRANCIS HENRY STRATMANN. *A New Edition*, Re-arranged, Revised, and Enlarged by HENRY BRADLEY, M.A. Small 4to, half-morocco, 1*l.* 11*s.* 6*d.*

Sweet. A New English Grammar, Logical and Historical. Part I. Introduction, Phonology, and Accidence. Crown 8vo, 10*s.* 6*d.*

—— A Short Historical English Grammar. Extra fcap. 8vo. 4*s.* 6*d.*

—— A Primer of Historical English Grammar. Extra fcap. 8vo, 2*s.*

—— History of English Sounds from the Earliest Period. With full Word-Lists. 8vo, 14*s.*

—— An Anglo-Saxon Primer, with Grammar, Notes, and Glossary. *Seventh Edition.* Extra fcap. 8vo, 2*s.* 6*d.*

—— An Anglo-Saxon Reader. In Prose and Verse. With Grammatical Introduction, Notes, and Glossary. *Sixth Edition, Revised and Enlarged.* Extra fcap. 8vo, 8*s.* 6*d.*

—— A Second Anglo-Saxon Reader. Extra fcap. 8vo, 4*s.* 6*d.*

—— Old English Reading Primers:

I. Selected Homilies of Ælfric. Stiff covers, 1*s.* 6*d.*

II. Extracts from Alfred's Orosius. *Second Edition*, 2*s.*

Sweet (*continued*). First Middle English Primer, with Grammar and Glossary. *Second Edition.* Extra fcap, 8vo, 2*s.*

—— Second Middle English Primer. Extracts from Chaucer, with Grammar and Glossary. *Second Edition.* Extra fcap. 8vo, 2*s.* 6*d.*

—— Elementarbuch des Gesprochenen Englisch. Grammatik, Texte und Glossar. *Third Edition.* Extra fcap. 8vo, stiff covers, 2*s.* 6*d.*

—— A Primer of Spoken English. Extra fcap. 8vo, 3*s.* 6*d.*

—— An Icelandic Primer, with Grammar, Notes and Glossary. Extra fcap. 8vo, 3*s.* 6*d.*

—— A Primer of Phonetics. Extra fcap. 8vo, 3*s.* 6*d.*

—— A Manual of Current Shorthand, Orthographic and Phonetic. Crown 8vo, 4*s.* 6*d.*

Tancock. An Elementary English Grammar and Exercise Book. By O. W. TANCOCK, M.A. *Third Edition.* Extra fcap. 8vo, 1*s.* 6*d.*

—— An English Grammar and Reading Book, for Lower Forms in Classical Schools. *Fourth Edition.* Extra fcap. 8vo, 3*s.* 6*d.*

Saxon Chronicles. Two of the Saxon Chronicles Parallel; with Supplementary Extracts from the others. A Revised Text. Edited, with Introduction, Notes, Appendices, and Glossary. By C. PLUMMER, M.A., and J. EARLE, M.A. Vol. I. Text, Appendices, and Glossary. 10*s.* 6*d.*

—— —— (787–1001 A.D.) Crown 8vo, stiff covers, 3*s.*

Specimens of Early English. A New and Revised Edition. With Introduction, Notes, and Glossarial Index.

Part I. From Old English Homilies to King Horn (A.D. 1150 to A.D. 1300). By R. MORRIS, LL.D. *Second Edition.* Extra fcap. 8vo, 9*s.*

Part II. From Robert of Gloucester to Gower (A.D. 1298 to A.D. 1393). By R. MORRIS, LL.D., and W. W. SKEAT, Litt. D. *Second Edition.* Extra fcap. 8vo, 7*s.* 6*d.*

Specimens of English Literature, from the 'Ploughman's Crede' to the 'Shepheardes Calender' (A.D. 1394 to A.D. 1579). With Introduction, Notes, and Glossarial Index. By W. W. SKEAT, Litt.D. *Fifth Edition.* Extra fcap. 8vo, 7*s.* 6*d.*

Typical Selections from the best English Writers, with Introductory Notices. In 2 vols. *Second Edition.* Extra fcap. 8vo, 3*s.* 6*d.* each.

Vol. I. Latimer to Berkeley. Vol. II. Pope to Macaulay.

A SERIES OF ENGLISH CLASSICS.

The Deeds of Beowulf. An English Epic of the Eighth Century done into Modern Prose. With an Introduction and Notes, by JOHN EARLE, M.A. Crown 8vo, 8*s.* 6*d.*

The Gospel of St. Luke in Anglo-Saxon. Edited from the MSS. With Introduction, Notes, and Glossary. By JAMES W. BRIGHT, Ph.D. Extra fcap. 8vo, 5*s.*

The Ormulum, with the Notes and Glossary of Dr. R. M. WHITE. Edited by R. HOLT, M.A. 2 vols. Extra fcap. 8vo, 1*l.* 1*s.*

CHAUCER.

I. The Prologue to the Canterbury Tales. (School Edition.) Edited by W. W. SKEAT, Litt.D. Extra fcap. 8vo, 1*s.*

II. The Prologue, the Knightes Tale, The Nonne Preestes Tale; from the Canterbury Tales. Edited by R. MORRIS, LL.D. A New Edition, with Collations and Additional Notes by W. W. SKEAT, Litt.D. Extra fcap. 8vo, 2*s.* 6*d.*

III. The Prioresses Tale; Sir Thopas; The Monkes Tale; The Clerkes Tale; The Squieres Tale, &c. Edited by W. W. SKEAT, Litt.D. *Fifth Edition.* Extra fcap. 8vo, 4*s.* 6*d.*

IV. The Tale of the Man of Lawe; The Pardoneres Tale; The Second Nonnes Tale; The Chanouns Yemannes Tale. By W. W. SKEAT, Litt.D. *New Edition.* Extra fcap. 8vo, 4*s.* 6*d.*

V. Minor Poems. Edited by W. W. SKEAT, Litt.D. Crown 8vo, 10*s.* 6*d.*

VI. The Legend of Good Women. Edited by W. W. SKEAT, Litt.D. Crown 8vo, 6*s.*

Langland, W. The Vision of William concerning Piers the Plowman, in three Parallel Texts; together with Richard the Redeless. By WILLIAM LANGLAND (about 1362–1399 A.D.). Edited from numerous Manuscripts, with Preface, Notes, and a Glossary, by W. W. SKEAT, Litt.D. 2 vols. 8vo, 1*l.* 11*s.* 6*d.*

—— The Vision of William concerning Piers the Plowman, by WILLIAM LANGLAND. Edited, with Notes, by W. W. SKEAT, Litt.D. *Sixth Edition.* Extra fcap. 8vo, 4*s.* 6*d.*

Gamelyn, The Tale of. Edited, with Notes, Glossary, &c., by W. W. SKEAT, Litt.D. Extra fcap. 8vo, stiff covers, 1*s.* 6*d.*

WYCLIFFE.

I. The Books of Job, Psalms, Proverbs, Ecclesiastes, and the Song of Solomon: according to the Wycliffite Version made by NICHOLAS DE HEREFORD, about A.D. 1381, and Revised by JOHN PURVEY, about A.D. 1388. With Introduction and Glossary by W. W. SKEAT, Litt.D. Extra fcap. 8vo, 3*s*. 6*d*.

II. The New Testament in English, according to the Version by JOHN WYCLIFFE, about A.D. 1380, and Revised by JOHN PURVEY, about A.D. 1388. With Introduction and Glossary by W. W. SKEAT, Litt.D. Extra fcap. 8vo, 6*s*.

Minot (Laurence). Poems. Edited, with Introduction and Notes, by JOSEPH HALL, M.A., Head Master of the Hulme Grammar School, Manchester. Extra fcap. 8vo, 4*s*. 6*d*.

Spenser's Faery Queene. Books I and II. Designed chiefly for the use of Schools. With Introduction and Notes by G. W. KITCHIN, D.D., and Glossary by A. L. MAYHEW, M.A. Extra fcap. 8vo, 2*s*. 6*d*. each.

Hooker. Ecclesiastical Polity, Book I. Edited by R. W. CHURCH, M.A. Extra fcap. 8vo, 2*s*. [See also p. 53.]

OLD ENGLISH DRAMA.

I. York Plays. The Plays performed by the Crafts or Mysteries of York, on the day of Corpus Christi, in the 14th, 15th, and 16th centuries; now first printed from the unique manuscript in the library of Lord Ashburnham. Edited, with Introduction and Glossary, by LUCY TOULMIN SMITH. 8vo, 1*l*. 1*s*.

II. English Miracle Plays, Moralities, and Interludes. Specimens of the Pre-Elizabethan Drama. Edited, with an Introduction, Notes, and Glossary, by ALFRED W. POLLARD, M.A. Crown 8vo, 7*s*. 6*d*.

III. The Pilgrimage to Parnassus, with the Two Parts of the Return from Parnassus. Three Comedies performed in St. John's College, Cambridge, A.D. MDXCVII–MDCI. Edited from MSS. by W. D. MACRAY, M.A., F.S.A. Medium 8vo, bevelled boards, gilt top, 8*s*. 6*d*.

IV. Marlowe's Edward II. With Introduction, Notes, &c. By O. W. TANCOCK, M.A. *Second Edition.* Extra fcap. 8vo, stiff covers, 2*s*.; cloth, 3*s*.

V. Marlowe and Greene. Marlowe's Tragical History of Dr. Faustus, and Greene's Honourable History of Friar Bacon and Friar Bungay. Edited by A. W. WARD, Litt. D. *New and enlarged Edition.* Crown 8vo, 6*s*. 6*d*.

SHAKESPEARE. Select Plays. Extra fcap. 8vo, stiff covers.

Edited by W. G. Clark, M.A., and W. Aldis Wright, D.C.L.

The Merchant of Venice. 1*s.* Macbeth. 1*s.* 6*d.*
Richard the Second. 1*s.* 6*d.* Hamlet. 2*s.*

Edited by W. Aldis Wright, D.C.L.

The Tempest. 1*s.* 6*d.* Midsummer Night's Dream. 1*s.* 6*d.*
As You Like It. 1*s.* 6*d.* Coriolanus. 2*s.* 6*d.*
Julius Caesar. 2*s.* Henry the Fifth. 2*s.*
Richard the Third. 2*s.* 6*d.* Twelfth Night. 1*s.* 6*d.*
King Lear. 1*s.* 6*d.* King John. 1*s.* 6*d.*
Henry the Eighth. 2*s.*

Shakespeare as a Dramatic Artist; a popular Illustration of the Principles of Scientific Criticism. By R. G. Moulton, M.A. *Third Edition, Enlarged.* Crown 8vo, 7*s.* 6*d.*

Bacon.

I. Advancement of Learning. Edited by W. Aldis Wright, D.C.L. *Third Edition.* Extra fcap. 8vo, 4*s.* 6*d.*

II. The Essays. Edited, with Introduction and Illustrative Notes, by S. H. Reynolds, M.A. 8vo, half-bound, 12*s.* 6*d.*

MILTON.

I. Areopagitica. With Introduction and Notes. By John W. Hales, M.A. *Third Edition.* Extra fcap. 8vo, 3*s.*

II. Poems. Edited by R. C. Browne, M.A. In two Volumes. *New Edition, Revised.* Extra fcap. 8vo, 6*s.* 6*d.*

Sold separately, Vol. I, 4*s.*; Vol. II, 3*s.*

In paper covers:

Lycidas, 3*d.* L'Allegro, 3*d.* Comus, 6*d.*

Edited with Notes, by O. Elton, B.A.

Lycidas, 6*d.* L'Allegro, 4*d.* Il Penseroso, 4*d.* Comus, 1*s.*

III. Paradise Lost. Book I. Edited by H. C. Beeching, M.A. Extra fcap. 8vo, stiff covers, 1*s.* 6*d.*; in Parchment, 3*s.* 6*d.*

IV. Paradise Lost. Book II. Edited by E. K. Chambers, B.A. Extra fcap. 8vo, 1*s.* 6*d.*

Books I and II combined, 2*s.* 6*d.*

V. Samson Agonistes. Edited, with Introduction and Notes, by J. Churton Collins, M.A. Extra fcap. 8vo, stiff covers, 1*s.*

Milton's Prosody. By Robert Bridges. Small 4to, 8*s.* 6*d.* *net.*

Bunyan.

I. The Pilgrim's Progress, Grace Abounding, Relation of the Imprisonment of Mr. JOHN BUNYAN. Edited, with Biographical Introduction and Notes, by E. VENABLES, M.A. Extra fcap. 8vo, cloth, 3*s*. 6*d*.; in Parchment, 4*s*. 6*d*.

II. The Holy War, and The Heavenly Footman. Edited by MABEL PEACOCK. Extra fcap. 8vo, 3*s*. 6*d*.

Fuller. Wise Words and Quaint Counsels of Thomas Fuller. Selected by AUGUSTUS JESSOPP, D.D. Crown 8vo, 6*s*.

Clarendon.

I. History of the Rebellion. Book VI. Edited by T. ARNOLD, M.A. Extra fcap. 8vo, 4*s*. 6*d*.

II. Characters and Episodes of the Great Rebellion. Selections from Clarendon. Edited by G. BOYLE, M.A., Dean of Salisbury. Crown 8vo, gilt top, 7*s*. 6*d*. [See also p. 55.]

Dryden. Select Poems. (Stanzas on the Death of Oliver Cromwell; Astraea Redux; Annus Mirabilis; Absalom and Achitophel; Religio Laici; The Hind and the Panther.) Edited by W. D. CHRISTIE, M.A. *Fifth Edition.* Revised by C. H. FIRTH, M.A. Extra fcap. 8vo, 3*s*. 6*d*.

—— An Essay of Dramatic Poesy. Edited, with Notes, by THOMAS ARNOLD, M.A. Extra fcap. 8vo, 3*s*. 6*d*.

Locke. Conduct of the Understanding. Edited, with Introduction, Notes, &c., by T. FOWLER, D.D. *Third Edition.* Extra fcap. 8vo, 2*s*. 6*d*.

Addison. Selections from Papers in the Spectator. With Notes. By T. ARNOLD, M.A. Extra fcap. 8vo, 4*s*. 6*d*.; in Parchment, 6*s*.

Steele. Selections from the Tatler, Spectator, and Guardian. Edited by AUSTIN DOBSON. Extra fcap. 8vo, 5*s*.; in Parchment, 7*s*. 6*d*.

Swift. Selections from his Works. Edited, with Life, Introductions, and Notes, by HENRY CRAIK. Two Vols. Crown 8vo, cloth extra, 15*s*.

Each volume may be had separately, price 7s. 6d.

Pope. Select Works. With Introduction and Notes. By MARK PATTISON, B.D.

I. Essay on Man. *Sixth Edition.* Extra fcap. 8vo, 1*s*. 6*d*.

II. Satires and Epistles. *Fourth Edition.* Extra fcap. 8vo, 2*s*.

Parnell. The Hermit. Paper coyers, 2*d*.

Thomson. The Seasons, and The Castle of Indolence. Edited by J. LOGIE ROBERTSON, M.A. Extra fcap. 8vo, 4*s*. 6*d*.

—— The Castle of Indolence. By the same Editor. Extra fcap. 8vo, 1*s*. 6*d*.

Gray. Selected Poems. Edited by EDMUND GOSSE, M.A. Extra fcap. 8vo. In Parchment, 3*s.*

—— *The same*, together with Supplementary Notes for Schools, by FOSTER WATSON, M.A. Stiff covers, 1*s.* 6*d.*

—— Elegy, and Ode on Eton College. Paper covers, 2*d.*

Chesterfield. Lord Chesterfield's Worldly Wisdom. Selections from his Letters and Characters. Edited by G. BIRKBECK HILL, D.C.L. Crown 8vo, 6*s.*

Goldsmith.

I. Selected Poems. Edited with Introduction and Notes, by AUSTIN DOBSON. Extra fcap. 8vo, 3*s.* 6*d.*; in Parchment, 4*s.* 6*d.*

II. The Traveller. Edited by G. BIRKBECK HILL, D.C.L. Stiff covers, 1*s.*

III. The Deserted Village. Paper covers, 2*d.*

JOHNSON.

I. Rasselas. Edited, with Introduction and Notes, by G. BIRKBECK HILL, D.C.L. Extra fcap. 8vo, bevelled boards, 3*s.* 6*d.*; in Parchment, 4*s.* 6*d.*

II. Rasselas; Lives of Dryden and Pope. Edited by ALFRED MILNES, M.A. (London). Extra fcap. 8vo, 4*s.* 6*d.*; or Lives of DRYDEN and POPE only, stiff covers, 2*s.* 6*d.*

III. Life of Milton. Edited by C. H. FIRTH, M.A. Extra fcap. 8vo, cloth, 2*s.* 6*d.*; stiff covers, 1*s.* 6*d.*

IV. Wit and Wisdom of Samuel Johnson. Edited by G. BIRKBECK HILL, D.C.L. Crown 8vo, 7*s.* 6*d.*

V. Vanity of Human Wishes. With Notes, by E. J. PAYNE, M.A. Paper covers, 4*d.*

VI. Letters of Samuel Johnson, LL.D. Collected and Edited by G. BIRKBECK HILL, D.C.L. 2 vols. Medium 8vo, half-roan, 28*s.*

BOSWELL.

Boswell's Life of Johnson. With the Journal of a Tour to the Hebrides. Edited by G. BIRKBECK HILL, D.C.L., Pembroke College. 6 vols. Medium 8vo, half-bound, 3*l.* 3*s.*

Cowper. Edited, with Life, Introductions, and Notes, by H. T. GRIFFITH, B.A.

I. The Didactic Poems of 1782, with Selections from the Minor Pieces, A.D. 1779–1783. Extra fcap. 8vo, 3*s.*

II. The Task, with Tirocinium, and Selections from the Minor Poems, A.D. 1784–1799. *Second Edition.* Extra fcap. 8vo, 3*s.*

Burke. Select Works. Edited, with Introduction and Notes, by E. J. PAYNE, M.A.

I. Thoughts on the Present Discontents; the two Speeches on America. *Second Edition.* Extra fcap. 8vo, 4*s.* 6*d.*

II. Reflections on the French Revolution. *Second Edition.* Extra fcap. 8vo, 5*s.*

III. Four Letters on the Proposals for Peace with the Regicide Directory of France. *Second Edition.* Extra fcap. 8vo, 5*s.*

Burns. Selected Poems. Edited, with Introduction, Notes, and a Glossary, by J. LOGIE ROBERTSON, M.A. Crown 8vo, 6*s.*

Keats. Hyperion, Book I. With Notes by W. T. ARNOLD, B.A. Paper covers, 4*d.*

Byron. Childe Harold. With Introduction and Notes, by H. F. TOZER, M.A. *Second Edition.* Extra fcap. 8vo, 3*s.* 6*d.*; in Parchment, 5*s.*

Scott. Lady of the Lake. Edited, with Preface and Notes, by W. MINTO, M.A. Extra fcap. 8vo, 3*s.* 6*d.*

—— Lay of the Last Minstrel. By the same Editor. With Map. *Second Edition.* Extra fcap. 8vo, 2*s.*; in parchment, 3*s.* 6*d.*

—— Lay of the Last Minstrel. Introduction and Canto I, with Preface and Notes, by the same Editor. 6*d.*

—— Lord of the Isles. Edited, with Introduction and Notes, by THOMAS BAYNE. Extra fcap. 8vo, 3*s.* 6*d.*

—— Marmion. Edited, with Introduction and Notes, by T. BAYNE. Extra fcap. 8vo, 3*s.* 6*d.*

Shelley. Adonais. Edited, with Introduction and Notes, by W. M. ROSSETTI. Crown 8vo, 5*s.*

Campbell. Gertrude of Wyoming. Edited, with Introduction and Notes, by H. MACAULAY FITZGIBBON, M.A. *Second Edition.* Extra fcap. 8vo, 1*s.*

Wordsworth. The White Doe of Rylstone, &c. Edited by WILLIAM KNIGHT, LL.D. Extra fcap. 8vo, 2*s.* 6*d.*

Shairp. Aspects of Poetry; being Lectures delivered at Oxford, by J. C. SHAIRP, LL.D. Crown 8vo, 10*s.* 6*d.*

Palgrave. The Treasury of Sacred Song. With Notes Explanatory and Biographical. By F. T. PALGRAVE, M.A. *Thirteenth Thousand.* Extra fcap. 8vo, 4*s.* 6*d.*

SECTION III.

EUROPEAN LANGUAGES, MEDIAEVAL AND MODERN.

(1) FRENCH AND ITALIAN.

Brachet's Etymological Dictionary of the French Language. Translated by G. W. KITCHIN, D.D. *Third Edition.* Crown 8vo, 7*s*. 6*d*.

—— Historical Grammar of the French Language. Translated by G. W. KITCHIN, D.D. *Seventh Edition.* Extra fcap. 8vo, 3*s*. 6*d*.

Saintsbury. Primer of French Literature. By GEORGE SAINTSBURY, M.A. *Third Edition, Revised.* Extra fcap. 8vo, 2*s*.

—— Short History of French Literature. *Fourth Edition.* Crown 8vo, 10*s*. 6*d*.

—— Specimens of French Literature, from Villon to Hugo. *Second Edition.* Crown 8vo, 9*s*.

Song of Dermot and the Earl. An Old French Poem. Edited, with Translation, Notes, &c., by G. H. ORPEN. Extra fcap. 8vo, 8*s*. 6*d*.

Toynbee. Specimens of Old French (ix–xv centuries). With Introduction, Notes, and Glossary. By PAGET TOYNBEE, M.A. Crown 8vo, 16*s*.

Beaumarchais' Le Barbier de Séville. Edited, with Introduction and Notes, by AUSTIN DOBSON. Extra fcap. 8vo, 2*s*. 6*d*.

Corneille's Horace. Edited, with Introduction and Notes, by GEORGE SAINTSBURY, M.A. Extra fcap. 8vo, 2*s*. 6*d*.

Molière's Les Précieuses Ridicules. Edited, with Introduction and Notes, by ANDREW LANG, M.A. *Second Edition.* Extra fcap. 8vo, 1*s*. 6*d*.

Musset's On ne badine pas avec l'Amour, and Fantasio. Edited, with Prolegomena, Notes, &c., by W. H. POLLOCK. Extra fcap. 8vo, 2*s*.

Racine's Esther. Edited, with Introduction and Notes, by GEORGE SAINTSBURY, M.A. Extra fcap. 8vo, *2s.*

Voltaire's Mérope. Edited, with Introduction and Notes, by GEORGE SAINTSBURY, M.A. Extra fcap. 8vo, *2s.*

*** *The above six Plays may be had in ornamental case, and bound in Imitation Parchment, price 12s. 6d.*

Molière. Le Misanthrope. Edited by H. W. G. MARKHEIM, M.A. Extra fcap. 8vo, *3s. 6d.*

MASSON'S FRENCH CLASSICS.

Edited by Gustave Masson, B.A.

Corneille's Cinna. With Notes, Glossary, &c. Extra fcap. 8vo, *2s.*; stiff covers, *1s. 6d.*

Louis XIV and his Contemporaries; as described in Extracts from the best Memoirs of the Seventeenth Century. With English Notes, Genealogical Tables, &c. Extra fcap. 8vo, *2s. 6d.*

Maistre, Xavier de, &c. Voyage autour de ma Chambre, by XAVIER DE MAISTRE; Ourika, by MADAME DE DURAS; Le Vieux Tailleur, by MM. ERCKMANN-CHATRIAN; La Veillée de Vincennes, by ALFRED DE VIGNY; Les Jumeaux de l'Hôtel Corneille, by EDMOND ABOUT; Mésaventures d'un Écolier, by RODOLPHE TÖPFFER. *Third Edition, Revised.* Extra fcap. 8vo, *2s. 6d.*

—— Voyage autour de ma Chambre. Limp, *1s. 6d.*

Molière's Les Fourberies de Scapin, and **Racine's** Athalie. With Voltaire's Life of Molière. Extra fcap. 8vo, *2s. 6d.*

—— Les Fourberies de Scapin. With Voltaire's Life of Molière. Extra fcap. 8vo, stiff covers, *1s. 6d.*

—— Les Femmes Savantes. With Notes, Glossary, &c. Extra fcap. 8vo, cloth, *2s.*; stiff covers, *1s. 6d.*

Racine's Andromaque, and **Corneille's** Le Menteur. With LOUIS RACINE'S Life of his Father. Extra fcap. 8vo, *2s. 6d.*

Regnard's Le Joueur, and **Brueys and Palaprat's** Le Grondeur. Extra fcap. 8vo, *2s. 6d.*

Sévigné, Madame de, and her chief Contemporaries. Selections from their Correspondence. Extra fcap. 8vo, *3s.*

Blouët. L'Éloquence de la Chaire et de la Tribune Françaises. Edited by PAUL BLOUËT, B.A. Vol. I. Sacred Oratory. Extra fcap. 8vo, 2*s*. 6*d*.

Gautier, Théophile. Scenes of Travel. Selected and Edited by GEORGE SAINTSBURY, M.A. *Second Edition.* Extra fcap. 8vo, 2*s*.

Perrault's Popular Tales. Edited from the Original Editions, with Introduction, &c., by A. LANG, M.A. Extra fcap. 8vo, 5*s*. 6*d*.

Quinet's Lettres à sa Mère. Selected and Edited by GEORGE SAINTSBURY, M.A. Extra fcap. 8vo, 2*s*.

Sainte-Beuve. Selections from the Causeries du Lundi. Edited by GEORGE SAINTSBURY, M.A. Extra fcap. 8vo, 2*s*.

A Primer of Italian Literature. By F. J. SNELL, M.A. Extra fcap. 8vo, 3*s*. 6*d*.

Dante. Selections from the Inferno. With Introduction and Notes. By H. B. COTTERILL, B.A. Extra fcap. 8vo, 4*s*. 6*d*.

Tasso. La Gerusalemme Liberata. Cantos i, ii. With Introduction and Notes. By the same Editor. Extra fcap. 8vo, 2*s*. 6*d*.

(2) GERMAN AND GOTHIC.

Max Müller. The German Classics, from the Fourth to the Nineteenth Century. With Biographical Notices, Translations into Modern German, and Notes. By F. MAX MÜLLER, M.A. A New Edition, Revised, Enlarged, and Adapted to WILHELM SCHERER'S 'History of German Literature,' by F. LICHTENSTEIN. 2 vols. Crown 8vo, 21*s*.

Scherer. A History of German Literature by WILHELM SCHERER. Translated from the Third German Edition by Mrs. F. C. CONYBEARE. Edited by F. MAX MÜLLER. 2 vols. 8vo, 21*s*.
Or, separately, 10*s*. 6*d*. each volume.

—— A History of German Literature, from the Accession of Frederick the Great to the Death of Goethe. By the same. Crown 8vo, 5*s*.

Skeat. The Gospel of St. Mark in Gothic. By W. W. SKEAT, Litt.D. Extra fcap. 8vo, cloth, 4*s*.

Wright. An Old High German Primer. With Grammar, Notes, and Glossary. By JOSEPH WRIGHT, Ph.D. Extra fcap. 8vo, 3*s*. 6*d*.

—— A Middle High German Primer. With Grammar, Notes, and Glossary. By the same Author. Extra fcap. 8vo, 3*s*. 6*d*.

—— A Primer of the Gothic Language. With Grammar, Notes, and Glossary. By the same Author. Extra fcap. 8vo, 4*s*. 6*d*.

LANGE'S GERMAN COURSE.

By HERMANN LANGE, Lecturer on French and German at the Manchester Technical School, and Lecturer on German at the Manchester Athenaeum.

I. Germans at Home; a Practical Introduction to German Conversation, with an Appendix containing the Essentials of German Grammar. *Third Edition.* 8vo, 2*s.* 6*d.*

II. German Manual; a German Grammar, Reading Book, and a Handbook of German Conversation. *Second Edition.* 8vo, 7*s.* 6*d.*

III. Grammar of the German Language. 8vo, 3*s.* 6*d.*

IV. German Composition; A Theoretical and Practical Guide to the Art of Translating English Prose into German. *Third Edition.* 8vo, 4*s.* 6*d.*

*** *A Key to the above,* price 5*s. net.*

German Spelling; A Synopsis of the Changes which it has undergone through the Government Regulations of 1880. 6*d.*

BUCHHEIM'S GERMAN CLASSICS.

Edited, with Biographical, Historical, and Critical Introductions, Arguments (to the Dramas), and Complete Commentaries, by C. A. Buchheim, *Phil. Doc., Professor in King's College, London.*

Becker (the Historian). Friedrich der Grosse. Edited, with Notes, an Historical Introduction, and a Map. *Second Edition.* 3*s.* 6*d.*

Goethe:

(*a*) Egmont. A Tragedy. *Fourth Edition.* 3*s.*
(*b*) Iphigenie auf Tauris. A Drama. *Third Edition.* 3*s.*

Heine:

(*a*) Prosa: being Selections from his Prose Writings. *Second Edition.* 4*s.* 6*d.*
(*b*) Harzreise. *Second Edition.* 2*s.* 6*d.*

Lessing:

(*a*) Nathan der Weise. A Dramatic Poem. *Second Edition.* 4*s.* 6*d.*
(*b*) Minna von Barnhelm. A Comedy. *Fifth Edition.* 3*s.* 6*d.*

Schiller:

(*a*) Wilhelm Tell. A Drama. Large Edition. With Map. *Seventh Edition.* 3*s.* 6*d.*
(*b*) Wilhelm Tell. School Edition. With Map. *Fourth Edition.* 2*s.*
(*c*) Historische Skizzen. With Map. *Fifth Edition.* 2*s.* 6*d.*
(*d*) Jungfrau von Orleans. 4*s.* 6*d.*
(*e*) Maria Stuart. [*Immediately.*]

Modern German Reader. A Graduated Collection of Extracts from Modern German Authors:—

Part I. **Prose Extracts.** With English Notes, a Grammatical Appendix, and a complete Vocabulary. *Seventh Edition.* 2*s.* 6*d.*

Part II. **Extracts in Prose and Poetry.** With English Notes and an Index. *Second Edition.* 2*s.* 6*d.*

German Poetry for Beginners. Edited with English Notes and a complete Vocabulary, by EMMA S. BUCHHEIM. Extra fcap. 8vo, 2*s.*

Elementary German Prose Composition. With Notes, Vocabulary, &c. By the same Editor. Cloth, 2*s.*; stiff covers, 1*s.* 6*d.*

Chamisso. Peter Schlemihl's Wundersame Geschichte. Edited with Notes and a complete Vocabulary, by EMMA S. BUCHHEIM. *Fourth Thousand.* Extra fcap. 8vo, 2*s.*

Lessing. The Laokoon; with English Notes by A. HAMANN, Phil. Doc., M.A. Revised, with an Introduction, by L. E. UPCOTT, M.A. Extra fcap. 8vo, 4*s.* 6*d.*

Niebuhr: Griechische Heroen-Geschichten (Tales of Greek Heroes). With English Notes and Vocabulary, by EMMA S. BUCHHEIM. Second Revised Edition. Extra fcap. 8vo, cloth, 2*s.*; stiff covers, 1*s.* 6*d.* Edition A. *Text in German Type.* Edition B. *Text in Roman Type.*

Riehl's Seines Vaters Sohn *and* Gespensterkampf. Edited with Notes by H. T. GERRANS. Extra fcap. 8vo, 2*s.*

Schiller's Wilhelm Tell. Translated into English Verse by E. MASSIE, M.A. Extra fcap. 8vo, 5*s.*

(3) SCANDINAVIAN.

Cleasby and Vigfússon. An Icelandic-English Dictionary, based on the MS. collections of the late RICHARD CLEASBY. Enlarged and completed by G. VIGFÚSSON, M.A. With an Introduction, and Life of Richard Cleasby, by G. WEBBE DASENT, D.C.L. 4to, 3*l.* 7*s.*

Sargent. Grammar of the Dano-Norwegian Language. By J. Y. SARGENT, M.A. Crown 8vo, 7*s.* 6*d.*

Sweet. Icelandic Primer, with Grammar, Notes, and Glossary. By HENRY SWEET, M.A. Extra fcap. 8vo, 3*s.* 6*d.*

Vigfússon. Sturlunga Saga, including the Islendinga Saga of Lawman STURLA THORDSSON and other works. Edited by GUÐBRAND VIGFÚSSON, M.A. In 2 vols. 8vo, 2*l.* 2*s.*

Vigfússon and Powell. Icelandic Prose Reader, with Notes, Grammar, and Glossary. By G. VIGFÚSSON, M.A., and F. YORK POWELL, M.A. Extra fcap. 8vo, 10*s.* 6*d.*

—— Corpvs Poeticvm Boreale. The Poetry of the Old Northern Tongue, from the Earliest Times to the Thirteenth Century. Edited, classified, and translated, with Introduction, Excursus, and Notes, by GUÐBRAND VIGFÚSSON, M.A., and F. YORK POWELL, M.A. 2 vols. 8vo, 2*l.* 2*s.*

SECTION IV.

CLASSICAL LANGUAGES.

(1) LATIN.

STANDARD WORKS AND EDITIONS.

King and **Cookson**. The Principles of Sound and Inflexion, as illustrated in the Greek and Latin Languages. By J. E. KING, M.A., and CHRISTOPHER COOKSON, M.A. 8vo, 18*s*.

Lewis and **Short**. A Latin Dictionary, founded on Andrews' edition of Freund's Latin Dictionary, revised, enlarged, and in great part rewritten by CHARLTON T. LEWIS, Ph.D., and CHARLES SHORT, LL.D. 4to, 1*l*. 5*s*.

Merry. Selected Fragments of Roman Poetry. Edited with Introduction and Notes by W. W. MERRY, D.D. Crown 8vo, 6*s*. 6*d*.

Nettleship. Contributions to Latin Lexicography. By HENRY NETTLESHIP, M.A. 8vo, 21*s*.

—— Lectures and Essays on Subjects connected with Latin Scholarship and Literature. Crown 8vo, 7*s*. 6*d*.

—— The Roman Satura. 8vo, sewed, 1*s*.

—— Ancient Lives of Vergil. 8vo, sewed, 2*s*.

Papillon. Manual of Comparative Philology. By T. L. PAPILLON, M.A. *Third Edition*. Crown 8vo, 6*s*.

Pinder. Selections from the less known Latin Poets. By NORTH PINDER, M.A. 8vo, 15*s*.

Rushforth. Latin Historical Inscriptions, illustrating the History of the Early Empire. By G. McN. RUSHFORTH, M.A. 8vo, 10*s*. *net*.

Sellar. Roman Poets of the Republic. By W. Y. SELLAR, M.A. *Third Edition*. Crown 8vo, 10*s*.

—— Roman Poets of the Augustan Age. VIRGIL. *Second Edition*. Crown 8vo, 9*s*.

—— —— HORACE and the ELEGIAC POETS. With a Memoir of the Author by ANDREW LANG, M.A., and a Portrait. 8vo, cloth, 14*s*.

Wordsworth. Fragments and Specimens of Early Latin. With Introductions and Notes. By J. WORDSWORTH, D.D. 8vo, 18*s*.

Avianus. The Fables. Edited, with Prolegomena, Critical Apparatus, Commentary, &c., by R. ELLIS, M.A., LL.D. 8vo, *8s. 6d.*

Catulli Veronensis Liber. Iterum recognovit, apparatum criticum prolegomena appendices addidit, ROBINSON ELLIS, A.M. 8vo, *16s.*

Catullus, a Commentary on. By ROBINSON ELLIS, M.A. *Second Edition.* 8vo, 18s.

Cicero. De Oratore Libri Tres. With Introduction and Notes. By A. S. WILKINS, Litt.D. 8vo, 18s.

Also separately:—

Book I, *Second Edition. 7s. 6d.* Book II, *Second Edition.* 5s. Book III, 6s.

—— Philippic Orations. With Notes. By J. R. KING, M.A. *Second Edition.* 8vo, *10s. 6d.*

—— Select Letters. With English Introductions, Notes, and Appendices. By ALBERT WATSON, M.A. *Fourth Edition.* 8vo, 18s.

Horace. With a Commentary. Vol. I. The Odes, Carmen Seculare, and Epodes. By E. C. WICKHAM, M.A. *Second Edition.* 8vo, 12s.

—— Vol. II. The Satires, Epistles, and De Arte Poetica. By the same Editor. 8vo, 12s.

Livy, Book I. With Introduction, Historical Examination, and Notes. By J. R. SEELEY, M.A. *Third Edition.* 8vo, 6s.

Manilius. Noctes Manilianae; sive Dissertationes in Astronomica Manilii. Accedvnt Coniectvrae in Germanici Aratea. Scripsit R. ELLIS. Crown 8vo, 6s.

Ovid. P. Ovidii Nasonis Ibis. Ex Novis Codicibus edidit, Scholia Vetera Commentarium cum Prolegomenis Appendice Indice addidit, R. ELLIS, A.M. 8vo, *10s. 6d.*

—— P. Ovidi Nasonis Tristium Libri V. Recensuit S. G. OWEN, A.M. 8vo, 16s.

Persius. The Satires. With a Translation and Commentary. By JOHN CONINGTON, M.A. Edited by HENRY NETTLESHIP, M.A. *Third Edition.* 8vo, 8s. 6d.

Plautus. Rudens. Edited, with Critical and Explanatory Notes, by E. A. SONNENSCHEIN, M.A. 8vo, 8s. 6d.

—— Bentley's Plautine Emendations. From his copy of Gronovius. By E. A. SONNENSCHEIN, M.A. (Anecdota Oxon.) 2s. 6d.

Quintilian. Institutionis Oratoriae Liber X. Edited by W. PETERSON, M.A. 8vo, *12s. 6d.*

Scriptores Latini rei Metricae. Ed. T. GAISFORD, S.T.P. 8vo, 5s.

Tacitus. The Annals. Books I–VI. Edited, with Introduction and Notes, by H. FURNEAUX, M.A. 8vo, 18*s*.

—— Books XI–XVI. By the same Editor. 8vo, 20*s*.

—— Dialogus De Oratoribus. A Revised Text, with Introductory Essays and Critical and Explanatory Notes. By W. PETERSON, M.A., LL.D. 8vo, 10*s*. 6*d*.

LATIN EDUCATIONAL WORKS.

GRAMMARS, EXERCISE BOOKS, &c.

ALLEN.

Rudimenta Latina. Comprising Accidence, and Exercises of a very Elementary Character, for the use of Beginners. By JOHN BARROW ALLEN, M.A. Extra fcap. 8vo, 2*s*.

An Elementary Latin Grammar. By the same Author. *Ninety-Seventh Thousand.* Extra fcap. 8vo, 2*s*. 6*d*.

A First Latin Exercise Book. By the same Author. *Seventh Edition.* Extra fcap. 8vo, 2*s*. 6*d*.

A Second Latin Exercise Book. By the same Author. *Second Edition.* Extra fcap. 8vo, 3*s*. 6*d*.

*** A Key to First and Second Latin Exercise Books, in one volume, price 5*s*. *net*. Supplied *to Teachers only*, on application to the Secretary, Clarendon Press.

An Introduction to Latin Syntax. By W. S. GIBSON, M.A. Extra fcap. 8vo, 2*s*.

First Latin Reader. By T. J. NUNNS, M.A. *Third Edition.* Extra fcap. 8vo, 2*s*.

A Latin Prose Primer. By J. Y. SARGENT, M.A. Extra fcap. 8vo, 2*s*. 6*d*.

Passages for Translation into Latin. Selected by J. Y. SARGENT, M.A. *Seventh Edition.* Extra fcap. 8vo, 2*s*. 6*d*.

*** A Key to the above, price 5*s*. *net*. Supplied *to Teachers only*, on application to the Secretary, Clarendon Press.

Latin Prose Composition. By G. G. RAMSAY, M.A., LL.D. *Third Edition.* Extra fcap. 8vo.

Vol. I. *Syntax, Exercises with Notes, &c.* 4*s*. 6*d*.

Vol. II. *Passages of Graduated Difficulty for Translation into Latin, together with an Introduction on Continuous Prose.* 4*s*. 6*d*.

*** A Key to Vol. I of the above, price 5*s*. *net*. Supplied *to Teachers only*, on application to the Secretary, Clarendon Press.

Hints and Helps for Latin Elegiacs. By H. LEE-WARNER, M.A. Extra fcap. 8vo, 3*s*. 6*d*.

*** A Key to the above, price 4*s*. 6*d*. *net*. Supplied *to Teachers only*, on application to the Secretary, Clarendon Press.

Reddenda Minora; or, Easy Passages, Latin and Greek, for Unseen Translation. For the use of Lower Forms. Composed and selected by C. S. JERRAM, M.A. *Third Edition*. Extra fcap. 8vo, 1*s*. 6*d*.

Anglice Reddenda; or, Extracts, Latin and Greek, for Unseen Translation. By C. S. JERRAM, M.A. *Fourth Edition*. Extra fcap. 8vo, 2*s*. 6*d*.

—— *Second Series*. By the same Editor. 3*s*.

Models and Exercises in Unseen Translation. By H. F. FOX, M.A., and T. M. BROMLEY, M.A. *Revised Edition*. Extra fcap. 8vo, 5*s*. 6*d*.

*** A Key to Passages quoted in the above, price 6*d*. Supplied *to Teachers only*, on application to the Secretary, Clarendon Press.

An Elementary Latin Dictionary. By CHARLTON T. LEWIS, Ph.D. Square 8vo, 7*s*. 6*d*.

A School Latin Dictionary. By CHARLTON T. LEWIS, Ph.D. Small 4to, 18*s*.

An Introduction to the Comparative Grammar of Greek and Latin. By J. E. KING, M.A., and C. COOKSON, M.A. Extra fcap. 8vo, 5*s*. 6*d*.

LATIN CLASSICS FOR SCHOOLS.

Caesar. The Commentaries (for Schools). With Notes and Maps. By CHARLES E. MOBERLY, M.A.

The Gallic War. *Second Edition*. Extra fcap. 8vo.

—— Books I and II, 2*s*.; III–V, 2*s*. 6*d*.; VI–VIII, 3*s*. 6*d*.

—— Books I–III, *stiff cover*, 2*s*.

The Civil War. Extra fcap. 8vo, 3*s*. 6*d*.

Catulli Veronensis Carmina Selecta, secundum recognitionem ROBINSON ELLIS, A.M. Extra fcap. 8vo, 3*s*. 6*d*.

CICERO. Selection of Interesting and Descriptive Passages. With Notes. By HENRY WALFORD, M.A. In three Parts. *Third Edition*. Extra fcap. 8vo, 4*s*. 6*d*.

Each Part separately, limp, 1*s*. 6*d*.

Part I. Anecdotes from Grecian and Roman History.

Part II. Omens and Dreams: Beauties of Nature.

Part III. Rome's Rule of her Provinces.

Cicero. De Amicitia. With Introduction and Notes. By St. George Stock, M.A. Extra fcap. 8vo, 3*s.*

—— De Senectute. Edited, with Introduction and Notes, by L. Huxley, M.A. Extra fcap. 8vo, 2*s.*

—— pro Cluentio. With Introduction and Notes. By W. Ramsay, M.A. Edited by G. G. Ramsay, M.A. *Second Edition.* Extra fcap. 8vo, 3*s.* 6*d.*

—— pro Marcello, pro Ligario, pro Rege Deiotaro. With Introduction and Notes. By W. Y. Fausset, M.A. Extra fcap. 8vo, 2*s.* 6*d.*

—— pro Milone. With Notes, &c. By A. B. Poynton, M.A. Extra fcap. 8vo, 2*s.* 6*d.*

—— pro Roscio. With Notes. By St. George Stock, M.A. Extra fcap. 8vo, 3*s.* 6*d.*

—— Select Orations (for Schools). In Verrem Actio Prima. De Imperio Gn. Pompeii. Pro Archia. Philippica IX. With Introduction and Notes by J. R. King, M.A. *Second Edition.* Extra fcap. 8vo, 2*s.* 6*d.*

—— In Q. Caecilium Divinatio, and In C. Verrem Actio Prima. With Introduction and Notes, by J. R. King, M.A. Extra fcap. 8vo, limp, 1*s.* 6*d.*

—— Speeches against Catilina. With Introduction and Notes, by E. A. Upcott, M.A. *Second Edition.* Extra fcap. 8vo, 2*s.* 6*d.*

—— Selected Letters (for Schools). With Notes. By the late C. E. Prichard, M.A., and E. R. Bernard, M.A. *Second Edition.* Extra fcap. 8vo, 3*s.*

—— Select Letters. Text. By Albert Watson, M.A. *Second Edition.* Extra fcap. 8vo, 4*s.*

Cornelius Nepos. With Notes. By Oscar Browning, M.A. *Third Edition.* Revised by W. R. Inge, M.A. Extra fcap. 8vo, 3*s.*

Horace. With a Commentary. (In a size suitable for the use of Schools.) Vol. I. The Odes, Carmen Seculare, and Epodes. By E. C. Wickham, M.A. *Second Edition.* Extra fcap. 8vo, 6*s.*

—— Odes, Book I. By the same Editor. Extra fcap. 8vo, 2*s.*

—— Selected Odes. With Notes for the use of a Fifth Form. By E. C. Wickham, M.A. Extra fcap. 8vo, 2*s.*

Juvenal. Thirteen Satires. Edited, with Introduction and Notes, by C. H. Pearson, M.A., and Herbert A. Strong, M.A., LL.D. *Second Edition.* Crown 8vo, 9*s.*

Livy. Books V–VII. With Introduction and Notes. By A. R. Cluer, B.A. *Second Edition.* Revised by P. E. Matheson, M.A. Extra fcap. 8vo, 5*s.*

—— Book V. By the same Editors. Extra fcap. 8vo, 2*s.* 6*d.*

—— Book VII. By the same Editors. Extra fcap. 8vo, 2*s.*

—— Books XXI–XXIII. With Introduction and Notes. By M. T. Tatham, M.A. *Second Edition, Enlarged.* Extra fcap. 8vo, 5*s.*

—— Book XXI. By the same Editor. Extra fcap. 8vo, 2*s.* 6*d.*

—— Book XXII. With Introduction, Notes, and Maps. By the same Editor. Extra fcap. 8vo, 2*s.* 6*d.*

—— Selections (for Schools). With Notes and Maps. By H. Lee-Warner, M.A. Extra fcap. 8vo. In Parts, limp, each 1*s.* 6*d.*

Part I. The Caudine Disaster.

Part II. Hannibal's Campaign in Italy.

Part III. The Macedonian War.

Ovid. Selections for the use of Schools. With Introductions and Notes, and an Appendix on the Roman Calendar. By W. Ramsay, M.A. Edited by G. G. Ramsay, M.A. *Third Edition.* Extra fcap. 8vo, 5*s.* 6*d.*

—— Tristia. Book I. The Text revised, with an Introduction and Notes. By S. G. Owen, B.A. *Second Edition.* Extra fcap. 8vo, 3*s.* 6*d.*

—— Tristia. Book III. With Introduction and Notes. By the same Editor. Extra fcap. 8vo, 2*s.*

Plautus. Captivi. Edited by Wallace M. Lindsay, M.A. Extra fcap. 8vo, 2*s.* 6*d.*

—— Trinummus. With Notes and Introductions. (Intended for the Higher Forms of Public Schools.) By C. E. Freeman, M.A., and A. Sloman, M.A. Extra fcap. 8vo, 3*s.*

Pliny. Selected Letters (for Schools). With Notes. By C. E. Prichard, M.A., and E. R. Bernard, M.A. *Third Edition.* Extra fcap. 8vo, 3*s.*

Quintilian. Institutionis Oratoriae. Liber X. By W. Peterson, M.A. Extra fcap. 8vo, 3*s.* 6*d.*

Sallust. With Introduction and Notes. By W. W. Capes, M.A. *Second Edition.* Extra fcap. 8vo, 4*s.* 6*d.*

Tacitus. The Annals. Books I–IV. Edited, with Introduction and Notes (for the use of Schools and Junior Students), by H. FURNEAUX, M.A. Extra fcap. 8vo, 5*s.*

—— The Annals. Book I. With Introduction and Notes, by the same Editor. Extra fcap. 8vo, limp, 2*s.*

Terence. Andria. With Notes and Introductions. By C. E. FREEMAN, M.A., and A. SLOMAN, M.A. Extra fcap. 8vo, 3*s.*

—— Adelphi. With Notes and Introductions. (Intended for the Higher Forms of Public Schools.) By A. SLOMAN, M.A. Extra fcap. 8vo, 3*s.*

—— Phormio. With Notes and Introductions. By A. SLOMAN, M.A. Extra fcap. 8vo, 3*s.*

Tibullus and **Propertius.** Selections. Edited by G. G. RAMSAY, M.A. (In one or two parts.) Extra fcap. 8vo, 6*s.*

Virgil. With an Introduction and Notes. By T. L. PAPILLON, M.A., and A. E. HAIGH, M.A. 2 vols. Crown 8vo, 12*s.*

—— Aeneid. By the same Editors. *In Four Parts.* Crown 8vo, 3*s. each.*

—— Bucolics and Georgics. By the same Editors. Crown 8vo, 3*s.* 6*d.*

—— Bucolics. Edited by C. S. JERRAM, M.A. Extra fcap. 8vo, 2*s.* 6*d.*

—— Georgics, Books I, II. By the same Editor. Extra fcap. 8vo, 2*s.* 6*d.*

—— Georgics, Books III, IV. By the same Editor. Extra fcap. 8vo, 2*s.* 6*d.*

—— Aeneid I. With Introduction and Notes. By the same Editor. Extra fcap. 8vo, limp, 1*s.* 6*d.*

—— Aeneid IX. Edited, with Introduction and Notes, by A. E. HAIGH, M.A. Extra fcap. 8vo, limp, 1*s.* 6*d.* In two Parts, 2*s.*

(2) GREEK.

STANDARD WORKS AND EDITIONS.

Allen. Notes on Abbreviations in Greek Manuscripts. By T. W. ALLEN, M.A., Queen's College, Oxford. Royal 8vo, 5*s.*

Chandler. A Practical Introduction to Greek Accentuation, by H. W. CHANDLER, M.A. *Second Edition.* 10*s.* 6*d.*

Haigh. The Attic Theatre. A Description of the Stage and Theatre of the Athenians, and of the Dramatic Performances at Athens. By A. E. HAIGH, M.A. 8vo, 12*s*. 6*d*.

Head. Historia Numorum: A Manual of Greek Numismatics. By BARCLAY V. HEAD, D.C.L. Royal 8vo, half-bound, 2*l*. 2*s*.

Hicks. A Manual of Greek Historical Inscriptions. By E. L. HICKS, M.A. 8vo, 10*s*. 6*d*.

King and **Cookson.** The Principles of Sound and Inflexion, as illustrated in the Greek and Latin Languages. By J. E. KING, M.A., and CHRISTOPHER COOKSON, M.A. 8vo, 18*s*.

Liddell and **Scott.** A Greek-English Lexicon, by H. G. LIDDELL, D.D., and ROBERT SCOTT, D.D. *Seventh Edition, Revised and Augmented throughout.* 4to, 1*l*. 16*s*.

Papillon. Manual of Comparative Philology. By T. L. PAPILLON, M.A. *Third Edition.* Crown 8vo, 6*s*.

Paton and **Hicks.** The Inscriptions of Cos. By W. R. PATON and E. L. HICKS. Royal 8vo, linen, with Map, 28*s*.

Veitch. Greek Verbs, Irregular and Defective. By W. VEITCH, LL.D. *Fourth Edition.* Crown 8vo, 10*s*. 6*d*.

Vocabulary, a copious Greek-English, compiled from the best authorities. 24mo, 3*s*.

Aeschinem et **Isocratem,** Scholia Graeca in. Edidit G. DINDORFIUS. 1852. 8vo, 4*s*.

Aeschines. See under **Oratores Attici,** and **Demosthenes.**

Aeschyli quae supersunt in Codice Laurentiano quoad effici potuit et ad cognitionem necesse est visum typis descripta edidit R. MERKEL. Small folio, 1*l*. 1*s*.

Aeschylus: Tragoediae et Fragmenta, ex recensione GUIL. DINDORFII. *Second Edition.* 1851. 8vo, 5*s*. 6*d*.

—— Annotationes GUIL. DINDORFII. Partes II. 1841. 8vo, 10*s*.

Anecdota Graeca Oxoniensia. Edidit J. A. CRAMER, S.T.P. Tomi IV. 1835. 8vo, 1*l*. 2*s*.

—— Graeca e Codd. MSS. Bibliothecae Regiae Parisiensis. Edidit J. A. CRAMER, S.T.P. Tomi IV. 1839. 8vo, 1*l*. 2*s*.

Apsinis et **Longini** Rhetorica. E Codicibus MSS. recensuit JOH. BAKIUS. 1849. 8vo, 3*s*.

Aristophanes. A Complete Concordance to the Comedies and Fragments. By HENRY DUNBAR, M.D. 4to, 1*l.* 1*s.*

—— J. Caravellae Index in Aristophanem. 8vo, 3*s.*

—— Comoediae et Fragmenta, ex recensione GUIL. DINDORFII. Tomi II. 1835. 8vo, 11*s.*

—— Annotationes GUIL. DINDORFII. Partes II. 8vo, 11*s.*

—— Scholia Graeca ex Codicibus aucta et emendata a GUIL. DINDORFIO. Partes III. 1838. 8vo, 1*l.*

ARISTOTLE.

—— Ex recensione IMMANUELIS BEKKERI. Accedunt Indices Sylburgiani. Tomi XI. 1837. 8vo, 2*l.* 10*s.*

The volumes (except vols. I and IX) may be had separately, price 5*s.* 6*d.* each.

—— **Ethica Nicomachea**, recognovit brevique Adnotatione critica instruxit I. BYWATER. 8vo, 6*s.*

—— **The same**, on 4to paper, for Marginal Notes, 10*s.* 6*d.*

—— Contributions to the Textual Criticism of Aristotle's Nicomachean Ethics. By INGRAM BYWATER. Stiff cover, 2*s.* 6*d.*

—— Notes on the Nicomachean Ethics of Aristotle. By J. A. STEWART, M.A. 2 vols. 8vo, 32*s.*

—— **The Politics**, with Introductions, Notes, &c., by W. L. NEWMAN, M.A., Fellow of Balliol College, Oxford. Vols. I and II. Medium 8vo, 28*s.*

—— **The Politics**, translated into English, with Introduction, Marginal Analysis, Notes, and Indices, by B. JOWETT, M.A. Medium 8vo. 2 vols. 21*s.*

—— **Aristotelian Studies.** I. On the Structure of the Seventh Book of the Nicomachean Ethics. By J. C. WILSON, M.A. 8vo, stiff covers, 5*s*

—— The English Manuscripts of the **Nicomachean Ethics**, described in relation to Bekker's Manuscripts and other Sources. By J. A. STEWART, M.A. (Anecdota Oxon.) Small 4to, 3*s.* 6*d.*

—— On the History of the process by which the **Aristotelian** Writings arrived at their present form. By R. SHUTE, M.A. 8vo, 7*s.* 6*d.*

—— **Physics.** Book VII. Collation of various MSS.; with Introduction by R. SHUTE, M.A. (Anecdota Oxon.) Small 4to, 2*s.*

Choerobosci Dictata in Theodosii Canones, necnon Epimerismi in Psalmos. E Codicibus MSS. edidit THOMAS GAISFORD, S.T.P. Tomi III. 8vo, 15*s.*

Demosthenes. Ex recensione GUIL. DINDORFII. Tomi IX. 8vo, 2*l.* 6*s.*

Separately:—

Textus, 1*l.* 1*s.* Annotationes, 15*s.* Scholia, 10*s.*

Demosthenes and Aeschines. The Orations of Demosthenes and Aeschines on the Crown. With Introductory Essays and Notes. By G. A. SIMCOX, M.A., and W. H. SIMCOX, M.A. 8vo, 12*s.*

Euripides. Tragoediae et Fragmenta, ex recensione GUIL. DINDORFII. Tomi II. 1833. 8vo, 10*s.*

—— Annotationes GUIL. DINDORFII. Partes II. 8vo, 10*s.*

—— Scholia Graeca, ex Codicibus aucta et emendata a GUIL. DINDORFIO. Tomi IV. 8vo, 1*l.* 16*s.*

—— Alcestis, ex recensione G. DINDORFII. 8vo, 2*s.* 6*d.*

Harpocrationis Lexicon. Ex recensione G. DINDORFII. Tomi II. 8vo, 10*s.* 6*d.*

Hephaestionis Enchiridion, Terentianus Maurus, Proclus, &c. Edidit T. GAISFORD, S.T.P. Tomi II. 10*s.*

Heracliti Ephesii Reliquiae. Recensuit I. BYWATER, M.A. Appendicis loco additae sunt Diogenis Laertii Vita Heracliti, Particulae Hippocratei De Diaeta Lib. I, Epistolae Heracliteae. 8vo, 6*s.*

Herodotus. Books V and VI. Terpsichore and Erato. Edited, with Notes and Appendices, by EVELYN ABBOTT, M.A., LL.D. 8vo, with two Maps, 10*s.* 6*d.*

HOMER.

—— A Complete Concordance to the Odyssey and Hymns of Homer; to which is added a Concordance to the Parallel Passages in the Iliad, Odyssey, and Hymns. By HENRY DUNBAR, M.D. 4to, 1*l.* 1*s.*

—— Seberi Index in Homerum. 1780. 8vo, 6*s.* 6*d.*

—— A Grammar of the Homeric Dialect. By D. B. MONRO, M.A. *Second Edition.* 8vo, 14*s.*

—— **Ilias**, cum brevi Annotatione C. G. HEYNII. Accedunt Scholia minora. Tomi II. 8vo, 15*s.*

HOMER (*continued*).

—— **Ilias**, ex rec. GUIL. DINDORFII. 8vo, 5*s.* 6*d.*

—— Scholia Graeca in Iliadem. Edited by W. DINDORF, after a new collation of the Venetian MSS. by D. B. MONRO, M.A., Provost of Oriel College. 4 vols. 8vo, 2*l.* 10*s.*

—— Scholia Graeca in Iliadem Townleyana. Recensuit ERNESTUS MAASS. 2 vols. 8vo, 1*l.* 16*s.*

—— **Odyssea**, ex rec. G. DINDORFII. 8vo, 5*s.* 6*d.*

—— Scholia Graeca in Odysseam. Edidit GUIL. DINDORFIUS. Tomi II. 8vo, 15*s.* 6*d.*

—— Odyssey. Books I–XII. Edited with English Notes, Appendices, &c. By W. W. MERRY, D.D., and the late JAMES RIDDELL, M.A. *Second Edition.* 8vo, 16*s.*

—— **Hymni Homerici.** Codicibus denuo collatis recensuit ALFREDUS GOODWIN. Small folio. With four Plates. 21*s. net.*

Oratores Attici, ex recensione BEKKERI:

I. Antiphon, Andocides, et Lysias. 8vo, 7*s.*

II. Isocrates. 8vo, 7*s.*

III. Isaeus, Aeschines, Lycurgus, Dinarchus, &c. 8vo, 7*s.*

Paroemiographi Graeci, quorum pars nunc primum ex Codd. MSS. vulgatur. Edidit T. GAISFORD, S.T.P. 8vo, 5*s.* 6*d.*

PLATO.

—— **Apology**, with a revised Text and English Notes, and a Digest of Platonic Idioms, by JAMES RIDDELL, M.A. 8vo, 8*s.* 6*d.*

—— **Philebus**, with a revised Text and English Notes, by EDWARD POSTE, M.A. 8vo, 7*s.* 6*d.*

—— **Sophistes** and **Politicus**, with a revised Text and English Notes, by L. CAMPBELL, M.A. 8vo, 18*s.*

—— **Theaetetus**, with a revised Text and English Notes, by L. CAMPBELL, M.A. *Second Edition.* 8vo, 10*s.* 6*d.*

—— **The Dialogues**, translated into English, with Analyses and Introductions, by B. JOWETT, M.A. *Third Edition.* 5 vols. medium 8vo, 4*l.* 4*s.* In half-morocco, 5*l.*

—— **The Republic**, translated into English, with Analysis and Introduction, by B. JOWETT, M.A. *Third Edition.* Medium 8vo, 12*s.* 6*d.*; half-roan, 14*s.*

—— Index to Plato. Compiled for Prof. Jowett's Translation of the Dialogues. By EVELYN ABBOTT, M.A. 8vo, paper covers, 2*s.* 6*d.*

Plotinus. Edidit F. CREUZER. Tomi III. 4to, 1*l.* 8*s.*

Plutarchi Moralia, id est, Opera, exceptis Vitis, reliqua. Edidit DANIEL WYTTENBACH. Accedit Index Graecitatis. Tomi VIII. Partes XV. 1795–1830. 8vo, cloth, 3*l.* 10*s.*

Polybius. Selections. Edited by J. L. STRACHAN-DAVIDSON, M.A. With Maps. Medium 8vo, buckram, 21*s.*

SOPHOCLES.

—— The Plays and Fragments. With English Notes and Introductions, by LEWIS CAMPBELL, M.A. 2 vols.

Vol. I. Oedipus Tyrannus. Oedipus Coloneus. Antigone. 8vo, 16*s.*

Vol. II. Ajax. Electra. Trachiniae. Philoctetes. Fragments. 8vo, 16*s.*

—— Tragoediae et Fragmenta, ex recensione et cum commentariis GUIL. DINDORFII. *Third Edition.* 2 vols. Fcap. 8vo, 1*l.* 1*s.*

Each Play separately, limp, 2*s.* 6*d.*

—— Tragoediae et Fragmenta cum Annotationibus GUIL. DINDORFII. Tomi II. 8vo, 10*s.*

The Text, Vol. I, 5*s.* 6*d.* The Notes, Vol. II, 4*s.* 6*d.*

Stobaei Florilegium. Ad MSS. fidem emendavit et supplevit T. GAISFORD, S.T.P. Tomi IV. 8vo, 1*l.*

—— Eclogarum Physicarum et Ethicarum libri duo. Accedit Hieroclis Commentarius in aurea carmina Pythagoreorum. Ad MSS. Codd. recensuit T. GAISFORD, S.T.P. Tomi II. 8vo, 11*s.*

STRABO, Selections from. With an Introduction on Strabo's Life and Works. By H. F. TOZER, M.A., F.R.G.S. With Maps and Plans. 8vo, cloth, 12*s.*

Thucydides. Translated into English, with Introduction, Marginal Analysis, Notes, and Indices. By B. JOWETT, M.A., Regius Professor of Greek. 2 vols. Medium 8vo, 1*l.* 12*s.*

XENOPHON. Ex rec. et cum annotatt. L. DINDORFII.

I. Historia Graeca. *Second Edition.* 8vo, 10*s.* 6*d.*

II. Expeditio Cyri. *Second Edition.* 8vo, 10*s.* 6*d.*

III. Institutio Cyri. 8vo, 10*s.* 6*d.*

IV. Memorabilia Socratis. 8vo, 7*s.* 6*d.*

V. Opuscula Politica Equestria et Venatica cum Arriani Libello de Venatione. 8vo, 10*s.* 6*d.*

GREEK EDUCATIONAL WORKS.

GRAMMARS, EXERCISE BOOKS, &c.

Chandler. The Elements of Greek Accentuation: abridged from his larger work by H. W. CHANDLER, M.A. Extra fcap. 8vo, 2*s*. 6*d*.

King and **Cookson.** An Introduction to the Comparative Grammar of Greek and Latin. By J. E. KING, M.A., and C. COOKSON, M.A. Extra fcap. 8vo, 5*s*. 6*d*.

Liddell and **Scott.** An Intermediate Greek-English Lexicon, founded upon the Seventh Edition of LIDDELL and SCOTT'S Greek Lexicon. Small 4to, 12*s*. 6*d*.

Liddell and **Scott.** A Greek-English Lexicon, abridged from LIDDELL and SCOTT'S 4to edition. Square 12mo, 7*s*. 6*d*.

Miller. A Greek Testament Primer. An Easy Grammar and Reading Book for the use of Students beginning Greek. By the Rev. E. MILLER, M.A. *Second Edition.* Extra fcap. 8vo, 3*s*. 6*d*.

Moulton. The Ancient Classical Drama. A Study in Literary Evolution. Intended for Readers in English and in the Original. By R. G. MOULTON, M.A. Crown 8vo, 8*s*. 6*d*.

Wordsworth. A Greek Primer, for the use of beginners in that Language. By the Right Rev. CHARLES WORDSWORTH, D.C.L. *Seventy-seventh Thousand.* Extra fcap. 8vo, 1*s*. 6*d*.

—— Graecae Grammaticae Rudimenta in usum Scholarum. Auctore CAROLO WORDSWORTH, D.C.L. *Nineteenth Edition.* 12mo, 4*s*.

A Primer of Greek Prose Composition. By J. Y. SARGENT, M.A. Extra fcap. 8vo, 3*s*. 6*d*.

*** A Key to the above, price 5*s*. *net.* Supplied *to Teachers only,* on application to the Secretary, Clarendon Press.

Passages for Translation into Greek Prose. By J. YOUNG SARGENT, M.A. Extra fcap. 8vo, 3*s*.

Exemplaria Graeca. Being Greek Renderings of Selected 'Passages for Translation into Greek Prose.' By the same Author. Extra fcap. 8vo, 3*s*.

Models and Materials for Greek Iambic Verse. By J. Y. Sargent, M.A. Extra fcap. 8vo, 4s. 6d.

Graece Reddenda. By C. S. Jerram, M.A. Extra fcap. 8vo, 2s. 6d.

Reddenda Minora; or, Easy Passages, Latin and Greek, for Unseen Translation. By C. S. Jerram, M.A. *Third Edition.* Extra fcap. 8vo, 1s. 6d.

Anglice Reddenda; or, Extracts, Latin and Greek, for Unseen Translation. By C. S. Jerram, M.A. Extra fcap. 8vo, 2s. 6d.

Anglice Reddenda. *Second Series.* By the same Author. Extra fcap. 8vo, 3s.

Models and Exercises in Unseen Translation. By H. F. Fox, M.A., and T. M. Bromley, M.A. Extra fcap. 8vo, 5s. 6d.

*** A Key to Passages quoted in the above, price 6d. Supplied *to Teachers only,* on application to the Secretary, Clarendon Press.

Golden Treasury of Ancient Greek Poetry. By R. S. Wright, M.A. *Second Edition.* Revised by Evelyn Abbott, M.A., LL.D. Extra fcap. 8vo, 10s. 6d.

Golden Treasury of Greek Prose, being a Collection of the finest passages in the principal Greek Prose Writers, with Introductory Notices and Notes. By R. S. Wright, M.A., and J. E. L. Shadwell, M.A. Extra fcap. 8vo, 4s. 6d.

Greek Readers.

Easy Greek Reader. By Evelyn Abbott, M.A. In one or two Parts. Extra fcap. 8vo, 3s.

First Greek Reader. By W. G. Rushbrooke, M.L. *Third Edition.* Extra fcap. 8vo, 2s. 6d.

Second Greek Reader. By A. M. Bell, M.A. *Second Edition.* Extra fcap. 8vo, 3s.

Specimens of Greek Dialects; being a Fourth Greek Reader. With Introductions, &c. By W. W. Merry, D.D. Extra fcap. 8vo, 4s. 6d.

Selections from Homer and the Greek Dramatists; being a Fifth Greek Reader. With Explanatory Notes and Introductions to the Study of Greek Epic and Dramatic Poetry. By Evelyn Abbott, M.A. Extra fcap. 8vo, 4s. 6d.

Greek Classics for Schools.

Aeschylus. In Single Plays. Extra fcap. 8vo.

I. Agamemnon. With Introduction and Notes, by ARTHUR SIDGWICK, M.A. *Fourth Edition.* 3s.

II. Choephoroi. By the same Editor. 3s.

III. Eumenides. By the same Editor. *New Edition.* 3s.

IV. Prometheus Bound. With Introduction and Notes, by A. O. PRICKARD, M.A. *Second Edition.* 2s.

Aristophanes. In Single Plays. Edited, with English Notes, Introductions, &c., by W. W. MERRY, D.D. Extra fcap. 8vo.

I. The Acharnians. *Third Edition,* 3s.

II. The Clouds. *Third Edition,* 3s.

III. The Frogs. *Third Edition,* 3s.

IV. The Knights. *Second Edition,* 3s.

V. The Birds. 3s. 6d.

VI. The Wasps. 3s. 6d.

Cebes. Tabula. With Introduction and Notes. By C. S. JERRAM, M.A. Extra fcap. 8vo, 2s. 6d.

Demosthenes. Orations against Philip. With Introduction and Notes, by EVELYN ABBOTT, M.A., and P. E. MATHESON, M.A.

Vol. I. Philippic I. Olynthiacs I–III. *Third Edition.* Extra fcap. 8vo, 3s.

Vol. II. De Pace, Philippic II, De Chersoneso, Philippic III. Extra fcap. 8vo, 4s. 6d.

Euripides. In Single Plays. Edited with Introduction and Notes. Extra fcap. 8vo.

I. Alcestis. By C. S. JERRAM, M.A. *Third Edition.* 2s. 6d.

II. Cyclops. By W. E. LONG, M.A. 2s. 6d.

III. Hecuba. By C. H. RUSSELL, M.A. 2s. 6d.

IV. Helena. By C. S. JERRAM, M.A. 3s.

V. Heracleidae. By C. S. JERRAM, M.A. 3s.

VI. Iphigenia in Tauris. By the same Editor. 3s.

VII. Medea. By C. B. HEBERDEN, M.A. *Second Edition.* 2s.

VIII. Bacchae. By A. H. CRUICKSHANK, M.A. 3s. 6d.

Herodotus. Book IX. Edited, with Notes, by EVELYN ABBOTT, M.A. Extra fcap. 8vo, 3*s*.

—— Selections. Edited, with Introduction and Notes, by W. W. MERRY, D.D. Extra fcap. 8vo, 2*s*. 6*d*.

Homer.

I. **For Beginners.** Iliad, Book III. By M. T. TATHAM, M.A. Extra fcap. 8vo, 1*s*. 6*d*.

II. Iliad, Books I–XII. With an Introduction and a brief Homeric Grammar, and Notes. By D. B. MONRO, M.A. *Third Edition.* Extra fcap. 8vo, 6*s*.

III. Iliad, Books XIII–XXIV. With Notes. By the same Editor. *Second Edition.* Extra fcap. 8vo, 6*s*.

IV. Iliad, Book I. By the same Editor. *Second Edition.* Extra fcap. 8vo, 2*s*.

V. Iliad, Book XXI. With Introduction and Notes. By HERBERT HAILSTONE, M.A. Extra fcap. 8vo, 1*s*. 6*d*.

VI. Odyssey, Books I–XII. By W. W. MERRY, D.D. *Fiftieth Thousand.* Extra fcap. 8vo, 5*s*.

Books I and II, separately, each 1*s*. 6*d*.
Books VI and VII. Extra fcap. 8vo. 1*s*. 6*d*.

VII. Odyssey, Books VII–XII. By the same Editor. Extra fcap. 8vo, 3*s*.

VIII. Odyssey, Books XIII–XXIV. By the same Editor. *Thirteenth Thousand.* Extra fcap. 8vo, 5*s*.

Lucian. Vera Historia. By C. S. JERRAM, M.A. *Second Edition.* Extra fcap. 8vo, 1*s*. 6*d*.

Lysias. Epitaphios. Edited, with Introduction and Notes, by F. J. SNELL, B.A. Extra fcap. 8vo, 2*s*.

Plato. With Introduction and Notes. By ST. GEORGE STOCK, M.A. Extra fcap. 8vo.

The Apology. *Second Edition.* 2*s*. 6*d*. Crito, 2*s*.
Meno. *Second Edition.* 2*s*. 6*d*.

—— Selections. With Introductions and Notes. By JOHN PURVES, M.A., and Preface by B. JOWETT, M.A. *Second Edition.* Extra fcap. 8vo, 5*s*.

Plutarch. Lives of the Gracchi. Edited, with Introduction, Notes, and Indices, by G. E. UNDERHILL, M.A. Crown 8vo. 4*s*. 6*d*.

Sophocles. Edited, with Introductions and English Notes, by LEWIS CAMPBELL, M.A., and EVELYN ABBOTT, M.A. *New Edition.* 2 vols. Extra fcap. 8vo, 10*s.* 6*d.*

Sold separately: Vol. I, Text, 4*s.* 6*d.*; Vol. II, Explanatory Notes, 6*s.*

Or in single Plays:—

Oedipus Coloneus, Antigone, 1*s.* 9*d.* each; Oedipus Tyrannus, Ajax, Electra, Trachiniae, Philoctetes, 2*s.* each.

—— Oedipus Rex: Dindorf's Text, with Notes by the present Bishop of St. David's. Extra fcap. 8vo, limp, 1*s.* 6*d.*

Theocritus (for Schools). With English Notes. By H. KYNASTON, D.D. (late SNOW). *Fifth Edition.* Extra fcap. 8vo, 4*s.* 6*d.*

XENOPHON. Easy Selections (for Junior Classes). With a Vocabulary, Notes, and Map. By J. S. PHILLPOTTS, B.C.L., and C. S. JERRAM, M.A. *Third Edition.* Extra fcap. 8vo, 3*s.* 6*d.*

—— Selections (for Schools). With Notes and Maps. By J. S. PHILLPOTTS, B.C.L. *Fourth Edition.* Extra fcap. 8vo, 3*s.* 6*d.*

—— Anabasis, Book I. Edited for the use of Junior Classes and Private Students. With Introduction, Notes, &c. By J. MARSHALL, M.A. Extra fcap. 8vo, 2*s.* 6*d.*

—— Anabasis, Book II. With Notes and Map. By C. S. JERRAM, M.A. Extra fcap. 8vo, 2*s.*

—— Anabasis, Book III. With Introduction, Analysis, Notes, &c. By J. MARSHALL, M.A. Extra fcap. 8vo, 2*s.* 6*d.*

—— Anabasis, Book IV. By J. MARSHALL, M.A. Extra fcap. 8vo, 2*s.*

—— Vocabulary to the Anabasis. By J. MARSHALL, M.A. Extra fcap. 8vo, 1*s.* 6*d.*

—— Cyropaedia, Book I. With Introduction and Notes. By C. BIGG, D.D. Extra fcap. 8vo, 2*s.*

—— Cyropaedia, Books IV and V. With Introduction and Notes. By C. BIGG, D.D. Extra fcap. 8vo, 2*s.* 6*d.*

—— Hellenica, Books I, II. With Introduction and Notes. By G. E. UNDERHILL, M.A. Extra fcap. 8vo, 3*s.*

—— Memorabilia. Edited with Introduction and Notes, &c., by J. MARSHALL, M.A. Extra fcap. 8vo, 4*s.* 6*d.*

SECTION V.

ORIENTAL LANGUAGES.*

THE SACRED BOOKS OF THE EAST.

TRANSLATED BY VARIOUS ORIENTAL SCHOLARS, AND EDITED BY F. MAX MÜLLER.

First Series, Vols. I—XXIV. Demy 8vo, cloth.

Vol. I. The Upanishads. Translated by F. MAX MÜLLER. Part I. 10*s*. 6*d*.

Vol. II. The Sacred Laws of the Âryas, as taught in the Schools of Âpastamba, Gautama, Vâsish*th*a, and Baudhâyana. Translated by Prof. GEORG BÜHLER. Part I. 10*s*. 6*d*.

Vol. III. The Sacred Books of China. The Texts of Confucianism. Translated by JAMES LEGGE. Part I. 12*s*. 6*d*.

Vol. IV. The Zend-Avesta. Part I. The Vendidâd. Translated by JAMES DARMESTETER. 10*s*. 6*d*.

Vol. V. The Pahlavi Texts. Translated by E. W. WEST. Part I. 12*s*. 6*d*.

Vols. VI and IX. The Qur'ân. Translated by E. H. PALMER. 21*s*.

Vol. VII. The Institutes of Vish*n*u. Translated by JULIUS JOLLY. 10*s*. 6*d*.

Vol. VIII. The Bhagavadgîtâ, with The Sanatsu*g*âtîya, and The Anugîtâ. Translated by KÂSHINÂTH TRIMBAK TELANG. 10*s*. 6*d*.

Vol. X. The Dhammapada, translated from Pâli by F. MAX MÜLLER; and The Sutta-Nipâta, translated from Pâli by V. FAUSBÖLL; being Canonical Books of the Buddhists. 10*s*. 6*d*.

Vol. XI. Buddhist Suttas. Translated from Pâli by T. W. RHYS DAVIDS. 10*s*. 6*d*.

Vol. XII. The *S*atapatha-Brâhma*n*a, according to the Text of the Mâdhyandina School. Translated by JULIUS EGGELING. Part I. Books I and II. 12*s*. 6*d*.

Vol. XIII. Vinaya Texts. Translated from the Pâli by T. W. RHYS DAVIDS and HERMANN OLDENBERG. Part I. 10*s*. 6*d*.

* See also ANECDOTA OXON., Series II, III, pp. 41–42, below.

The Sacred Books of the East (*continued*).

Vol. XIV. The Sacred Laws of the Âryas, as taught in the Schools of Âpastamba, Gautama, Vâsish*th*a and Baudhâyana. Translated by GEORG BÜHLER. Part II. 10*s*. 6*d*.

Vol. XV. The Upanishads. Translated by F. MAX MÜLLER. Part II. 10*s*. 6*d*.

Vol. XVI. The Sacred Books of China. The Texts of Confucianism. Translated by JAMES LEGGE. Part II. 10*s*. 6*d*.

Vol. XVII. Vinaya Texts. Translated from the Pâli by T. W. RHYS DAVIDS and HERMANN OLDENBERG. Part II. 10*s*. 6*d*.

Vol. XVIII. Pahlavi Texts. Translated by E. W. WEST. Part II. 12*s*. 6*d*.

Vol. XIX. The Fo-sho-hing-tsan-king. A Life of Buddha by A*s*vaghosha Bodhisattva, translated from Sanskrit into Chinese by Dharmaraksha, A.D. 420, and from Chinese into English by SAMUEL BEAL. 10*s*. 6*d*.

Vol. XX. Vinaya Texts. Translated from the Pâli by T. W. RHYS DAVIDS and HERMANN OLDENBERG. Part III. 10*s*. 6*d*.

Vol. XXI. The Saddharma-pu*nd*arîka; or, the Lotus of the True Law. Translated by H. KERN. 12*s*. 6*d*.

Vol. XXII. *G*aina-Sûtras. Translated from Prâkrit by HERMANN JACOBI. Part I. 10*s*. 6*d*.

Vol. XXIII. The Zend-Avesta. Part II. Translated by JAMES DARMESTETER. 10*s*. 6*d*.

Vol. XXIV. Pahlavi Texts. Translated by E. W. WEST. Part III. 10*s*. 6*d*.

Second Series.

Vol. XXV. Manu. Translated by GEORG BÜHLER. 21*s*.

Vol. XXVI. The *S*atapatha-Brâhma*n*a. Translated by JULIUS EGGELING. Part II. 12*s*. 6*d*.

Vols. XXVII and XXVIII. The Sacred Books of China. The Texts of Confucianism. Translated by JAMES LEGGE. Parts III and IV. 25*s*.

Vols. XXIX and XXX. The G*ri*hya-Sûtras, Rules of Vedic Domestic Ceremonies. Translated by HERMANN OLDENBERG.

Part I (Vol. XXIX). 12*s*. 6*d*.
Part II (Vol. XXX). 12*s*. 6*d*.

The Sacred Books of the East (*continued*).

Vol. XXXI. The Zend-Avesta. Part III. Translated by L. H. MILLS. 12*s*. 6*d*.

Vol. XXXII. Vedic Hymns. Translated by F. MAX MÜLLER. Part I. 18*s*. 6*d*.

Vol. XXXIII. Nârada, and some Minor Law-books. Translated by JULIUS JOLLY. 10*s*. 6*d*.

Vol. XXXIV. The Vedânta-Sûtras, with *S*aṅkara's Commentary. Translated by G. THIBAUT. 12*s*. 6*d*.

Vol. XXXV. The Questions of King Milinda. Part I. Translated from the Pâli by T. W. RHYS DAVIDS. 10*s*. 6*d*.

Vols. XXXIX and XL. The Sacred Books of China. The Texts of Tâoism. Translated by JAMES LEGGE. 21*s*.

Vol. XXXVII. The Contents of the Nasks, as stated in the Eighth and Ninth Books of the Dînkard. Part I. Translated by E. W. WEST. 15*s*.

Vol. XLI. *S*atapatha-Brâhma*n*a. Part III. Translated by JULIUS EGGELING. 12*s*. 6*d*.

In the Press:—

Vol. XXXVI. The Questions of King Milinda. Part II. Translated by T. W. RHYS DAVIDS.

Vol. XXXVIII. The Vedânta-Sûtras. Part II.

Vol. XLII. The Buddha-*k*arita. Translated by E. B. COWELL. The Sukhâvatî-vyûha. Translated by F. MAX MÜLLER.

ARABIC. A Practical Arabic Grammar. Compiled by A. O. GREEN, Brigade Major, Royal Engineers.

Part I. *Third Edition. Revised and Enlarged.* Crown 8vo, 7*s*. 6*d*.
Part II. *Third Edition. Revised and Enlarged.* 10*s*. 6*d*.

BENGALI. Grammar of the Bengali Language; Literary and Colloquial. By JOHN BEAMES. Crown 8vo, cloth, 4*s*. 6*d*.

CHINESE. The Chinese Classics: with a Translation, Critical and Exegetical Notes, Prolegomena, and Copious Indexes. By JAMES LEGGE, D.D., LL.D. In Eight Volumes. Royal 8vo.

Vol. I. Confucian Analects, &c. *New Edition.* 1*l*. 10*s*.

Vol. II. The Works of Mencius. 1*l*. 10*s*.

Vol. III. The Shoo-King; or, The Book of Historical Documents. In two Parts. 1*l*. 10*s*. each.

Vol. IV. The She-King; or, The Book of Poetry. In two Parts. 1*l*. 10*s*. each.

Vol. V. The Ch'un Ts'ew, with the Tso Chuen. In two Parts. 1*l*. 10*s*. each.

CHINESE. The Nestorian Monument of Hsî-an Fû in Shen-hsî, China, relating to the Diffusion of Christianity in China in the Seventh and Eighth Centuries. By JAMES LEGGE, D.D. 2*s*. 6*d*.

—— Record of Buddhistic Kingdoms; being an Account by the Chinese Monk FÂ-HIEN of his travels in India and Ceylon (A.D. 399–414). Translated and annotated, with a Corean recension of the Chinese Text, by JAMES LEGGE, D.D. Crown 4to, boards, 10*s*. 6*d*.

—— Catalogue of the Chinese Translation of the Buddhist Tripiṭaka, the Sacred Canon of the Buddhists in China and Japan. Compiled by BUNYIU NANJIO. 4to, 1*l*. 12*s*. 6*d*.

—— Handbook of the Chinese Language. Parts I and II. Grammar and Chrestomathy. By JAMES SUMMERS. 8vo, 1*l*. 8*s*.

CHALDEE. Book of Tobit. A Chaldee Text, from a unique MS. in the Bodleian Library. Edited by AD. NEUBAUER, M.A. Crown 8vo, 6*s*.

COPTIC. Libri Prophetarum Majorum, cum Lamentationibus Jeremiae, in Dialecto Linguae Aegyptiacae Memphitica seu Coptica. Edidit cum Versione Latina H. TATTAM, S.T.P. Tomi II. 8vo, 17*s*.

—— Libri duodecim Prophetarum Minorum in Ling. Aegypt. vulgo Coptica. Edidit H. TATTAM, A.M. 8vo, 8*s*. 6*d*.

—— Novum Testamentum Coptice, cura D. WILKINS. 12*s*. 6*d*.

HEBREW. Psalms in Hebrew (without points). Cr. 8vo, 2*s*.

Driver. Notes on the Hebrew Text of the Books of Samuel. By S. R. DRIVER, D.D. 8vo, 14*s*.

—— Treatise on the use of the Tenses in Hebrew. By S. R. DRIVER, D.D. *Third Edition.* Crown 8vo, 7*s*. 6*d*.

—— Commentary on the Book of Proverbs. Attributed to Abraham Ibn Ezra. Edited from a Manuscript in the Bodleian Library by S. R. DRIVER, D.D. Crown 8vo, paper covers, 3*s*. 6*d*.

A Hebrew and English Lexicon of the Old Testament, with an Appendix containing the Biblical Aramaic, based on the Thesaurus and Lexicon of GESENIUS, by FRANCIS BROWN, D.D., S. R. DRIVER, D.D., and C. A. BRIGGS, D.D. Parts I and II. Small 4to, each, 2*s*. 6*d*.

Neubauer. Book of Hebrew Roots, by Abu 'l-Walîd Marwân ibn Janâh, otherwise called Rabbi Yônâh. Now first edited, with an Appendix, by AD. NEUBAUER. 4to, 2*l*. 7*s*. 6*d*.

Spurrell. Notes on the Hebrew Text of the Book of Genesis. By G. J. SPURRELL, M.A. Crown 8vo, 10*s*. 6*d*.

Wickes. Hebrew Accentuation of Psalms, Proverbs, and Job. By WILLIAM WICKES, D.D. 8vo, 5*s*.

—— Hebrew Prose Accentuation. 8vo, 10*s*. 6*d*.

SANSKRIT.—Sanskrit-English Dictionary, Etymologically and Philologically arranged, with special reference to Greek, Latin, German, Anglo-Saxon, English, and other cognate Indo-European Languages. By Sir M. MONIER-WILLIAMS, D.C.L. 4to, 4*l.* 14*s.* 6*d.*

—— Practical Grammar of the Sanskrit Language, arranged with reference to the Classical Languages of Europe, by Sir M. MONIER-WILLIAMS, D.C.L. *Fourth Edition.* 8vo, 15*s.*

—— Nalopákhyánam. Story of Nala, an Episode of the Mahá-bhárata: Sanskrit Text, with a copious Vocabulary, and an improved version of Dean Milman's Translation, by Sir M. MONIER-WILLIAMS, D.C.L. *Second Edition, Revised and Improved.* 8vo, 15*s.*

—— Sakuntalā. A Sanskrit Drama, in seven Acts. Edited by SIR M. MONIER-WILLIAMS, D.C.L. *Second Edition.* 8vo, 1*l.* 1*s.*

SYRIAC.—**Thesaurus Syriacus:** collegerunt Quatremère, Bernstein, Lorsbach, Arnoldi, Agrell, Field, Roediger: edidit R. PAYNE SMITH, S.T.P. Vol. I, containing Fasc. I–V. Sm. fol. 5*l.* 5*s.*
Fasc. VI, 1*l.* 1*s.*; VII, 1*l.* 11*s.* 6*d.*; VIII, 1*l.* 16*s.*; IX, 1*l.* 5*s.*

—— **The Book of Kalīlah and Dimnah.** Translated from Arabic into Syriac. Edited by W. WRIGHT, LL.D. 8vo. 1*l.* 1*s.*

—— **Cyrilli** Archiepiscopi Alexandrini Commentarii in Lucae Evangelium quae supersunt Syriace. E MSS. apud Mus. Britan. edidit R. PAYNE SMITH, A.M. 4to, 1*l.* 2*s.*

—— —— Translated by R. PAYNE SMITH, M.A. 2 vols. 8vo, 14*s.*

—— **Ephraemi Syri, Rabulae** Episcopi Edesseni, **Balaei**, &c., Opera Selecta. E Codd. Syriacis MSS. in Museo Britannico et Bibliotheca Bodleiana asservatis primus edidit J. J. OVERBECK. 8vo, 1*l.* 1*s.*

—— **John**, Bishop of Ephesus. The Third Part of his Ecclesiastical History. [In Syriac.] Now first edited by WILLIAM CURETON, M.A. 4to, 1*l.* 12*s.*

—— —— Translated by R. PAYNE SMITH, M.A. 8vo, 10*s.*

TAMIL. First Lessons in Tamil. By G. U. POPE, D.D. *Fifth Edition.* Crown 8vo, 7*s.* 6*d.*

—— The Nālaḍiyār, or Four Hundred Quatrains in Tamil. Edited by G. U. POPE, D.D. 8vo, 18*s.* *Large Paper*, 2*l.* *half Roxburgh.*

ZEND. **The Ancient MS. of the Yasna,** with its Pahlavi Translation (A.D. 1323), generally quoted as J2, and now in the possession of the Bodleian Library. Reproduced in Facsimile, and Edited with an Introductory Note by L. H. MILLS, D.D. Half-bound, Imperial 4to, 10*l.* 10*s.* *net.*

SECTION VI.

ANECDOTA OXONIENSIA.

(Crown 4to, stiff covers.)

I. CLASSICAL SERIES.

I. The English Manuscripts of the Nicomachean Ethics. By J. A. STEWART, M.A. 3*s.* 6*d.*

II. Nonius Marcellus, de Compendiosa Doctrina, Harleian MS. 2719. Collated by J. H. ONIONS, M.A. 3*s.* 6*d.*

III. Aristotle's Physics. Book VII. With Introduction by R. SHUTE, M.A. 2*s.*

IV. Bentley's Plautine Emendations. From his copy of Gronovius. By E. A. SONNENSCHEIN, M.A. 2*s.* 6*d.*

V. Harleian MS. 2610; Ovid's Metamorphoses I, II, III. 1–622; XXIV Latin Epigrams from Bodleian or other MSS.; Latin Glosses on Apollinaris Sidonius from MS. Digby 172. Collated and Edited by ROBINSON ELLIS, M.A., LL.D. 4*s.*

VI. A Collation with the Ancient Armenian Versions of the Greek Text of Aristotle's Categories, De Interpretatione, De Mundo, De Virtutibus et Vitiis, and of Porphyry's Introduction. By F. C. CONYBEARE, M.A. 14*s.*

VII. Collations from the Harleian MS. of Cicero 2682. By ALBERT C. CLARK, M.A. 7*s.* 6*d.*

II. SEMITIC SERIES.

I. Commentary on Ezra and Nehemiah. By Rabbi Saadiah. Edited by H. J. MATHEWS, M.A. 3*s.* 6*d.*

II. The Book of the Bee. Edited by ERNEST A. WALLIS BUDGE, M.A. 21*s.*

III. A Commentary on the Book of Daniel. By Japhet Ibn Ali. Edited and Translated by D. S. MARGOLIOUTH, M.A. 21*s.*

IV. Mediaeval Jewish Chronicles and Chronological Notes. Edited by AD. NEUBAUER, M.A. 14*s.*

V. The Palestinian Version of the Holy Scriptures. Five more Fragments recently acquired by the Bodleian Library. Edited by G. H. GWILLIAM, B.D. 6*s.*

London: HENRY FROWDE, Amen Corner, E.C.

ANECDOTA OXONIENSIA (*continued*).

III. ARYAN SERIES.

I. Buddhist Texts from Japan. 1. Va*g*ra*kkh*edikâ. Edited by F. MAX MÜLLER. 3*s.* 6*d.*

II. Buddhist Texts from Japan. 2. Sukhâvatî Vyûha. Edited by F. MAX MÜLLER, M.A., and BUNYIU NANJIO. 7*s.* 6*d.*

III. Buddhist Texts from Japan. 3. The Ancient Palm-leaves containing the Pra*g*ñâ-Pâramitâ-H*r*idaya-Sûtra and the Ush*n*îsha-Vigaya-Dhâra*n*î, edited by F. MAX MÜLLER, M.A., and BUNYIU NANJIO, M.A. With an Appendix by G. BÜHLER. 10*s.*

IV. Kâtyâyana's Sarvânukrama*n*î of the *R*igveda. With Extracts from Sha*d*guru*s*ishya's Commentary entitled Vedârthadîpikâ. Edited by A. A. MACDONELL, M.A., Ph.D. 16*s.*

V. The Dharma Sa*m*graha. Edited by KENJIU KASAWARA, F. MAX MÜLLER, and H. WENZEL. 7*s.* 6*d.*

VII. The Buddha-*K*arita of A*s*vaghosha. Edited, from three MSS., by E. B. COWELL, M.A. 12*s.* 6*d.*

IV. MEDIAEVAL AND MODERN SERIES.

I. Sinonoma Bartholomei. Edited by J. L. G. MOWAT, M.A. 3*s.* 6*d.*

II. Alphita. Edited by J. L. G. MOWAT, M.A. 12*s.* 6*d.*

III. The Saltair Na Rann. Edited from a MS. in the Bodleian Library, by WHITLEY STOKES, D.C.L. 7*s.* 6*d.*

IV. The Cath Finntrága, or Battle of Ventry. Edited by KUNO MEYER, Ph.D., M.A. 6*s.*

V. Lives of Saints, from the Book of Lismore. Edited, with Translation, by WHITLEY STOKES, D.C.L. 1*l.* 11*s.* 6*d.*

II. THEOLOGY.

A. THE HOLY SCRIPTURES, APOCRYPHA, &c.

COPTIC. Libri Prophetarum Majorum, cum Lamentationibus Jeremiae, in Dialecto Linguae Aegyptiacae Memphitica seu Coptica. Edidit cum Versione Latina H. TATTAM, S.T.P. Tomi II. 8vo, 17*s.*

—— Libri duodecim Prophetarum Minorum in Ling. Aegypt. vulgo Coptica. Edidit H. TATTAM, A.M. 8vo, 8*s.* 6*d.*

—— Novum Testamentum Coptice, cura D. WILKINS. 1716. 4to, 12*s.* 6*d.*

ENGLISH. The Holy Bible in **the Earliest English Versions,** made from the Latin Vulgate by JOHN WYCLIFFE and his followers: edited by FORSHALL and MADDEN. 4 vols. Royal 4to, 3*l.* 3*s.*

Also reprinted from the above, with Introduction and Glossary by W. W. SKEAT, Litt.D.

I. The Books of Job, Psalms, Proverbs, Ecclesiastes, and the Song of Solomon. Extra fcap. 8vo, 3*s.* 6*d.*

II. The New Testament. Extra fcap. 8vo, 6*s.*

—— **The Holy Bible: an exact reprint, page for page, of** the Authorised Version published in the year 1611. Demy 4to, half-bound. 1*l.* 1*s.*

—— **The Holy Bible, Revised Version*.**

Cheap editions for School Use.

Revised Bible. Pearl 16mo, cloth boards, 1*s.* 6*d.*

Revised New Testament. Nonpareil 32mo, 6*d.*; Brevier 16mo, 1*s.* Long Primer 8vo, 1*s.* 6*d.*

—— **The Oxford Bible for Teachers,** containing the Holy Scriptures, together with a new, enlarged, and illustrated edition of the OXFORD HELPS TO THE STUDY OF THE BIBLE, comprising Introductions to the several Books, the History and Antiquities of the Jews, the results of Modern Discoveries, and the Natural History of Palestine, with copious Tables, Concordance and Indices, and a series of Maps. Prices in various sizes and bindings from 7*s.* 6*d.* to 2*l.* 2*s.*

* *The Revised Version is the joint property of the Universities of Oxford and Cambridge.*

ENGLISH (*continued*).

—— **Helps to the Study of the Bible**, taken from the OXFORD BIBLE FOR TEACHERS. *New, Enlarged, and Illustrated Edition.* Crown 8vo, 4*s*. 6*d*.

—— **The Psalter**, or Psalms of David, and certain Canticles, with a Translation and Exposition in English, by RICHARD ROLLE of Hampole. Edited by H. R. BRAMLEY, M.A., Fellow of S. M. Magdalen College, Oxford. With an Introduction and Glossary. Demy 8vo, 1*l*. 1*s*.

—— **Studia Biblica et Ecclesiastica.** Essays in Biblical and Patristic Criticism, and kindred subjects. By Members of the University of Oxford. 8vo.

Vol. I, 10*s*. 6*d*. Vol. II, 12*s*. 6*d*. Vol. III, 16*s*.

—— **Lectures on the Book of Job.** Delivered in Westminster Abbey by the Very Rev. G. G. BRADLEY, D.D. *Second Edition.* Crown 8vo, 7*s*. 6*d*.

—— **Lectures on Ecclesiastes.** By the same Author. Cr. 8vo, 4*s*. 6*d*.

—— **The Book of Wisdom:** the Greek Text, the Latin Vulgate, and the Authorised English Version; with an Introduction, Critical Apparatus, and a Commentary. By W. J. DEANE, M.A. 4to, 12*s*. 6*d*.

—— **The Five Books of Maccabees**, in English, with Notes and Illustrations by HENRY COTTON, D.C.L. 8vo, 10*s*. 6*d*.

—— **The Book of Enoch.** Translated from Dillmann's Ethiopic Text (emended and revised), and Edited by R. H. CHARLES, M.A. 8vo, 16*s*.

—— **List of Editions of the Bible in English.** By HENRY COTTON, D.C.L. *Second Edition.* 8vo, 8*s*. 6*d*.

—— **Rhemes and Doway.** An attempt to show what has been done by Roman Catholics for the diffusion of the Holy Scriptures in English. By HENRY COTTON, D.C.L. 8vo, 9*s*.

GOTHIC. Evangeliorum Versio Gothica, cum Interpr. et Annott. E. BENZELII. Edidit E. LYE, A.M. 4to, 12*s*. 6*d*.

—— **The Gospel of St. Mark in Gothic**, according to the translation made by WULFILA in the Fourth Century. Edited by W. W. SKEAT, Litt.D. Extra fcap. 8vo, 4*s*.

GREEK. Old Testament. Vetus Testamentum ex Versione Septuaginta Interpretum secundum exemplar Vaticanum Romae editum. Accedit potior varietas Codicis Alexandrini. Tomi III. 18mo, 18*s*.

—— Vetus Testamentum Graece cum Variis Lectionibus. Editionem a R. HOLMES, S.T.P. inchoatam continuavit J. PARSONS, S.T.B. Tomi V. folio, 7*l*.

GREEK (*continued*).

—— **A Concordance to the Septuagint** and the other Greek Versions of the Old Testament (including the Apocryphal Books). By the late EDWIN HATCH, M.A., and H. A. REDPATH, M.A. Parts I–III. Α–Ἰωβήλ. Imperial 4to, *each*, 21*s*. Part IV. *In the Press*.

—— Origenis Hexaplorum quae supersunt; sive, Veterum Interpretum Graecorum in totum Vetus Testamentum Fragmenta. Edidit FREDERICUS FIELD, A.M. 2 vols. 1875. 4to, 5*l*. 5*s*.

—— Essays in Biblical Greek. By EDWIN HATCH, M.A., D.D. 8vo, 10*s*. 6*d*.

—— An Essay on the Place of Ecclesiasticus in Semitic Literature. By D. S. MARGOLIOUTH, M.A., Laudian Professor of Arabic in the University of Oxford. Small 4to, 2*s*. 6*d*.

—— **New Testament**. Novum Testamentum Graece. Antiquissimorum Codicum Textus in ordine parallelo dispositi. Edidit E. H. HANSELL, S.T.B. Tomi III. 8vo, 24*s*.

—— Novum Testamentum Graece. Accedunt parallela S. Scripturae loca, &c. Edidit CAROLUS LLOYD, S.T.P.R. 18mo, 3*s*. *On writing paper, with wide margin*, 7*s*. 6*d*.

Critical Appendices to the above, by W. SANDAY, M.A. Extra fcap. 8vo, cloth, 3*s*. 6*d*.

—— Novum Testamentum Graece. Accedunt parallela S. Scripturae loca, &c. Ed. C. LLOYD, with SANDAY'S Appendices. Cloth, 6*s*.; paste grain, 7*s*. 6*d*.; morocco, 10*s*. 6*d*.

—— Novum Testamentum Graece juxta Exemplar Millianum. 18mo, 2*s*. 6*d*. *On writing paper, with wide margin*, 7*s*. 6*d*.

—— Evangelia Sacra Graece. Fcap. 8vo, limp, 1*s*. 6*d*.

—— The Greek Testament, with the Readings adopted by the Revisers of the Authorised Version:—

(1) Pica type, with Marginal References. Demy 8vo, 10*s*. 6*d*.
(2) Long Primer type. Fcap. 8vo, 4*s*. 6*d*.
(3) *The same, on writing paper, with wide margin*, 15*s*.

—— The New Testament in Greek and English. Edited by E. CARDWELL, D.D. 2 vols. 1837. Crown 8vo, 6*s*.

—— The Parallel New Testament, Greek and English; being the Authorised Version, 1611; the Revised Version, 1881; and the Greek Text followed in the Revised Version. 8vo, 12*s*. 6*d*.

—— Diatessaron; sive Historia Jesu Christi ex ipsis Evangelistarum verbis apte dispositis confecta. Ed. J. WHITE. 3*s*. 6*d*.

GREEK (*continued*).

—— Outlines of Textual Criticism applied to the New Testament. By C. E. HAMMOND, M.A. *Fifth Edition.* Crown 8vo, 4*s.* 6*d.*

—— A Greek Testament Primer. An Easy Grammar and Reading Book for the use of Students beginning Greek. By E. MILLER, M.A. Extra fcap. 8vo, 3*s.* 6*d.*

—— Canon Muratorianus. Edited, with Notes and Facsimile, by S. P. TREGELLES, LL.D. 4to, 10*s.* 6*d.*

HEBREW, &c. A Hebrew and English Lexicon of the Old Testament, with an Appendix containing the Biblical Aramaic, based on the Thesaurus and Lexicon of GESENIUS, by FRANCIS BROWN, D.D., S. R. DRIVER, D.D., and C. A. BRIGGS, D.D. Parts I and II. Small 4to, each 2*s.* 6*d.*

—— Notes on the Hebrew Text of the Book of Genesis. By G. J. SPURRELL, M.A. Crown 8vo, 10*s.* 6*d.*

—— Notes on the Hebrew Text of the Books of Samuel. By S. R. DRIVER, D.D. 8vo, 14*s.*

—— The Psalms in Hebrew without points. Stiff covers, 2*s.*

—— A Commentary on the Book of Proverbs. Attributed to ABRAHAM IBN EZRA. Edited from a MS. in the Bodleian Library by S. R. DRIVER, D.D. Crown 8vo, paper covers, 3*s.* 6*d.*

—— The Book of Tobit. A Chaldee Text, from a unique MS. in the Bodleian Library; with other Rabbinical Texts, English Translations, and the Itala. Edited by AD. NEUBAUER, M.A. Crown 8vo, 6*s.*

—— Hebrew Accentuation of Psalms, Proverbs, and Job. By WILLIAM WICKES, D.D. 8vo, 5*s.*

—— Hebrew Prose Accentuation. By the same. 8vo, 10*s.* 6*d.*

—— Horae Hebraicae et Talmudicae, a J. LIGHTFOOT. A new Edition, by R. GANDELL, M.A. 4 vols. 8vo, 1*l.* 1*s.*

LATIN. Libri Psalmorum Versio antiqua Latina, cum Paraphrasi Anglo-Saxonica. Edidit B. THORPE, F.A.S. 8vo, 10*s.* 6*d.*

—— Nouum Testamentum Domini Nostri Iesu Christi Latine, secundum Editionem Sancti Hieronymi. Ad Codicum Manuscriptorum fidem recensuit IOHANNES WORDSWORTH, S.T.P., Episcopus Sarisburiensis; in operis societatem adsumto HENRICO IULIANO WHITE, A.M. 4to.

Fasc. I. Euangelium secundum Mattheum. 12*s.* 6*d.*
Fasc. II. Euangelium secundum Marcum. 7*s.* 6*d.*
Fasc. III. Euangelium secundum Lucam. 12*s.* 6*d.*

LATIN (*continued*).

—— Old-Latin Biblical Texts: No. I. The Gospel according to St. Matthew, from the St. Germain MS. (g_1). Edited by JOHN WORDSWORTH, D.D. Small 4to, stiff covers, 6*s*.

—— Old-Latin Biblical Texts: No. II. Portions of the Gospels according to St. Mark and St. Matthew, from the Bobbio MS. (k), &c. Edited by JOHN WORDSWORTH, D.D., W. SANDAY, M.A., D.D., and H. J. WHITE, M.A. Small 4to, stiff covers, 21*s*.

—— Old-Latin Biblical Texts: No. III. The Four Gospels, from the Munich MS. (q), now numbered Lat. 6224 in the Royal Library at Munich. With a Fragment from St. John in the Hof-Bibliothek at Vienna (Cod. Lat. 502). Edited, with the aid of Tischendorf's transcript (under the direction of the Bishop of Salisbury), by H. J. WHITE, M.A. Small 4to, stiff covers, 12*s*. 6*d*.

OLD-FRENCH. Libri Psalmorum Versio antiqua Gallica e Cod. MS. in Bibl. Bodleiana adservato, una cum Versione Metrica aliisque Monumentis pervetustis. Nunc primum descripsit et edidit FRANCISCUS MICHEL, Phil. Doc. 8vo, 10*s*. 6*d*.

B. FATHERS OF THE CHURCH, &c.

St. Athanasius: Orations against the Arians. With an Account of his Life by WILLIAM BRIGHT, D.D. Crown 8vo, 9*s*.

—— Historical Writings, according to the Benedictine Text. With an Introduction by W. BRIGHT, D.D. Crown 8vo, 10*s*. 6*d*.

St. Augustine: Select Anti-Pelagian Treatises, and the Acts of the Second Council of Orange. With an Introduction by WILLIAM BRIGHT, D.D. Crown 8vo, 9*s*.

St. Basil: The Book of St. Basil on the Holy Spirit. A Revised Text, with Notes and Introduction by C. F. H. JOHNSTON, M.A. Crown 8vo, 7*s*. 6*d*.

Barnabas, The Editio Princeps of the Epistle of, by Archbishop Ussher, as printed at Oxford, A.D. 1642, and preserved in an imperfect form in the Bodleian Library. With a Dissertation by J. H. BACKHOUSE, M.A. Small 4to, 3*s*. 6*d*.

Canons of the First Four General Councils of Nicaea, Constantinople, Ephesus, and Chalcedon. With Notes, by W. BRIGHT, D.D. *Second Edition.* Crown 8vo, 7*s*. 6*d*.

Catenae Graecorum Patrum in Novum Testamentum. Edidit J. A. CRAMER, S.T.P. Tomi VIII. 8vo, 2*l*. 4*s*.

Clementis Alexandrini Opera, ex recensione Guil. Dindorfii. Tomi IV. 8vo, 3*l*.

Cyrilli Archiepiscopi Alexandrini in XII Prophetas. Edidit P. E. Pusey, A.M. Tomi II. 8vo, 2*l*. 2*s*.

—— in D. Joannis Evangelium. Accedunt Fragmenta Varia necnon Tractatus ad Tiberium Diaconum Duo. Edidit post Aubertum P. E. Pusey, A.M. Tomi III. 8vo, 2*l*. 5*s*.

—— Commentarii in Lucae Evangelium quae supersunt Syriace. E mss. apud Mus. Britan. edidit R. Payne Smith, A.M. 4to, 1*l*. 2*s*.

—— —— Translated by R. Payne Smith, M.A. 2 vols, 14*s*.

Ephraemi Syri, Rabulae Episcopi Edesseni, Balaei, aliorumque Opera Selecta. E Codd. Syriacis mss. in Museo Britannico et Bibliotheca Bodleiana asservatis primus edidit J. J. Overbeck. 8vo, 1*l*. 1*s*.

Eusebii Pamphili Evangelicae Praeparationis Libri XV. Ad Codd. mss. recensuit T. Gaisford, S.T.P. Tomi IV. 8vo, 1*l*. 10*s*.

—— Evangelicae Demonstrationis Libri X. Recensuit T. Gaisford, S.T.P. Tomi II. 8vo, 15*s*.

—— contra Hieroclem et Marcellum Libri. Recensuit T. Gaisford, S.T.P. 8vo, 7*s*.

Eusebius' Ecclesiastical History, according to the text of Burton, with an Introduction by W. Bright, D.D. *Second Edition.* Crown 8vo, 8*s*. 6*d*.

—— —— Annotationes Variorum. Tomi II. 8vo, 17*s*.

Evagrii Historia Ecclesiastica, ex recensione H. Valesii. 1844. 8vo, 4*s*.

Irenaeus: The Third Book of St. Irenaeus, Bishop of Lyons, against Heresies. With short Notes and a Glossary by H. Deane, B.D. Crown 8vo, 5*s*. 6*d*.

Origenis Philosophumena; sive omnium Haeresium Refutatio. E Codice Parisino nunc primum edidit Emmanuel Miller. 8vo, 10*s*.

Patrum Apostolicorum, S. Clementis Romani, S. Ignatii, S. Polycarpi, quae supersunt. Edidit Guil. Jacobson, S.T.P.R. Tomi II. *Fourth Edition.* 8vo, 1*l*. 1*s*.

Reliquiae Sacrae secundi tertiique saeculi. Recensuit M. J. Routh, S.T.P. Tomi V. *Second Edition.* 8vo, 1*l*. 5*s*.

Scriptorum Ecclesiasticorum Opuscula. Recensuit M. J. Routh, S.T.P. Tomi II. *Third Edition.* 8vo, 10*s*.

Socratis Scholastici Historia Ecclesiastica. Gr. et Lat. Edidit R. HUSSEY, S.T.B. Tomi III. 1853. 8vo, 15*s*.

Socrates' Ecclesiastical History, according to the Text of HUSSEY, with an Introduction by WILLIAM BRIGHT, D.D. *Second Edition*. Crown 8vo, 7*s*. 6*d*.

Sozomeni Historia Ecclesiastica. Edidit R. HUSSEY, S.T.B. Tomi III. 8vo, 15*s*.

Tertulliani Apologeticus adversus Gentes pro Christianis. Edited, with Introduction and Notes, by T. HERBERT BINDLEY, M.A. Crown 8vo, 6*s*.

De Praescriptione Haereticorum ad Martyras: ad Scapulam. With Introductions and Notes. By the same Editor. Crown, 8vo, [illegible]. 6/-

Theodoreti Ecclesiasticae Historiae Libri V. Recensuit T. GAISFORD, S.T.P. 8vo, 7*s*. 6*d*.

—— Graecarum Affectionum Curatio. Ad Codices MSS. recensuit T. GAISFORD, S.T.P. 8vo, 7*s*. 6*d*.

C. ECCLESIASTICAL HISTORY, &c.

Baedae Historia Ecclesiastica. Edited, with English Notes, by G. H. MOBERLY, M.A. Crown 8vo, 10*s*. 6*d*.

Bigg. The Christian Platonists of Alexandria; being the Bampton Lectures for 1886. By CHARLES BIGG, D.D. 8vo, 10*s*. 6*d*.

Bingham's Antiquities of the Christian Church, and other Works. 10 vols. 8vo, 3*l*. 3*s*.

Bright. Chapters of Early English Church History. By W. BRIGHT, D.D. *Second Edition*. 8vo, 12*s*.

Burnet's History of the Reformation of the Church of England. *A new Edition*. Carefully revised, and the Records collated with the originals, by N. POCOCK, M.A. 7 vols. 8vo, 1*l*. 10*s*.

Cardwell's Documentary Annals of the Reformed Church of England; being a Collection of Injunctions, Declarations, Orders, Articles of Inquiry, &c., from 1546 to 1716. 2 vols. 8vo, 18*s*.

Councils and Ecclesiastical Documents relating to Great Britain and Ireland. Edited, after SPELMAN and WILKINS, by A. W. HADDAN, B.D., and W. STUBBS, D.D. Vols. I and III. Medium 8vo, each 1*l*. 1*s*.

Vol. II, Part I. Medium 8vo, 10*s*. 6*d*.

Vol. II, Part II. Church of Ireland; Memorials of St. Patrick. Stiff covers, 3*s*. 6*d*.

Formularies of Faith set forth by the King's authority during the Reign of Henry VIII. 8vo, 7*s*.

Fuller's Church History of Britain. Edited by J. S. BREWER, M.A. 6 vols. 8vo, 1*l*. 19*s*.

Gibson's Synodus Anglicana. Edited by E. CARDWELL, D.D. 8vo, 6*s*.

Hamilton's (Archbishop John) Catechism, 1552. Edited, with Introduction and Glossary, by THOMAS GRAVES LAW, Librarian of the Signet Library, Edinburgh. With a Preface by the Right Hon. W. E. GLADSTONE. Demy 8vo, 12*s*. 6*d*.

Inett's Origines Anglicanae (in continuation of Stillingfleet). Edited by J. GRIFFITHS, M.A. 3 vols. 8vo, 15*s*.

John, Bishop of Ephesus. The Third Part of his Ecclesiastical History. [In Syriac.] Now first edited by WILLIAM CURETON, M.A. 4to, 1*l*. 12*s*.

—— The same, translated by R. PAYNE SMITH, M.A. 8vo, 10*s*.

Le Neve's Fasti Ecclesiae Anglicanae. Corrected and continued from 1715 to 1853 by T. DUFFUS HARDY. 3 vols. 8vo, 1*l*. 1*s*.

Noelli (A.) Catechismus sive prima institutio disciplinaque Pietatis Christianae Latine explicata. Editio nova cura GUIL. JACOBSON, A.M. 8vo, 5*s*. 6*d*.

Prideaux's Connection of Sacred and Profane History. 2 vols. 8vo, 10*s*.

Primers put forth in the Reign of Henry VIII. 8vo, 5*s*.

Records of the Reformation. The Divorce, 1527–1533. Mostly now for the first time printed from MSS. in the British Museum and other Libraries. Collected and arranged by N. POCOCK, M.A. 2 vols. 8vo, 1*l*. 16*s*.

Reformatio Legum Ecclesiasticarum. The Reformation of Ecclesiastical Laws, as attempted in the reigns of Henry VIII, Edward VI, and Elizabeth. Edited by E. CARDWELL, D.D. 8vo, 6*s*. 6*d*.

Shirley. Some Account of the Church in the Apostolic Age. By W. W. SHIRLEY, D.D. *Second Edition*. Fcap. 8vo, 3*s*. 6*d*.

Shuckford's Sacred and Profane History connected (in continuation of Prideaux). 2 vols. 8vo, 10*s*.

Stillingfleet's Origines Britannicae, with LLOYD'S Historical Account of Church Government. Edited by T. P. PANTIN, M.A. 2 vols. 8vo, 10*s*.

Stubbs. Registrum Sacrum Anglicanum. An attempt to exhibit the course of Episcopal Succession in England. By W. STUBBS, D.D. Small 4to, 8*s.* 6*d.*

Strype's Memorials of Cranmer. 2 vols. 8vo, 11*s.*

Life of Aylmer. 8vo, 5*s.* 6*d.*

Life of Whitgift. 3 vols. 8vo, 16*s.* 6*d.*

General Index. 2 vols. 8vo, 11*s.*

Sylloge Confessionum sub tempus Reformandae Ecclesiae editarum. Subjiciuntur Catechismus Heidelbergensis et Canones Synodi Dordrechtanae. 8vo, 8*s.*

D. LITURGIOLOGY.

Cardwell's Two Books of Common Prayer, set forth by authority in the Reign of King Edward VI, compared with each other. *Third Edition.* 8vo, 7*s.*

—— History of Conferences on the Book of Common Prayer from 1551 to 1690. *Third Edition.* 8vo, 7*s.* 6*d.*

Hammond. Liturgies, Eastern and Western. Edited, with Introduction, Notes, and a Liturgical Glossary, by C. E. HAMMOND, M.A. *New Edition in the Press.*

Helps to the Study of the Book of Common Prayer. Being a Companion to Church Worship. Crown 8vo, 3*s.* 6*d.*

Leofric Missal, The; together with some Account of the Red Book of Derby, the Missal of Robert of Jumièges, &c. Edited, with Introduction and Notes, by F. E. WARREN, B.D., F.S.A. 4to, half-morocco, 1*l.* 15*s.*

Maskell. Ancient Liturgy of the Church of England, according to the uses of Sarum, York, Hereford, and Bangor, and the Roman Liturgy arranged in parallel columns, with preface and notes. By W. MASKELL, M.A. *Third Edition.* 8vo, 15*s.*

—— Monumenta Ritualia Ecclesiae Anglicanae. The occasional Offices of the Church of England according to the old use of Salisbury, the Prymer in English, and other prayers and forms, with dissertations and notes. *Second Edition.* 3 vols. 8vo, 2*l.* 10*s.*

Warren. The Liturgy and Ritual of the Celtic Church. By F. E. WARREN, B.D. 8vo, 14*s.*

E. ENGLISH THEOLOGY.

Bradley. Lectures on the Book of Job. By George Granville Bradley, D.D., Dean of Westminster. *Second Edition.* Crown 8vo, *7s. 6d.*

—— Lectures on Ecclesiastes. By G. G. Bradley, D.D. Crown 8vo, *4s. 6d.*

Bull's Works, with Nelson's Life. Edited by E. Burton, D.D. 8 vols. 8vo, *2l. 9s.*

Burnet's Exposition of the XXXIX Articles. 8vo, *7s.*

Burton's (Edward) Testimonies of the Ante-Nicene Fathers to the Divinity of Christ. 1829. 8vo, *7s.*

—— Testimonies of the Ante-Nicene Fathers to the Doctrine of the Trinity and of the Divinity of the Holy Ghost. 1831. 8vo, *3s. 6d.*

Butler's Works. 2 vols. 8vo, *11s.*

—— Sermons. *5s. 6d.* Analogy of Religion. *5s. 6d.*

Chillingworth's Works. 3 vols. 8vo, *1l. 1s. 6d.*

Clergyman's Instructor. *Sixth Edition.* 8vo, *6s. 6d.*

Cranmer's Works. Collected and arranged by H. Jenkyns, M.A., Fellow of Oriel College. 4 vols. 8vo, *1l. 10s.*

Enchiridion Theologicum Anti-Romanum.

Vol. I. Jeremy Taylor's Dissuasive from Popery, and Treatise on the Real Presence. 8vo, *8s.*

Vol. II. Barrow on the Supremacy of the Pope, with his Discourse on the Unity of the Church. 8vo, *7s. 6d.*

Vol. III. Tracts selected from Wake, Patrick, Stillingfleet, Clagett, and others. 8vo, *11s.*

Greswell's Harmonia Evangelica. *Fifth Edition.* 8vo, *9s. 6d.*

Hall's Works. Edited by P. Wynter, D.D. 10 vols. 8vo, *3l. 3s.*

Heurtley. Harmonia Symbolica: Creeds of the Western Church. By C. Heurtley, D.D. 8vo, *6s. 6d.*

Homilies appointed to be read in Churches. Edited by J. Griffiths, M.A. 8vo, *7s. 6d.*

HOOKER'S WORKS, with his Life by WALTON, arranged by JOHN KEBLE, M.A. *Seventh Edition.* Revised by R. W. CHURCH, M.A., Dean of St. Paul's, and F. PAGET, D.D. 3 vols. medium 8vo, 1*l.* 16*s.*

—— the Text as arranged by J. KEBLE, M.A. 2 vols. 8vo, 11*s.*

Hooper's Works. 2 vols. 8vo, 8*s.*

Jackson's (Dr. Thomas) Works. 12 vols. 8vo, 3*l.* 6*s.*

Jewel's Works. Edited by R. W. JELF, D.D. 8 vols. 8vo, 1*l.* 10*s.*

Martineau. A Study of Religion: its Sources and Contents. By JAMES MARTINEAU, D.D. *Second Edition.* 2 vols. crown 8vo, 15*s.*

Patrick's Theological Works. 9 vols. 8vo, 1*l.* 1*s.*

Pearson's Exposition of the Creed. Revised and corrected by E. BURTON, D.D. *Sixth Edition.* 8vo, 10*s.* 6*d.*

—— Minor Theological Works. Edited with a Memoir, by EDWARD CHURTON, M.A. 2 vols. 8vo, 10*s.*

Sanderson's Works. Edited by W. JACOBSON, D.D. 6 vols. 8vo, 1*l.* 10*s.*

Stillingfleet's Origines Sacrae. 2 vols. 8vo, 9*s.*

—— Rational Account of the Grounds of Protestant Religion. 2 vols. 8vo, 10*s.*

Wall's History of Infant Baptism. Edited by HENRY COTTON, D.C.L. 2 vols. 8vo, 1*l.* 1*s.*

Waterland's Works, with Life, by Bp. VAN MILDERT. *A new Edition*, with copious Indexes. 6 vols. 8vo, 2*l.* 11*s.*

—— Review of the Doctrine of the Eucharist, with a Preface by the late Bishop of London. Crown 8vo, 6*s.* 6*d.*

Wheatly's Illustration of the Book of Common Prayer. 8vo, 5*s.*

Wyclif. A Catalogue of the Original Works of John Wyclif. By W. W. SHIRLEY, D.D. 8vo, 3*s.* 6*d.*

—— Select English Works. By T. ARNOLD, M.A. 3 vols. 8vo, 1*l.* 1*s.*

—— Trialogus. With the Supplement now first edited. By GOTTHARD LECHLER. 8vo, 7*s.*

III. HISTORY, BIOGRAPHY,
POLITICAL ECONOMY, &c.

Arbuthnot. The Life and Works of John Arbuthnot. By GEORGE A. AITKEN. 8vo, cloth extra, with Portrait, 16*s.*

Baker's Chronicle. Chronicon Galfridi le Baker de Swynebroke. Edited with Notes by EDWARD MAUNDE THOMPSON, LL.D., D.C.L., F.S.A. Small 4to, stiff covers, 18*s.*; cloth, gilt top, 21*s.*

Bentham. A Fragment on Government. By JEREMY BENTHAM. Edited by F. C. MONTAGUE, M.A. 8vo, 7*s.* 6*d.*

Bluntschli. The Theory of the State. By J. K. BLUNTSCHLI. Translated from the Sixth German Edition. Second Edition, Revised. Crown 8vo, half-bound, 8*s.* 6*d.*

Boswell's Life of Samuel Johnson, LL.D.; including BOSWELL'S Journal of a Tour to the Hebrides, and JOHNSON'S Diary of a Journey into North Wales. Edited by G. BIRKBECK HILL, D.C.L. In six vols., 8vo. With Portraits and Facsimiles. Half-bound, 3*l.* 3*s.*

Burnet's History of James II. 8vo, 9*s.* 6*d.*

—— Life of Sir M. Hale, and **Fell's** Life of Dr. Hammond. Small 8vo, 2*s.* 6*d.*

Calendar of the Clarendon State Papers, preserved in the Bodleian Library. In three volumes. 1869–76.

Vol. I. From 1523 to January 1649. 8vo, 18*s.*
Vol. II. From 1649 to 1654. 8vo, 16*s.*
Vol. III. From 1655 to 1657. 8vo, 14*s.*

Calendar of Charters and Rolls preserved in the Bodleian Library. 8vo, 1*l.* 11*s.* 6*d.*

Carte's Life of James Duke of Ormond. A new Edition, carefully compared with the original MSS. 6 vols. 8vo, 1*l.* 5*s.*

Casaubon (Isaac), Life of, by MARK PATTISON, B.D. *Second Edition.* 8vo, 16*s.*

Casauboni Ephemerides, cum praefatione et notis J. RUSSELL, S.T.P. Tomi II. 8vo, 15*s.*

Chesterfield. Letters of Philip Dormer Fourth Earl of Chesterfield, to his Godson and Successor. Edited from the Originals, with a Memoir of Lord Chesterfield, by the late EARL OF CARNARVON. *Second Edition.* With Appendix of Additional Correspondence. Royal 8vo, cloth extra, 21*s*.

CLARENDON'S History of the Rebellion and Civil Wars in England. Re-edited from a fresh collation of the original MS. in the Bodleian Library, with marginal dates and occasional notes, by W. DUNN MACRAY, M.A., F.S.A. 6 vols. Crown 8vo, 2*l*. 5*s*.

—— History of the Rebellion and Civil Wars in England. To which are subjoined the Notes of BISHOP WARBURTON. 1849. 7 vols. Medium 8vo, 2*l*. 10*s*.

—— History of the Rebellion and Civil Wars in England. Also his Life, written by himself, in which is included a Continuation of his History of the Grand Rebellion. Royal 8vo, 1*l*. 2*s*.

Clarendon's Life, including a Continuation of his History. 2 vols. 1857. Medium 8vo, 1*l*. 2*s*.

Clinton's Fasti Hellenici. The Civil and Literary Chronology of Greece, from the LVIth to the CXXIIIrd Olympiad. *Third Edition.* 4to, 1*l*. 14*s*. 6*d*.

—— Fasti Hellenici. The Civil and Literary Chronology of Greece, from the CXXIVth Olympiad to the Death of Augustus. *Second Edition.* 4to, 1*l*. 12*s*.

—— Epitome of the Fasti Hellenici. 8vo, 6*s*. 6*d*.

—— Fasti Romani. The Civil and Literary Chronology of Rome and Constantinople, from the Death of Augustus to the Death of Heraclius. 2 vols. 4to, 2*l*. 2*s*.

—— Epitome of the Fasti Romani. 8vo, 7*s*.

Codrington. The Melanesians. Studies in their Anthropology and Folk-Lore. By R. H. CODRINGTON, D.D. 8vo, 16*s*.

Cramer's Geographical and Historical Description of Asia Minor. 2 vols. 8vo, 11*s*.

—— Description of Ancient Greece. 3 vols. 8vo, 16*s*. 6*d*.

Earle. Handbook to the Land-Charters, and other Saxonic Documents. By JOHN EARLE, M.A., Professor of Anglo-Saxon in the University of Oxford. Crown 8vo, 16*s*.

Elizabethan Seamen, Voyages of, to America. Edited by E. J. PAYNE, M.A. *First Series.* HAWKINS. FROBISHER. DRAKE. *Second Edition.* Crown 8vo, 5*s*.

Finlay. A History of Greece from its Conquest by the Romans to the present time, B.C. 146 to A.D. 1864. By GEORGE FINLAY, LL.D. A new Edition, revised throughout, and in part re-written, with considerable additions, by the Author, and edited by H. F. TOZER, M.A. 7 vols. 8vo, 3*l.* 10*s.*

Fortescue. The Governance of England: otherwise called The Difference between an Absolute and a Limited Monarchy. By Sir JOHN FORTESCUE, Kt. A Revised Text. Edited, with Introduction, Notes, &c., by CHARLES PLUMMER, M.A. 8vo, half-bound, 12*s.* 6*d.*

Freeman. The History of Sicily from the Earliest Times. Vols. I and II. 8vo, 2*l.* 2*s.*

Vol. III. The Athenian and Carthaginian Invasions. 1*l.* 4*s.*

—— History of the Norman Conquest of England; its Causes and Results. By E. A. FREEMAN, D.C.L. In Six Volumes, 8vo, 5*l.* 9*s.* 6*d.*

—— The Reign of William Rufus and the Accession of Henry the First. 2 vols. 8vo, 1*l.* 16*s.*

—— A Short History of the Norman Conquest of England. *Third Edition.* Extra fcap. 8vo, 2*s.* 6*d.*

French Revolutionary Speeches. See STEPHENS, H. Morse.

Gardiner. The Constitutional Documents of the Puritan Revolution. 1628–1660. Selected and Edited by SAMUEL RAWSON GARDINER, M.A. Crown 8vo, 9*s.*

Gascoigne's Theological Dictionary ('Liber Veritatum'): Selected Passages, illustrating the Condition of Church and State, 1403–1458. With an Introduction by JAMES E. THOROLD ROGERS, M.A. Small 4to, 10*s.* 6*d.*

George. Genealogical Tables illustrative of Modern History. By H. B. GEORGE, M.A. *Third Edition.* Small 4to, 12*s.*

Greswell's Fasti Temporis Catholici. 4 vols. 8vo, 2*l.* 10*s.*

—— Tables to Fasti, 4to, and Introduction to Tables, 8vo, 15*s.*

—— Origines Kalendariæ Italicæ. 4 vols. 8vo, 2*l.* 2*s.*

—— Origines Kalendariæ Hellenicæ. 6 vols. 8vo, 4*l.* 4*s.*

Greswell (W. Parr). History of the Dominion of Canada. By W. PARR GRESWELL, M.A., under the Auspices of the Royal Colonial Institute. With Eleven Maps. Crown 8vo, 7*s.* 6*d.*

—— Geography of the Dominion of Canada and Newfoundland. By the same Author. With Ten Maps. Crown 8vo, 6*s.*

—— Geography of Africa South of the Zambesi. With Maps. Crown 8vo, 7*s.* 6*d.*

Gross. The Gild Merchant: a Contribution to British Municipal History. By C. GROSS, Ph.D. 2 vols. 8vo, half-bound, 24*s.*

Hastings. Hastings and The Rohilla War. By Sir JOHN STRACHEY, G.C.S.I. 8vo, cloth, 10*s.* 6*d.*

Hodgkin. Italy and her Invaders. With Plates and Maps. By THOMAS HODGKIN, D.C.L. (A.D. 376–553).

Vols. I–II. The Visigothic Invasions. The Hunnish Invasion. The Vandal Invasion, and the Herulian Mutiny. *Second Edition*, 2*l.* 2*s.*

Vols. III–IV. The Ostrogothic Invasion. The Imperial Restoration. 36*s.*

—— The Dynasty of Theodosius; or, Seventy Years' Struggle with the Barbarians. By the same Author. Crown 8vo, 6*s.*

Hume. Letters of David Hume to William Strahan. Edited with Notes, Index, &c., by G. BIRKBECK HILL, D.C.L. 8vo, 12*s.* 6*d.*

Hunter (Sir W. W.). A Brief History of the Indian Peoples. By Sir W. W. HUNTER, K.C.S.I. *Eightieth Thousand.* Crown 8vo, 3*s.* 6*d.*

Jackson. Dalmatia, the Quarnero, and Istria; with Cettigne in Montenegro and the Island of Grado. By T. G. JACKSON, M.A. 3 vols. With many Plates and Illustrations. 8vo, half-bound, 2*l.* 2*s.*

Johnson. Letters of Samuel Johnson, LL.D. Collected and Edited by G. BIRKBECK HILL, D.C.L. In two volumes. Medium 8vo, half-roan (uniform with Boswell's Life of Johnson,) 28*s.*

Kitchin. A History of France. With numerous Maps, Plans, and Tables. By G. W. KITCHIN, D.D. In three Volumes. Crown 8vo, each 10*s.* 6*d.*

Vol. I, to 1453. *Third Edition.*
Vol. II, 1453–1624. *Second Edition.*
Vol. III, 1624–1793. *Second Edition.*

Knight's Life of Dean Colet. 1823. 8vo, 7*s.* 6*d.*

Lloyd's Prices of Corn in Oxford, 1583–1830. 8vo, 1*s.*

Lewes, The Song of. Edited, with Introduction and Notes, by C. L. KINGSFORD, M.A. Extra fcap. 8vo, 5*s.*

Lewis (Sir G. Cornewall). An Essay on the Government of Dependencies. Edited by C. P. LUCAS, B.A. 8vo, half-roan, 14*s*.

Lucas. Introduction to a Historical Geography of the British Colonies. By C. P. LUCAS, B.A. With Eight Maps. Crown 8vo, 4*s*. 6*d*.

—— Historical Geography of the British Colonies. By the same Author:

Vol. I. The Mediterranean and Eastern Colonies (exclusive of India). With Eleven Maps. 5*s*.

Vol. II. The West Indian Colonies. With Twelve Maps. 7*s*. 6*d*.

Luttrell's (Narcissus) Diary. A Brief Historical Relation of State Affairs, 1678–1714. 6 vols. 8vo, 1*l*. 4*s*.

Machiavelli (Niccolò). Il Principe. Edited by L. ARTHUR BURD. With an Introduction by LORD ACTON. 8vo, 14*s*.

Macray (W. D.). Annals of the Bodleian Library, Oxford, with a Notice of the Earlier Library of the University. By W. DUNN MACRAY, M.A., F.S.A. *Second Edition, enlarged and continued from* 1868 to 1880. Medium 8vo, half-bound, 25*s*.

Magna Carta, a careful Reprint. Edited by W. STUBBS, D.D., Lord Bishop of Oxford. 4to, stitched, 1*s*.

Metcalfe. Passio et Miracula Beati Olaui. Edited from a Twelfth-Century MS. by F. METCALFE, M.A. Small 4to, 6*s*.

OXFORD, University of.

Oxford University Calendar for 1894. Crown 8vo, 6*s*.

The Historical Register of the University of Oxford. Being a Supplement to the Oxford University Calendar, with an Alphabetical Record of University Honours and Distinctions, completed to the end of Trinity Term, 1888. Crown 8vo, 5*s*.

Student's Handbook to the University and Colleges of Oxford. *Twelfth Edition.* Crown 8vo, 2*s*. 6*d*.

The Examination Statutes; together with the Regulations of the Boards of Studies and Boards of Faculties for the Academical Year 1893–94. Revised to June 21, 1893. 8vo, paper covers, 1*s*.

Statuta Universitatis Oxoniensis. 1893. 8vo, 5*s*.

Statutes made for the University of Oxford, and the Colleges therein, by the University of Oxford Commissioners. 8vo, 12*s*. 6*d*.

Also separately—University Statutes, 2*s*.; College Statutes, 1*s*. each.

Supplementary Statutes made by the University of Oxford, and by certain of the Colleges therein, in pursuance of the Universities of Oxford and Cambridge Act, 1877; approved by the Queen in Council. 8vo, paper covers, 2*s*. 6*d*.

OXFORD, University of (*continued*).

Statutes of the University of Oxford, codified in the year 1636 under the Authority of ARCHBISHOP LAUD, Chancellor of the University. Edited by the late JOHN GRIFFITHS, D.D. With an Introduction on the History of the Laudian Code by C. L. SHADWELL, M.A., B.C.L. 4to, 1*l*. 1*s*.

Enactments in Parliament, specially concerning the Universities of Oxford and Cambridge. Collected and arranged by J. GRIFFITHS, D.D. 1869. 8vo, 12*s*.

Catalogue of Oxford Graduates, 1659 to 1850. 7*s*. 6*d*.

Index to Wills proved in the Court of the Chancellor of the University of Oxford, &c. Compiled by J. GRIFFITHS, D.D. 3*s*. 6*d*.

Manuscript Materials relating to the History of Oxford; contained in the Printed Catalogues of the Bodleian and College Libraries. By F. MADAN, M.A. 8vo, 7*s*. 6*d*.

Pattison. Essays by the late MARK PATTISON, sometime Rector of Lincoln College. Collected and arranged by HENRY NETTLESHIP, M.A. 2 vols. 8vo, 24*s*.

—— Life of Isaac Casaubon (1559–1614). By the same Author. *Second Edition.* 8vo, 16*s*.

Payne. History of the New World called America. By E. J. PAYNE, M.A. Vol. I, 8vo, 18*s*. Vol. II. *In the Press.*

—— Voyages of the Elizabethan Seamen to America. Edited by E. J. PAYNE, M.A. *First Series.* HAWKINS. FROBISHER. DRAKE. *Second Edition.* Crown 8vo, 5*s*.

Ralegh. Sir Walter Ralegh. A Biography. By W. STEBBING, M.A. 8vo, 10*s*. 6*d*.

Ramsay (Sir James H.). **Lancaster and York.** A Century of English History (A.D. 1399–1485). 2 vols. 8vo, 1*l*. 16*s*.

Ranke. A History of England, principally in the Seventeenth Century. By L. VON RANKE. Translated under the superintendence of G. W. KITCHIN, D.D., and C. W. BOASE, M.A. 6 vols. 8vo, 3*l*. 3*s*.

Rawlinson. A Manual of Ancient History. By GEORGE RAWLINSON, M.A. *Second Edition.* Demy 8vo, 14*s*.

Rhŷs. Studies in the Arthurian Legend. By JOHN RHŶS, M.A., Professor of Celtic in the University of Oxford. 8vo, 12*s*. 6*d*.

Ricardo. Letters of David Ricardo to T. R. Malthus (1810–1823). Edited by JAMES BONAR, M.A. 8vo, 10*s*. 6*d*.

Rogers. History of Agriculture and Prices in England, A.D. 1259–1793. By JAMES E. THOROLD ROGERS, M.A.

Vols. I and II (1259–1400). 8vo, *2l. 2s.*

Vols. III and IV (1401–1582). 8vo, *2l. 10s.*

Vols. V and VI (1583–1702). 8vo, *2l. 10s.*

Vols. VII and VIII. *In the Press.*

—— First Nine Years of the Bank of England. 8vo, *8s. 6d.*

—— Protests of the Lords, including those which have been expunged, from 1624 to 1874; with Historical Introductions. In three volumes. 8vo, *2l. 2s.*

Selden. The Table Talk of JOHN SELDEN. Edited, with an Introduction and Notes, by SAMUEL HARVEY REYNOLDS, M.A. 8vo, half-roan, *8s. 6d.*

Smith's Wealth of Nations. A new Edition, with Notes, by J. E. THOROLD ROGERS, M.A. 2 vols. 8vo, *21s.*

Sprigg's England's Recovery; being the History of the Army under Sir Thomas Fairfax. 8vo, *6s.*

RULERS OF INDIA: The History of the Indian Empire in a carefully planned succession of Political Biographies. Edited by Sir WILLIAM WILSON HUNTER, K.C.S.I. In crown 8vo. Half-crown volumes.

Now Ready:

The Marquess of Dalhousie. By Sir W. W. HUNTER.

Akbar. By COLONEL MALLESON, C.S.I.

Dupleix. By COLONEL MALLESON, C.S.I.

Warren Hastings. By CAPTAIN L. J. TROTTER.

The Marquess of Cornwallis. By W. S. SETON-KARR.

The Earl of Mayo. By Sir W. W. HUNTER, K.C.S.I.

Viscount Hardinge. By his son, VISCOUNT HARDINGE.

Clyde and Strathnairn. By Major-General Sir OWEN TUDOR BURNE, K.C.S.I.

Earl Canning. By Sir H. S. CUNNINGHAM, K.C.I.E.

Mádhava Ráo Sindhia. By H. G. KEENE, M.A., C.I.E.

Mountstuart Elphinstone. By J. S. COTTON, M.A.

Lord William Bentinck. By DEMETRIUS C. BOULGER.

Ranjit Singh. By Sir LEPEL GRIFFIN, K.C.S.I.

Lord Lawrence. By Sir C. AITCHISON, K.C.S.I., LL.D.

Albuquerque. By H. MORSE STEPHENS.

Marquess of Hastings. By Major ROSS-OF-BLADENSBURG, C.B.

RULERS OF INDIA (*continued*).

Aurangzíb. By STANLEY LANE-POOLE, B.A.

The Earl of Auckland. By Captain L. J. TROTTER.

Lord Clive. By COLONEL MALLESON, C.S.I.

The Marquess Wellesley, K.G. By W. H. HUTTON, M.A.

Haidar Alí and Tipú Sultán. By L. B. BOWRING, C.S.I.

SUPPLEMENTARY VOLUMES.

James Thomason. By Sir RICHARD TEMPLE, Bart. 3*s.* 6*d.*

A Brief History of the Indian Peoples. By Sir W. W. HUNTER, K.C.S.I. *Eightieth Thousand.* Crown 8vo, 3*s.* 6*d.*

Stephens. The Principal Speeches of the Statesmen and Orators of the French Revolution, 1789–1795. With Introductions, Notes, &c. By H. MORSE STEPHENS. 2 vols. Crown 8vo, 21*s.*

Stubbs. Select Charters and other Illustrations of English Constitutional History, from the Earliest Times to the Reign of Edward I. Arranged and edited by W. STUBBS, D.D., Lord Bishop of Oxford. *Seventh Edition.* Crown 8vo, 8*s.* 6*d.*

—— The Constitutional History of England, in its Origin and Development. *Library Edition.* 3 vols. Demy 8vo, 2*l.* 8*s.*

Also in 3 vols. crown 8vo, price 12*s.* each.

—— Seventeen Lectures on the Study of Mediaeval and Modern History. *Second Edition.* Crown 8vo, 8*s.* 6*d.*

Tozer. The Islands of the Aegean. By H. FANSHAWE TOZER, M.A., F.R.G.S. Crown 8vo, 8*s.* 6*d.*

Vinogradoff. Villainage in England. Essays in English Mediaeval History. By PAUL VINOGRADOFF, Professor in the University of Moscow. 8vo, half-bound, 16*s.*

Wellesley. A Selection from the Despatches, Treaties, and other Papers of the MARQUESS WELLESLEY, K.G., during his Government of India. Edited by S. J. OWEN, M.A. 8vo, 1*l.* 4*s.*

Wellington. A Selection from the Despatches, Treaties, and other Papers relating to India of Field-Marshal the DUKE OF WELLINGTON, K.G. Edited by S. J. OWEN, M.A. 8vo, 1*l.* 4*s.*

Whitelock's Memorials of English Affairs from 1625 to 1660. 4 vols. 8vo, 1*l.* 10*s.*

Cannan. Elementary Political Economy. By EDWIN CANNAN, M.A. Extra fcap. 8vo, stiff covers, 1*s.*

Raleigh. Elementary Politics. By THOMAS RALEIGH, M.A. *Sixth Edition.* Extra fcap. 8vo, stiff covers, 1*s.*

IV. LAW.

Anson. Principles of the English Law of Contract, and of Agency in its Relation to Contract. By SIR W. R. ANSON, D.C.L. *Seventh Edition*. 8vo, 10s. 6d.

—— Law and Custom of the Constitution. In two Parts.

Part I. Parliament. *Second Edition.* 8vo, 12s. 6d.

Part II. The Crown. 8vo, 14s.

Baden-Powell. Land-Systems of British India; being a Manual of the Land-Tenures, and of the Systems of Land-Revenue Administration prevalent in the several Provinces. By B. H. BADEN-POWELL, C.I.E., F.R.S.E., M.R.A.S. 3 vols. 8vo, with Maps, 3l. 3s.

—— Land-Revenue and Tenure in British India. By the same Author. With Map. Crown 8vo, 5s.

Bentham. An Introduction to the Principles of Morals and Legislation. By JEREMY BENTHAM. Crown 8vo, 6s. 6d.

Digby. An Introduction to the History of the Law of Real Property. By KENELM E. DIGBY, M.A. *Fourth Edition.* 8vo, 12s. 6d.

Grueber. Lex Aquilia. The Roman Law of Damage to Property: being a Commentary on the Title of the Digest 'Ad Legem Aquiliam' (ix. 2). With an Introduction to the Study of the Corpus Iuris Civilis. By ERWIN GRUEBER, Dr. Jur., M.A. 8vo, 10s. 6d.

Hall. International Law. By W. E. HALL, M.A. *Third Edition.* 8vo, 22s. 6d.

Holland. Elements of Jurisprudence. By T. E. HOLLAND, D.C.L. *Sixth Edition.* 8vo, 10s. 6d.

—— The European Concert in the Eastern Question, a Collection of Treaties and other Public Acts. Edited, with Introductions and Notes, by T. E. HOLLAND, D.C.L. 8vo, 12s. 6d.

—— Gentilis, Alberici, I.C.D., I.C.P.R., de Iure Belli Libri Tres. Edidit T. E. HOLLAND, I.C.D. Small 4to, half-morocco, 21s.

—— The Institutes of Justinian, edited as a recension of the Institutes of GAIUS, by T. E. HOLLAND, D.C.L. *Second Edition.* Extra fcap. 8vo, 5s.

Holland and **Shadwell**. Select Titles from the Digest of Justinian. By T. E. Holland, D.C.L., and C. L. Shadwell, B.C.L. 8vo, 14*s*.

Also sold in Parts, in paper covers, as follows:—

Part I. Introductory Titles. 2*s*. 6*d*.

Part II. Family Law. 1*s*.

Part III. Property Law. 2*s*. 6*d*.

Part IV. Law of Obligations (No. 1). 3*s*. 6*d*.

Part IV. Law of Obligations (No. 2). 4*s*. 6*d*.

Markby. Elements of Law considered with reference to Principles of General Jurisprudence. By Sir William Markby, D.C.L. *Fourth Edition*. 8vo, 12*s*. 6*d*.

Moyle. Imperatoris Iustiniani Institutionum Libri Quattuor; with Introductions, Commentary, Excursus, and Translation. By J. B. Moyle, D.C.L. *Second Edition*. 2 vols. 8vo, 22*s*.

—— Contract of Sale in the Civil Law. By J. B. Moyle, D.C.L. 8vo, 10*s*. 6*d*.

Pollock and **Wright**. An Essay on Possession in the Common Law. By Sir F. Pollock, M.A., and Sir R. S. Wright, B.C.L. 8vo, 8*s*. 6*d*.

Poste. Gaii Institutionum Juris Civilis Commentarii Quattuor; or, Elements of Roman Law by Gaius. With a Translation and Commentary by Edward Poste, M.A. *Third Edition*. 8vo, 18*s*.

Raleigh. An Outline of the Law of Property. By Thomas Raleigh, M.A. 8vo, cloth, 7*s*. 6*d*.

Sohm. Institutes of Roman Law. By Rudolph Sohm, Professor in the University of Leipzig. Translated (from the Fourth Edition of the German) by J. C. Ledlie, B.C.L., M.A. With an Introductory Essay by Erwin Grueber, Dr. Jur., M.A. 8vo, 18*s*.

Stokes. Anglo-Indian Codes. By Whitley Stokes, LL.D. Vol. I. Substantive Law. 8vo, 30*s*. Vol. II. Adjective Law. 8vo, 35*s*.

—— First Supplement to the above, 1887, 1888. 2*s*. 6*d*.

—— Second Supplement, to May 31, 1891. 4*s*. 6*d*.

—— First and Second Supplements in one volume, price 6*s*. 6*d*.

Twiss. The Law of Nations considered as Independent Political Communities. By Sir Travers Twiss, D.C.L.

Part I. On the rights and Duties of Nations in time of Peace. New Edition, Revised and Enlarged. 8vo, 15*s*.

V. PHILOSOPHY, LOGIC, &c.

Bacon. Novum Organum. Edited, with Introduction, Notes, &c., by T. Fowler, D.D. *Second Edition.* 8vo, 15*s.*

—— Novum Organum. Edited, with English Notes, by G. W. Kitchin, D.D. 8vo, 9*s.* 6*d.*

—— The Essays. Edited, with Introduction and Illustrative Notes, by S. H. Reynolds, M.A. Demy 8vo, half-bound, 12*s.* 6*d.*

Berkeley. The works of George Berkeley, D.D., formerly Bishop of Cloyne; including many of his writings hitherto unpublished. With Prefaces, Annotations, and an Account of his Life and Philosophy, by Alexander Campbell Fraser, LL.D. 4 vols. 8vo, 2*l.* 18*s.*

The Life, Letters, &c., separately, 16*s.*

Berkeley. Selections. With Introduction and Notes. For the use of Students in the Universities. By Alexander Campbell Fraser, LL.D. *Fourth Edition.* Crown 8vo, 8*s.* 6*d.*

Bosanquet. Logic; or, The Morphology of Knowledge. By B. Bosanquet, M.A. 8vo, 21*s.*

Butler's Works, with Index to the Analogy. 2 vols. 8vo, 11*s.*

Fowler. The Elements of Deductive Logic, designed mainly for the use of Junior Students in the Universities. By T. Fowler, D.D. *Ninth Edition,* with a Collection of Examples. Extra fcap. 8vo, 3*s.* 6*d.*

Fowler. The Elements of Inductive Logic, designed mainly for the use of Students in the Universities. *Fifth Edition.* Extra fcap. 8vo, 6*s.*

—— The Principles of Morals (Introductory Chapters). By T. Fowler, D.D., and J. M. Wilson, B.D. 8vo, boards, 3*s.* 6*d.*

—— The Principles of Morals. Part II. By T. Fowler, D.D. 8vo, 10*s.* 6*d.*

Green. Prolegomena to Ethics. By T. H. Green, M.A. Edited by A. C. Bradley, M.A. *Third Edition.* 8vo, 12*s.* 6*d.*

Hegel. The Logic of Hegel; translated from the Encyclopaedia of the Philosophical Sciences. By William Wallace, M.A., LL.D. *Second Edition, Revised and Augmented.* Crown 8vo, 10*s.* 6*d.*

The Volume containing the Prolegomena is under Revision, and will be issued shortly.

Hume's Treatise of Human Nature. Reprinted from the Original Edition in Three Volumes, and Edited by L. A. Selby-Bigge, M.A. Crown 8vo, 9*s.*

Locke's Conduct of the Understanding. Edited by T. FOWLER, D.D. *Third Edition.* Extra fcap. 8vo, 2*s.* 6*d.*

Lotze's Logic, in Three Books; of Thought, of Investigation, and of Knowledge. English Translation; Edited by B. BOSANQUET, M.A. *Second Edition.* 2 vols. Crown 8vo, 12*s.*

—— Metaphysic, in Three Books; Ontology, Cosmology, and Psychology. English Translation; Edited by B. BOSANQUET, M.A. *Second Edition.* 2 vols. Crown 8vo, 12*s.*

Martineau. Types of Ethical Theory. By JAMES MARTINEAU, D.D. *Third Edition.* 2 vols. Crown 8vo, 15*s.*

—— A Study of Religion: its Sources and Contents. *Second Edition.* 2 vols. Crown 8vo, 15*s.*

VI. PHYSICAL SCIENCE AND MATHEMATICS, &c.

Acland. Synopsis of the Pathological Series in the Oxford Museum. By Sir H. W. ACLAND, M.D., F.R.S. 8vo, 2*s.* 6*d.*

Aldis. A Text-Book of Algebra: with Answers to the Examples. By W. S. ALDIS, M.A. Crown 8vo, 7*s.* 6*d.*

Aplin. The Birds of Oxfordshire. By O. V. APLIN. 8vo. with a Map and one coloured Plate, 10*s.* 6*d.*

Archimedis quae supersunt omnia cum Eutocii commentariis ex recensione J. TORELLI, cum nova versione latina. 1792. Fol. 1*l.* 5*s.*

Baynes. Lessons on Thermodynamics. By R. E. BAYNES, M.A. Crown 8vo, 7*s.* 6*d.*

BIOLOGICAL SERIES. (Translations of Foreign Memoirs.)

I. Memoirs on the Physiology of Nerve, of Muscle, and of the Electrical Organ. Edited by J. BURDON-SANDERSON, M.D., F.R.SS.L. & E. Medium 8vo, 1*l.* 1*s.*

II. The Anatomy of the Frog. By Dr. ALEXANDER ECKER, Professor in the University of Freiburg. Translated, with numerous Annotations and Additions, by GEORGE HASLAM, M.D. Medium 8vo, 21*s.*

IV. Essays upon Heredity and kindred Biological Problems. By Dr. AUGUST WEISMANN. Authorised Translation. Edited by EDWARD B. POULTON, M.A., F.R.S., SELMAR SCHÖNLAND, PH.D., and ARTHUR E. SHIPLEY, M.A., F.L.S. Crown 8vo.

Vol. I. *Second Edition*, 7*s.* 6*d.*

Vol. II. Edited by E. B. POULTON and A. E. SHIPLEY. 5*s.*

BOTANICAL SERIES.

History of Botany (1530–1860). By JULIUS VON SACHS. Authorised Translation, by H. E. F. GARNSEY, M.A. Revised by ISAAC BAYLEY BALFOUR, M.A., M.D., F.R.S. Crown 8vo, 10*s*.

Comparative Anatomy of the Vegetative Organs of the Phanerogams and Ferns. By Dr. A. DE BARY. Translated and Annotated by F. O. BOWER, M.A., F.L.S., and D. H. SCOTT, M.A., Ph.D., F.L.S. Royal 8vo, half-morocco, 1*l*. 2*s*. 6*d*.

Outlines of Classification and Special Morphology of Plants. By Dr. K. GOEBEL. Translated by H. E. F. GARNSEY, M.A., and Revised by ISAAC BAYLEY BALFOUR, M.A., M.D., F.R.S. Royal 8vo, half-morocco, 1*l*. 1*s*.

Lectures on the Physiology of Plants. By JULIUS VON SACHS. Translated by H. MARSHALL WARD, M.A., F.L.S. Royal 8vo, half-morocco, 1*l*. 11*s*. 6*d*.

Comparative Morphology and Biology of Fungi, Mycetozoa and Bacteria. By Dr. A. DE BARY. Translated by H. E. F. GARNSEY, M.A., Revised by ISAAC BAYLEY BALFOUR, M.A., M.D., F.R.S. Royal 8vo, half-morocco, 1*l*. 2*s*. 6*d*.

Lectures on Bacteria. By Dr. A. DE BARY. *Second Improved Edition.* Translated by H. E. F. GARNSEY, M.A. Revised by ISAAC BAYLEY BALFOUR, M.A., M.D., F.R.S. Crown 8vo, 6*s*.

Introduction to Fossil Botany. By Count H. ZU SOLMS-LAUBACH. Translated by H. E. F. GARNSEY, M.A. Revised by ISAAC BAYLEY BALFOUR, M.A., M.D., F.R.S. Royal 8vo, half-morocco, 18*s*.

Index Kewensis; an enumeration of the Genera and Species of Flowering Plants from the time of Linnaeus to the year 1885 inclusive. Edited by Sir J. D. HOOKER and B. D. JACKSON. Part I. 4to. Price to Subscribers, 2*l*. 2*s*. *net*.

*** *The Work will be completed in Four Parts, to be issued to Subscribers at Eight Guineas net.*

Annals of Botany. Edited by ISAAC BAYLEY BALFOUR, M.A., M.D., F.R.S., SYDNEY H. VINES, D.Sc., F.R.S., D. H. SCOTT, M.A., Ph.D., F.L.S., and W. G. FARLOW, M.D.; assisted by other Botanists. Royal 8vo, half-morocco, gilt top.

Vol. I. Parts I–IV. 1*l*. 16*s*. — Vol. II. Parts V–VIII. 2*l*. 2*s*.
Vol. III. Parts IX–XII. 2*l*. 12*s*. 6*d*. — Vol. IV. Parts XIII–XVI. 2*l*. 5*s*.
Vol. V. Parts XVII–XX. 2*l*. 10*s*. — Vol. VI. Part XXI–XXIV. 2*l*. 4*s*.
Vol. VII. Part XXV. 12*s*. — Part XXVI. 12*s*.

Reprints from the 'Annals of Botany.'

A Summary of the New Ferns which have been Discovered or Described since 1874. A Supplement to the *Synopsis Filicum*, bringing that work up to 1890. By J. G. BAKER, F.R.S. Royal 8vo, with one Plate, price 5*s*. *net*.

A Revised List of the British Marine Algae. With an Appendix, by E. M. HOLMES, F.L.S., and E. A. L. BATTERS, B.A., LL.B., F.L.S. Royal 8vo, paper covers, price 2*s*. 6*d*. *net*.

Bradley's Miscellaneous Works and Correspondence. With an Account of Harriot's Astronomical Papers. 4to, 17*s*.

Chambers. A Handbook of Descriptive Astronomy. By G. F. CHAMBERS, F.R.A.S. *Fourth Edition.*

Vol. I. The Sun, Planets, and Comets. 8vo, 21*s*.
Vol. II. Instruments and Practical Astronomy. 8vo, 21*s*.
Vol. III. The Starry Heavens. 8vo, 14*s*.

Clarke. Geodesy. By Col. A. R. CLARKE, C.B., R.E. 8vo, 12*s*. 6*d*.

Cremona. Elements of Projective Geometry. By LUIGI CREMONA. Translated by C. LEUDESDORF, M.A. *Second Edition.* 8vo, 12*s*. 6*d*.

—— Graphical Statics. Two Treatises on the Graphical Calculus and Reciprocal Figures in Graphical Statics. By the same Author. Translated by T. HUDSON BEARE. Demy 8vo, 8*s*. 6*d*.

Daubeny's Introduction to the Atomic Theory. 16mo, 6*s*.

Dixey. Epidemic Influenza, a Study in Comparative Statistics. By F. A. DIXEY, M.A., D.M. Medium 8vo, 7*s*. 6*d*.

Donkin. Acoustics. By W. F. DONKIN, M.A., F.R.S. *Second Edition.* Crown 8vo, 7*s*. 6*d*.

Emtage. An Introduction to the Mathematical Theory of Electricity and Magnetism. By W. T. A. EMTAGE, M.A. Crown 8vo, 7*s*. 6*d*.

Etheridge. Fossils of the British Islands, Stratigraphically and Zoologically arranged. Part I. PALAEOZOIC. By R. ETHERIDGE, F.R.SS.L. & E., F.G.S. 4to, 1*l*. 10*s*.

EUCLID REVISED. Containing the Essentials of the Elements of Plane Geometry as given by Euclid in his first Six Books. Edited by R. C. J. NIXON, M.A. *Second Edition.* Crown 8vo, 6*s*.

Supplement to *Euclid Revised.* 6*d*.

Sold separately as follows:—

Book I. 1*s*. Books I, II. 1*s*. 6*d*.
Books I–IV. 3*s*. Books V, VI. 3*s*.

Euclid. Geometry in Space. Containing parts of Euclid's Eleventh and Twelfth Books. By R. C. J. NIXON, M.A. Crown 8vo, 3*s*. 6*d*.

Fisher. Class-Book of Chemistry. By W. W. FISHER, M.A., F.C.S. Second Edition. Crown 8vo, 4*s*. 6*d*.

Galton. The Construction of Healthy Dwellings. By Sir DOUGLAS GALTON, K.C.B., F.R.S. 8vo, 10*s*. 6*d*.

—— Healthy Hospitals. Observations on some points connected with Hospital Construction. With Illustrations. 8vo, 10*s*. 6*d*.

Greenwell. British Barrows, a Record of the Examination of Sepulchral Mounds in various parts of England. By W. GREENWELL, M.A., F.S.A. Together with Description of Figures of Skulls, General Remarks on Prehistoric Crania, and an Appendix by GEORGE ROLLESTON, M.D., F.R.S. Medium 8vo, 25*s*.

Gresswell. A Contribution to the Natural History of Scarlatina, derived from Observations on the London Epidemic of 1887–1888. By D. ASTLEY GRESSWELL, M.D. Medium 8vo, 10*s*. 6*d*.

Hamilton and **Ball.** Book-keeping. New and enlarged Edition. By Sir R. G. C. HAMILTON and JOHN BALL. Cloth, 2*s*.

Ruled Exercise books adapted to the above may be had, price 1*s*. 6*d*.*; also, adapted to the Preliminary Course only, price* 4*d*.

Harcourt and **Madan.** Exercises in Practical Chemistry. Vol. I. Elementary Exercises. By A. G. VERNON HARCOURT, M.A., and H. G. MADAN, M.A. *Fourth Edition.* Crown 8vo, 10*s*. 6*d*.

Madan. Tables of Qualitative Analysis. By H. G. MADAN, M.A. Large 4to, paper covers, 4*s*. 6*d*.

Hensley. Figures made Easy. A first Arithmetic Book. By LEWIS HENSLEY, M.A. Crown 8vo, 6*d*. Answers, 1*s*.

—— The Scholar's Arithmetic. 2*s*. 6*d*. Answers, 1*s*. 6*d*.

—— The Scholar's Algebra. Crown 8vo, 2*s*. 6*d*.

Hughes. Geography for Schools. By ALFRED HUGHES, M.A. Part I. Practical Geography. With Diagrams. Crown 8vo, 2*s*. 6*d*.

Johnston. An Elementary Treatise on Analytical Geometry. By W. J. JOHNSTON, M.A. Crown 8vo, 10*s*. 6*d*.

Maclaren. A System of Physical Education: Theoretical and Practical. By ARCHIBALD MACLAREN. Extra fcap. 8vo, 7*s*. 6*d*.

Maxwell. A Treatise on Electricity and Magnetism. By J. CLERK MAXWELL, M.A. *Third Edition.* 2 vols. 8vo, 1*l*. 12*s*.

—— An Elementary Treatise on Electricity. Edited by WILLIAM GARNETT, M.A. 8vo, 7*s*. 6*d*.

Minchin. A Treatise on Statics with Applications to Physics. By G. M. MINCHIN, M.A. *Fourth Edition.*

Vol. I. Equilibrium of Coplanar Forces. 8vo, 10*s*. 6*d*.
Vol. II. Non-Coplanar Forces. 8vo, 16*s*.

—— Uniplanar Kinematics of Solids and Fluids. Crown 8vo, 7*s*. 6*d*.

—— Hydrostatics and Elementary Hydrokinetics. Crown 8vo, 10*s*. 6*d*.

Müller. On certain Variations in the Vocal Organs of the Passeres. By J. MÜLLER. Translated by F. J. BELL, B.A., and edited by A. H. GARROD, M.A., F.R.S. With Plates. 4to, 7*s*. 6*d*.

Nixon. Elementary Plane Trigonometry. By R. C. J. NIXON, M.A. Crown 8vo, 7*s*. 6*d*. (See EUCLID REVISED.)

Phillips. Geology of Oxford and the Valley of the Thames. By JOHN PHILLIPS, M.A., F.R.S. 8vo, 21*s*.

—— Vesuvius. Crown 8vo, 10*s*. 6*d*.

Powell. The Surgical Aspect of Traumatic Insanity. By H. A. POWELL, M.A., M.D. 8vo, stiff cover, 2*s*. 6*d*.

Prestwich. Geology, Chemical, Physical, and Stratigraphical. By JOSEPH PRESTWICH, M.A., F.R.S. In two Volumes.

Vol. I. Chemical and Physical. Royal 8vo, 1*l*. 5*s*.
Vol. II. Stratigraphical and Physical. With a new Geological Map of Europe. Royal 8vo, 1*l*. 16*s*.
New Geological Map of Europe. In case or on roller. 5*s*.

Price. Treatise on Infinitesimal Calculus. By BARTHOLOMEW PRICE, M.A., F.R.S.

Vol. I. Differential Calculus. *Second Edition.* 8vo, 14*s*. 6*d*.
Vol. II. Integral Calculus, Calculus of Variations, and Differential Equations. *Reprinting.*
Vol. III. Statics, including Attractions; Dynamics of a Material Particle. *Second Edition.* 8vo, 16*s*.
Vol. IV. Dynamics of Material Systems. *Second Edition.* 8vo, 18*s*.

Pritchard. Astronomical Observations made at the University Observatory, Oxford, under the direction of C. PRITCHARD, D.D. No. I. Royal 8vo, paper covers, 3*s*. 6*d*.

—— No. II. Uranometria Nova Oxoniensis. A Photometric determination of the magnitudes of all Stars visible to the naked eye, from the Pole to ten degrees south of the Equator. Royal 8vo, 8*s*. 6*d*.

—— No. III. Researches in Stellar Parallax by the aid of Photography. Royal 8vo, 7*s*. 6*d*.

—— No IV. Researches in Stellar Parallax by the aid of Photography. Part II. Royal 8vo, 4*s*. 6*d*.

Rigaud's Correspondence of Scientific Men of the 17th Century, with Table of Contents by A. de MORGAN, and Index by J. RIGAUD, M.A. 2 vols. 8vo, 18*s*. 6*d*.

Rolleston and Jackson. Forms of Animal Life. A Manual of Comparative Anatomy, with descriptions of selected types. By GEORGE ROLLESTON, M.D., F.R.S. *Second Edition.* Revised and enlarged by W. HATCHETT JACKSON, M.A. Medium 8vo, 1*l*. 16*s*.

Russell. An Elementary Treatise on Pure Geometry. With numerous Examples. By J. WELLESLEY RUSSELL, M.A. Crown 8vo, 10*s*. 6*d*.

Rolleston. Scientific Papers and Addresses. By GEORGE ROLLESTON, M.D., F.R.S. Arranged and edited by WILLIAM TURNER, M.B., F.R.S. With a Biographical Sketch by EDWARD TYLOR, F.R.S. 2 vols. 8vo, 1*l*. 4*s*.

Selby. Elementary Mechanics of Solids and Fluids. By A. L. SELBY, M.A. Crown 8vo, 7*s*. 6*d*.

Smyth. A Cycle of Celestial Objects. Observed, Reduced, and Discussed by Admiral W. H. SMYTH, R.N. Revised, condensed, and greatly enlarged by G. F. CHAMBERS, F.R.A.S. 8vo, 12*s*.

Stewart. An Elementary Treatise on Heat, with numerous Woodcuts and Diagrams. By BALFOUR STEWART, LL.D., F.R.S. *Fifth Edition.* Extra fcap. 8vo, 7*s*. 6*d*.

Strabo, Selections from. With an Introduction on Strabo's Life and Works. By H. F. TOZER, M.A., F.R.G.S. With Maps and Plans. [*Immediately.*]

Swinhoe. Catalogue of Eastern and Australian Lepidoptera Heterocera in the Collection of the Oxford University Museum. By Colonel C. Swinhoe, F.L.S., F.Z.S., &c. Part I. Sphinges and Bombyces. 8vo, with eight Plates, 21*s*.

Thomson. Notes on Recent Researches in Electricity and Magnetism, intended as a sequel to Professor CLERK MAXWELL'S 'Treatise on Electricity and Magnetism.' By J. J. THOMSON, M.A., F.R.S., Professor of Experimental Physics in the University of Cambridge. 8vo, 18*s*. 6*d*.

Van 't Hoff. Chemistry in Space. Translated and Edited by J. E. MARSH, B.A. Crown 8vo, 4*s*. 6*d*.

Vernon-Harcourt. Treatise on Rivers and Canals, relating to Control and Improvement of Rivers, and Design, Construction, and Development of Canals. By L. F. VERNON-HARCOURT, M.A. 2 vols. 8vo, 1*l*. 1*s*.

—— Harbours and Docks; their Physical Features, History, Construction, Equipment, and Maintenance. 2 vols. 8vo, 25*s*.

Walker. The Theory of a Physical Balance. By JAMES WALKER, M.A. 8vo, stiff cover, 3s. 6d.

Watson. A Treatise on the Kinetic Theory of Gases. By H. W. WATSON, D.Sc., F.R.S. *Second Edition.* Crown 8vo, 4s. 6d.

Watson and **Burbury.** A Treatise on the Application of Generalised Co-ordinates to the Kinetics of a Material System. By H. W. WATSON, D.Sc., and S. H. BURBURY, M.A. 8vo, 6s.

—— The Mathematical Theory of Electricity and Magnetism. Vol. I. Electrostatics. 8vo, 10s. 6d.
Vol. II. Magnetism and Electrodynamics. 8vo, 10s. 6d.

Westwood. Thesaurus Entomologicus Hopeianus. By J. O. WESTWOOD, M.A., F.R.S. With 40 Plates. Small folio, 7l. 10s.

Williamson. Chemistry for Students. With Solutions. By A. W. WILLIAMSON, Phil. Doc., F.R.S. Extra fcap. 8vo, 8s. 6d.

Woollcombe. Practical Work in Heat. By W. G. WOOLLCOMBE, M.A., B.Sc. Crown 8vo, 3s.

VII. ART AND ARCHAEOLOGY.

Butler. Ancient Coptic Churches of Egypt. By A. J. BUTLER, M.A., F.S.A. 2 vols. 8vo, 30s.

Head. Historia Numorum. A Manual of Greek Numismatics. By BARCLAY V. HEAD, D.C.L., Keeper of the Department of Coins and Medals in the British Museum. Royal 8vo, half-morocco, 42s.

Jackson. Dalmatia, the Quarnero and Istria; with Cettigne in Montenegro and the Island of Grado. By T. G. JACKSON, M.A. 3 vols. 8vo. With many Illustrations. Half-bound, 42s.

—— Wadham College, Oxford; Its Foundation, Architecture and History. With an Account of the Family of Wadham, and their seats in Somerset and Devon. By T. G. JACKSON, M.A., A.R.A. 4to, half-persian, 2l. 2s. *net.*

Gardner. Catalogue of the Greek Vases in the Ashmolean Museum. By PERCY GARDNER, M.A., Litt. D. Small folio, linen, with 26 Plates. Price 3l. 3s. *net.*

Three hundred and fifty copies only printed, all of which are numbered.

MUSIC.—Farmer. Hymns and Chorales for Schools and Colleges. Edited by JOHN FARMER, Organist of Balliol College. 5s.

☞ *The Hymns without the Tunes*, 2s.

Hullah. Cultivation of the Speaking Voice. By JOHN HULLAH. *Second Edition.* Extra fcap. 8vo, 2s. 6d.

MUSIC (*continued*).

Ouseley. Treatise on Harmony. By Sir F. A. Gore Ouseley, Bart. *Third Edition.* 4to, 10*s.*

—— Treatise on Counterpoint, Canon, and Fugue, based upon that of Cherubini. *Second Edition.* 4to, 16*s.*

—— Treatise on Musical Form and General Composition. *Second Edition.* 4to, 10*s.*

Troutbeck and Dale. Music Primer. By J. Troutbeck, D.D., and F. Dale, M.A. *Second Edition.* Crown 8vo, 1*s.* 6*d.*

Robinson. A Critical Account of the Drawings by Michel Angelo and Raffaello in the University Galleries, Oxford. By J. C. Robinson, F.S.A. Crown 8vo, 4*s.*

Tyrwhitt. Handbook of Pictorial Art. With Illustrations, and a chapter on Perspective by A. Macdonald. By R. St. J. Tyrwhitt, M.A. *Second Edition.* 8vo, half-morocco, 18*s.*

Upcott. Introduction to Greek Sculpture. By L. E. Upcott, M.A. Crown 8vo, 4*s.* 6*d.*

Vaux. Catalogue of the Castellani Collection in the University Galleries, Oxford. By W. S. W. Vaux, M.A. Crown 8vo, 1*s.*

VIII. PALAEOGRAPHY.

Allen. Notes on Abbreviations in Greek Manuscripts. By T. W. Allen, M.A., Queen's College, Oxford. Royal 8vo, 5*s.*

Gardthausen. Catalogus Codicum Graecorum Sinaiticorum. Scripsit V. Gardthausen Lipsiensis. With Facsimiles. 8vo, *linen*, 25*s.*

Fragmenta Herculanensia. A Descriptive Catalogue of the Oxford copies of the Herculanean Rolls, together with the texts of several papyri. Edited by Walter Scott, M.A. Royal 8vo, 21*s.*

—— Thirty-six Engravings of Texts and Alphabets from the Herculanean Fragments, taken from the original Copper-plates executed under the direction of the Rev. John Hayter, M.A., and now in the Bodleian Library. With an Introductory Note by Bodley's Librarian. Folio, *small paper*, 10*s.* 6*d.*; *large paper*, 21*s.*

Herculanensium Voluminum Partes II. 1824. 8vo, 10*s.*

Oxford:
AT THE CLARENDON PRESS.
LONDON: HENRY FROWDE,
OXFORD UNIVERSITY PRESS WAREHOUSE, AMEN CORNER, E.C.

Made in the USA
Monee, IL
13 September 2026

62976743R00185